Praise for Wordstruck!

Susanna Janssen is one of the most wordstruck, word-besotted, word-bethumped women riding our planet. Reading *Wordstruck!*, one basks in the luminous presence of learning dressed up to have fun.

—**Richard Lederer,** author of *Anguished English* and *Amazing Words*

Hang on to your hats and enjoy your ride with Susanna Janssen, an astute observer of people, customs, and language. Janssen's debut gem sparkles with laugh-out-loud humor and shared insights that will delight your imagination and instill in you a sense of, "I'm so glad I know that now!" Her personality, wit, charm, and fierce intelligence shine into and burst forth from each page.

—**Richard Gardiner, MD,** author and editor

Janssen's crisp, elegant prose leaps off the page. Her skill in weaving humor, etymology, and cultural insights will make her a hit with fans of Lynne Truss and Karen Elizabeth Gordon. Each paragraph has the playful, wry humor of your favorite linguistics professor and the grace of a tango dancer. This gem is not to be missed!

—**Jody Gehrman,** author of *Watch Me*

Facts made fun! I'm wordstruck by Janssen's tell-all truth about lies, time, money, open kimonos, and godly goodbyes. I want a classroom set!

—**E. Hale,** high school teacher and author of *Birthing Orgasms, Time, & Money*

"It's hard to imagine 'a gram of prevention' becoming worth 'a kilo of cure' in one's lifetime."—True, but it's fun to try, aided by Susanna Janssen's light-hearted (but fundamentally serious) and experience-based tour of global culture and language. Pack it in your old kit bag, and smile at her anecdotes, etymologies and wit.

—**Jonathan Middlebrook,** columnist ("It's All Good")

Susanna Janssen has been writing about language for the *Ukiah Daily Journal* in California and our readers have come to look forward to her fun plays on words, her personal stories, her travels, and mostly her vast knowledge of our language and how it gives us myriad ways to express ourselves. Get ready to be delighted at what you'll learn. You're in for a treat!

—**K.C. Meadows,** Editor, Ukiah Daily Journal

My interest was "peaked," "peeked," and "piqued" in the first paragraph of this intelligent, high-speed and frequently zany romp through the alternately charming and mind-boggling babel of our language. From personal anecdotes to Shakespeare creations, Susanna has crafted a page-turner.

—**Laura Fogg,** artist and author of *Traveling Blind*

What a delightful and insightful book! Susanna Janssen's *Wordstruck!* unveils fantastic aspects of language, all across the spectrum from the linguistic perspective to the bilingual brain. Your awareness of the significance of words and how the inner and outer worlds are affected by them will certainly increase as you enjoy her reader-friendly and fun style.

—**Ricardo Stocker,** Ph.D., Professor of Communication
and author of *Our Compassionate Kosmos*

With wit and wonder Susanna Janssen lures and captures the reader into her world of words in *Wordstruck!* Her passion for origins, historical context, metaphors and hilarious adventures is infectious from one memorable passage to the next.

—**Heidi Cusick Dickerson,** author of *Soul &
Spice: African Cooking in the New World*

Anyone with an interest in language and culture will enjoy and learn from this book. *Wordstruck!* presents an amusing, eye-opening, and well-informed array of anecdotes, examples, historical vignettes, and observations about the history, usage, and even the neuropsychology of language.

—**H. Stephen Straight,** Professor Emeritus of Anthropology
and of Linguistics, Binghamton University of New York

Wordstruck!

Wordstruck!

The Fun and Fascination of Language

SUSANNA JANSSEN

ISBN: 978-0-9983048-2-3

Book Design: AuthorSupport.com

To my father, Friedjof Johannes Christie (Fred) Janssen,
and to my mother, Caterina (Kay) Crai Janssen Bowman.
Their multilingual, multicultural union is to blame
and bless for all that follows.

Contents

AUTHOR'S NOTE FOR THE SECOND EDITION

Much has happened in the world of words, language, and culture since I published the first edition of *Wordstruck!* in October of 2016. I had no sooner finalized the manuscript, when Oxford University Press made a momentous announcement: the name of Christopher Marlowe will henceforth join that of William Shakespeare on the title pages of the three *Henry VI* plays. That shot a cannonball at my stubborn stance against theories of multiple authorship of the Shakespeare plays.

A month later, a new U.S. president was elected, and it became evident that the course of Cuban-American relations would not continue in the direction I had cheerfully projected. As old years end and new ones begin, all the important sources announce their latest picks for Word of the Year, and this too is compelling news to offer readers in a new edition of *Wordstruck!*

We're all still speaking our native languages, but we pause to notice that they contain new words, new meanings for old words, and even whole new concepts. A hashtag (still a relatively new word) before the phrase "me too" now speaks volumes about the prevalence of sexual assault and harassment. We are on high alert for "fake news" and "truthiness," but sometimes get so sick of ferreting out what's really happening that we "binge-watch" a whole season of *Grace and Frankie.*

The world of words is ever-changing, dynamic, and alive with the times as we constantly invent vocabulary to talk about new realities. By now, everyone is conversant with terms like "Brexit" and "bromance," and even my mother slings the word "bling," though she still prefers to call it her "hardware," as in when she looks down at her naked hands and hollers, "Turn the car around—I forgot my hardware!" It's impossible to absorb every new word coined in English, nor would we want to. New slang like "po-po" meaning "police" may not catch on—but maybe they said that about "cop" in the mid-1800s too.

Before I get carried too away with words here, as is my wont, let me conclude this Note by saying that I added, updated, corrected, and also wrote some new pieces, all of which I hope will excite your brain, warm your heart, and tickle your funny bone. May your love of language and delight in words grow deeper, wider, and wilder with each season of your life.

Susanna Janssen, May 2018

PREFACE

W*ordstruck!* It's not a disease or a mental imbalance, but certainly a lifelong condition of which I hope never to be cured. Of all human creations, I rate words and language in top place. There are some 46 alphabets in the world today, but let's take just our Roman (also called Latin) one, and consider how many different alphabet soups have been concocted throughout the past 3,000 years with a couple dozen letters.

The number of letters varies slightly among the over 500 languages that use this alphabet, mostly in Europe and the Americas, but basically everything that ever has been and ever will be written with it is just various combinations of a couple dozen symbols linked to specific sounds. If one is speaking, then well-placed pauses and inflections round out the meaning. When writing, a dozen punctuation symbols are all this alphabet soup needs for clarity and flavor. Given the endless possibilities for construction and communication with so few building blocks and tools, what a miracle language is!

One could make a similar claim to supremacy for the creation of music out of a mere twelve basic notes and their endless combinations. Chapter Five, "The Wonders of the Bilingual Brain," explores how the brain is strengthened and how many cognitive abilities are developed by learning a foreign language. It's worth mentioning here that studies of the effects of music on the human brain have uncovered similar enhancements and labeled them "The Mozart Effect."

Words and music—I would not want to be without either. My appreciation of music is huge, but my personal accomplishment in that field is limited despite a decade of piano lessons and the conviction that I was born to sing opera, though not gifted with the voice. Banish me to a desert isle, but let me have words and music. If I must choose between the two, I'll take words, because Nature creates her own music and, in solitude, I can screech out opera to my heart's (if not ears') content. Whenever I think about solitary confinement, it's the horror of having nothing to read that floods my mind and grips my heart. I do seem to be able to generate a lot of words of my own, but what if in my cell I had neither books to read nor tools with which to write? That is a fate that gives me nightmares, while an abundance of words is always a promise of sweet dreams.

I did not set out to write a book, so I think I should tell you how this came to be. As a child, I wanted three things: to have a pet monkey, to play the harp, and to be a poet. I was perhaps 10 years old when, on a family trip to the San Diego Zoo, I was smitten at first sight by a golden marmoset monkey, as enchanted by the velvety sound of its name as by the hairy little mammal itself. As the family finished touring the zoo, I clung to the monkey cage begging and cajoling for what I was sure was my birthright. We got a dachshund puppy instead.

I also knew becoming a harpist was my destiny, and I was convinced I was meant for a starring role in the orchestra with that huge, graceful instrument rocking in my arms. I made it clear to my parents that *that* was the musical instrument with my name on it, and I got . . . 10 years of piano lessons with Grandma.

As for poetry, at least I had more control over that dream. I wrote goofy rhyming lines about the Easter Bunny, Mom's routine of routing us all to bed, and what a meanie my big sister was. I thought brushing my teeth, disliking liver and onions, and watching my little brother belly-flop off the high dive were verse-worthy inspirations. In adolescence, I poured out the requisite righteous angst over self-discovery, social woes, and unrequited infatuations. During the middle years, my creative pen was mostly still. I wrote an occasional poem, essay, and impassioned letter to the editor, but mostly and daily, I wrote lesson plans, homework and composition corrections, to-do lists, and birthday cards—oh, and of course musings on scraps of paper about what I might write . . . someday.

One day, that *someday* came. It was not long after I retired from teaching college Spanish that I retrieved that pile of scraps. On a yellow pad, I wrote one idea at the top of each page. All were topics related to words, languages, and cultures that I thought might be article-worthy: what I was fascinated by, knew a lot about, had an inkling of and wanted to explore, found hilarious, found deeply moving, wanted to share. From off the top of my head and down to the bottom of that pile of scribbled scraps, there were dozens of topics:

- Captivating word derivations
- Crazy English pronunciations
- Collective terms for animals, like "a murder of crows." (I didn't know then that these are called "terms of venery.")

- Sputnik and the lingo of the Cold War
- How Shakespeare's originality changed English forever and for better
- The Word of the Year
- Untranslatable words from other languages
- Arabic words in English
- Translations gone hysterically awry

Well, you get the idea. These and several dozen more are in the table of contents of this book.

I willed myself to emulate the dedication of master storyteller Isabel Allende, who graciously declined my invitation to speak at Mendocino College, adding that she closets herself in her studio in early January every year and writes daily with as few interruptions as possible, until she finishes the project. Perhaps if I had a turret guarded by a jailer to repair to, or if a friend insisted I take over his Italian villa for six months. But no, I lacked Isabel Allende's focus and discipline.

My solution was to propose a column on words, language, and cultures called "A Word in Edgewise" to the local newspaper editor and, once accepted, write an article of 900 to 1,200 words for publication every two weeks. This became a huge and highly satisfying part of my life, and I never missed a deadline, writing during the better part of Fridays, Saturdays, and Sundays twice a month. My social life dwindled as my number of published words grew. When I wrote an article about prepositions (*to, with, for, in, out, on,* etc.) that readers found funny and worthwhile or, more to the point, that people actually *read*, I knew I had found firm footing on the terrain of words and language.

These essays, originally launched to readers of my local newspaper column, have now been released to a wider audience (you!)

in book form for your enjoyment and entertainment. In the writing and publication of them, I had more fun and satisfaction than I ever thought I had a right to. I hope you will smile a lot, that you will laugh too, nod in resonance, and come across things you find wondrous, compelling, annoying, provocative, moving. Most of all, I hope you come away loving words and language all the more.

Susanna Janssen, October 2016

CHAPTER ONE

Life and Language in the USA

The Tower of Scrabble Babel

The official Scrabble lexicon of playable words recently grew by over 5,000 entries. Even if I memorized and strategized every single one, I still couldn't beat a certain formidable opponent at the game. Experience and treachery will always overcome university degrees and a big vocabulary—in Scrabble, that is.

You Say Goodbye and I Say Hello

Is there "good" in *goodbye*? Is there "hell" in *hello*? The origin of these words goes deeper than you might think. And why *do* we answer the phone with "hello"?

The "U.S. and Them" View of the World

Besides our non-use of the metric system, there are about a half dozen other areas in which the U.S. operates differently than most countries, including how we write dates and numbers, how we tell time and eat our food, and even how we do bathrooms.

Minding the Metaphor, Part I

Am I opening a can of worms, a box of chocolates, or reaching for a forbidden fruit? Metaphor engages the imagination through the five senses and can create an unexpected jolt, a deeper understanding, or simply a fresh way of perceiving a well-worn subject.

Minding the Metaphor, Part II

Herein are metaphors on love from some superbly creative writers, metaphors that motivate us to part with our money, and mixed metaphors that might have you "burning the midnight oil from both ends."

Let's Play the Dictionary Game

This word game costs nothing but builds biceps and brain cells, critical-thinking skills and funny bones, and also lets you practice making friends and influencing people. (Author not responsible for split sides or busted guts.)

Pants on Fire

The statistics on how many times a day a lie comes our way are hair-raising. Herein will be revealed a baker's dozen of verbal clues that can tip you off when someone is lying to you.

How Are You Fixed for Time and Money?

So much energy is invested in suffering over the scarcity of these two "commodities." What if they aren't absolutes but creations following the mold of cultural conditioning?

The Tower of Scrabble Babel

Well, it's about time. I've spent years "chillaxing" on Sunday afternoons, "mojito" in one hand and "Sudoku" puzzle in the other, pausing now and then to snap a "selfie" for social media self-promotion, yet only recently has America's leading dictionary publisher canonized these as bona fide words in the English language.

Merriam-Webster's youth-friendly update to the college dictionary with thousands of new, trendy words created nary a ripple. After that, however, M-W's next new edition release created a tsunami of interest and media attention. As soon as new words appear in a standard dictionary, they are already fair game in Scrabble, as long as they are not abbreviations, proper nouns, or words with hyphens or apostrophes. Merriam-Webster's Fifth Edition of *The Official Scrabble Players Dictionary* was published on August 6, 2015, and its more than 5,000 new words became fair game for official club and tournament Scrabble matches as of December 1, 2015.

With my sweet mother's birthday coming up, it crossed my mind to gift her a copy of that dictionary, the first new edition in nearly 10 years, because she is an avid Scrabble player. And a ruthless one. I have accused her of cheating more than once when she plunks down two tiles to connect with two existing words on the board, and then counts out her score for that move both horizontally and vertically, increasing her lead over me by about 48 points. Or when she plays one tile (usually a J, Q, X, or Z) to make a two-letter word that I would have bet money didn't exist.

SJ: "Mom, what does 'zu' mean??"

Mom: "I don't know, but it's a word."

SJ: "But Mom, it's not among the bazillion words in my American Heritage dictionary."

Mom: "No, dear, use the Scrabble book."

SJ: "Oh, of course! It's 'a monetary unit of Vietnam.'"

To add injury to insult, she played that *Z* for a triple-word score: 33 points. *Grrr!*

With only a few tiles left in the bag, I am playing with a mixture of anticipation for my suffering to end and ardent effort to lose by as few points as possible. There are seven tiles in my tray, and all I can manage to do is add a T under an A: "at," for two measly points.

Mom's turn, and she pops a Q in front of my meager move.

SJ: "Q-a-t? Qat?? That's not a word!"

Mom: "It's a variation of k-a-t."

SJ: "That's not how to spell 'cat'!"

Mom: "No, nothing to do with that. It's k-a-t."

SJ: "And what does that mean?"

Mom: "I don't know. Look it up."

And she pushes the fat Merriam-Webster paperback my way.

This isn't the first time I have felt deep hatred for *The Official Scrabble Players Dictionary*, and I refuse to take it in hand. I look up *"qat"* and *"kat"* in every dictionary in the house. Nothing. I look online and . . . oh, but of course: "*qat*—the leaves of the shrub *Catha edulis,* native to the Horn of Africa and the Arabian Peninsula, which are chewed like tobacco or used to make tea; has the effect of a euphoric stimulant." I'm not a happy player; I could use some of that *qat* right now. Game over. Mom has beat me not by dozens of points, but by over 100.

According to the rules of the game, Mom is playing fair and square. Nowhere does it state a player has to know what a word means before playing it. She's not cheating. It pains me to confess that I, on the other hand, cheat often and abundantly. The rules are clear: "Consult the dictionary for challenges only," yet I troll the M-W Scrabble bible at practically every turn seeking inspiration for what to do with my tray of letters. This has provided me with no advantage.

Embarrassingly, there is no correlation between my performance at Scrabble with Mom and my university degrees plus over four decades in academia. In my final attempt at self-justification, I will reveal my adversary's most potent secret weapon: Mom has created her very own Scrabble "dictionary" consisting of tiny 2 x 2" pages stapled together and containing every playable two-letter word in the universe alphabetized A through Z. She rarely consults it, for nearly every word is committed to her crafty memory. It's enough to sizzle my cerebrum.

I don't know that I'll ever be a Scrabble fan, let alone approach Mom's echelon of skill (and did I mention cunning?), but I am fascinated by the 5,000-plus new words that have been inducted into the game's official dictionary. The four in my first paragraph are known even to terminally "unhip" me, so they must be known to you, too. (I suspect anyone who uses the terms "hip" or "unhip" is terminally in the latter category.) I originally had to google the meaning of the following additions to the *Scrabble Dictionary,* but now they seem to pop up everywhere:

- ***Beatbox:*** A form of vocal percussion primarily involving the art of producing drum beats, rhythm, and musical sounds using one's mouth, lips, tongue, and voice.

- ***Bromance:*** A close, nonsexual relationship between two men. (This might be so rare that someone felt it needed a name. Female friendships, on the other hand . . .)
- ***Catfish:*** A person who sets up a fake social media profile.
- ***Frenemy:*** Can refer to either an enemy pretending to be a friend or someone who really *is* a friend but is also a rival.
- ***Geocache:*** An outdoor recreational activity in which participants use a GPS and other navigational techniques to hide and seek containers anywhere in the world. (Unlike Pokémon Go, you are hunting for an actual cache deposited by a real, live person.)
- ***Quinzhee:*** A shelter made by hollowing out a pile of settled snow. This is in contrast to an igloo, which is made from blocks of hard snow. (This word has been in our language since 1984 but absent from the *Scrabble Dictionary* until now, proving, at least to me, that said tool is capricious and unreliable, though official.)*
- ***Vlog:*** A blog with content primarily consisting of videos.†

In addition to these, fair play on the Scrabble board includes the interjections "oof," "yessiree," "aiyee," and "meh," the last being

---

* This makes me think of my all-time-favorite Far Side cartoon by Gary Larsen: Picture two polar bears standing next to an igloo. One says to the other, "I just love these things, crunchy on the outside, and chewy on the inside."

† If these already seem stale as you read this, ponder for a moment the breakneck speed at which English precipitously adopts and often abandons neologisms. In a recent interview, a radio talk show host asked me which slang words meaning "great" have survived the test of time. After discarding boss, bad, bitchin', jake, righteous, tubular, wicked, sweet, on fleek, slaying, and snatched (by the time you read this, more will have come and gone), we agreed the survivor is "cool." Not only does it have many shades of meaning, it leaps socio-cultural fences and has been around for several generations—so long, in fact, that we don't even think of it as slang anymore. We decided it passes the test because it's still cool to say "Cool!"

a verbal shrug of the shoulders. Just don't breathe a word about any of this to my mom. I rejected the thought of buying her the new dictionary. She'd have no use for any of these new words in her vocabulary anyway, and as for her Scrabble game, she doesn't need any more ammunition! She's already a lexical savant, as long as she doesn't have to produce any definitions.

You Say Goodbye and I Say Hello

If you can get through a day without ever saying "Hello" and "Goodbye" (or any of the many variations, like "Hi/G'bye/Bye/Bye-bye/etc."), you might be a hermit in the desert or a nun committed to a life of silent prayer. Where do these words come from? Did someone once decree them to be the official American formulas for our greeting and leave-taking? Is there "good" in "goodbye"? Is there "hell" in "hello"? No and no, and the country western song with those lyrics has already been written.

Let's start with "goodbye" because it's simpler, and because Paul McCartney *didn't* in his catchy song "Hello Goodbye." ("You say yes, I say no. You say stop, and I say go, go, go . . .") The original phrase was "God be with ye," an archaic way of wishing one well as you took your leave. Folks in the 15th century said every syllable of that sweet expression, but by the late 16th century, it had contracted to "Godbwye." (I've no idea how that jumble was pronounced.) With everyone already saying, "Good day" and "Good evening," it was inevitable that the phrase would soon become completely secularized to "Goodbye."

Losing "God" to "Goodbye" did not sit well with everyone; many viewed it as a trendy and degenerate utterance popular only among certain slices of society. However, as is our human bent, one year's scandal becomes another's status quo, and we've been saying "Goodbye" ever since (though the argument whether it should be written "Goodbye" or "Good-bye" persists).

I am struck by the similarity of "God be with ye" to the archaic but still widely known Spanish parting phrase, *Vaya con Dios* ("Go with God"). God has also survived in the standard Spanish goodbye, *Adiós*, commending one "to God" for safekeeping. I suppose this is why *Adiós* is sometimes reserved for more permanent or meaningful partings, while *Hasta luego* works for "Bye, see you later." *Hasta la vista* is a less common expression among Spanish speakers, but is about as familiar in America as Cinco de Mayo and enchiladas, thanks to Arnold Schwarzenegger in his 1991 action flick, *Terminator 2: Judgment Day*. "Ahnold" made $15 million for that role even though his entire dialogue consisted of only 700 words. Let's see . . . that comes out to $21,429 per word—and $85,714 just for saying, "*Hasta la vista*, baby." One stunning linguistic accomplishment!

In parts of South America, it's common to say *Ciao* as a goodbye, but there it's spelled *chau* or *chao*. In Italy, it's both a greeting and a farewell, and it came into the language via Medieval Latin as *s-ciàvo>sclavus,* meaning "(I am your) slave," a rather weighty commitment to proffer when all you really mean is "Hi" or "See you later."

"Hello" is a somewhat newer word than "goodbye," but its roots do go way back. According to the *Oxford English Dictionary*, "hello" first appeared in print in 1827, but its usage then was not as a greeting, rather as a way of getting someone's attention ("Hello, look what you just did!") or showing surprise ("Hello, Tom! Can your dog really shoplift?") In its many variations throughout time and place (beginning around 1400 in Old High German and also in Old French), it was a shout to attract attention, especially to hail a ferryboat: "halloo/hallo/halloa/hillo/holla/holler/hollo/hollow/hullo/holà," and so on. Yes, the Spanish word for "hello," *hola*, comes from this lexical lineage as well.

Now let's examine the history of how "hello" became our formula for answering the phone. These things rarely happen by chance alone, and this one has a good backstory. Alexander

Graham Bell and Thomas Alva Edison were both born in 1847, and leapfrogged each other through the U.S. Patent Office with their world-changing inventions. Among his many patents, Bell is credited with the metal detector, the hydrofoil boat, the harmonic telegraph, and in 1876 the telephone. Edison invented the phonograph (just imagine what it meant to replay sound!), the motion-picture camera (and movement!), the incandescent light bulb, and the microphone that made Mr. Bell's telephone into an apparatus that quickly revolutionized business communication. The early telephone was used exclusively in commerce, and the line was open on both ends at all times.

For the caller to be able to get the attention of someone on the other end, several strategies were considered. The president of the Central District and Printing Telegraph Company of Pittsburg pondered the merits of a call bell, but Thomas Edison convinced him that the perfect word, spoken "cheerfully and firmly," could be heard 10 to 20 feet away. Alexander Graham Bell was adamant that word should be "Ahoy!" and stubbornly used it for the rest of his life.

Today, "Ahoy" is used to answer the phone in parts of Eastern Europe, spelled "*Ahoj.*" Other early contenders included "What is wanted?", "Are you there?", and "Are you ready to talk?" Thomas Edison's *perfect* word won out, though, and the first telephone books recommended it in their instructions to users. Just like that, "Hello" was the official way to start a telephone conversation, and it soon became the most popular way to greet people as well, altering forever the proscriptive 19th-century etiquette of not speaking unless you were first introduced. "Hello" or a variation close in sound (as "*Aló*") is used to answer the phone in nearly 40 languages, as diverse as Arabic, Cantonese, Danish, French,

German, Hungarian, Hebrew, Hindi, Japanese, Persian, Polish, Russian, Thai, and Vietnamese.

The Greek philosopher Heraclitus said, "The only thing constant in life is change," and now we have the game-changer of caller ID. While we're not yet saying "Goodbye" to the telephone greeting "Hello," for many of us it has become rare to answer the phone if we don't know who is calling. When I do, I tend to say a rather questioning, suspicious, and totally unsatisfying "Hello?" So, in honor of the amazingly inventive duo Bell and Edison, who pioneered the electronic revolution that has progressed beyond wild imagination, I hereby resolve to make all my future hellos "cheerful and firm," and perhaps I'll even throw in an occasional "Ahoy" just for colorful good measure.

The "U.S. and Them" View of the World

Not only is American English the fastest-growing language on the planet, but for better or worse we are also exporting our culture to the world's insatiable appetite for American music, movies, cultural trends, fast food, and big-box retail. What they want nothing to do with is our measuring system. In the U.S., the metric system is consistently used in the scientific, military, and manufacturing sectors, but in everyday life we stubbornly cling to our ounces, gallons, acres, and 212-degree boiling point, unable to think in any other terms than miles per hour, tablespoons of sugar, and 102 degrees Fahrenheit on the Fourth of July. So here we are, a huge island of 10-gallon hats in a sea of metric-users wearing the 37.8541-liter version.

Ah, but we are not entirely alone! Myanmar and Liberia don't use the metric system either, though both have declared its future adoption. Our nonmetric system was inherited by the 13 colonies as a legacy from the British Empire. Today, the United Kingdom and Canada use the metric system—if not exclusively, at least dominantly. In 1971, the U.S. National Bureau of Standards proposed that metrics be phased in over a period of 10 years, but when lawmakers took action, they legislated out "deadline" in favor of "voluntary adoption." Since shifting to metric would be akin to everyone having to read, write, think, and speak a foreign language, there were predictably few "volunteers."

Like most Americans, I can't think in metric. If a pancake recipe calls for 200 ml of milk and 180 gm of flour, I'm having scrambled eggs and toast for breakfast. When my aunties used to exclaim over the extremely rare 35 degrees of heat they were having in northern Holland, I had to get out the calculator and do the math: 35°C x 9/5 + 32 = 95°F. I never got a speeding ticket driving Aunt Vena's car along the Dutch canals because going 80 to 100 seemed plenty fast to me. Of course, that's kilometers per hour, and only 50–62 in miles per hour, but those bigger numbers made me feel I was flying toward the next quaint, steepled village at Grand Prix racing velocity.

With water freezing at 0 degrees and boiling at 100 degrees Celsius, the elegance of the metric system is inarguable. And it truly is a *system,* because there is the same ratio (1,000:1) for millimeters to meter, meters to kilometer, grams to kilogram, and kilograms to tonne (or "ton" to North Americans). Our American way does not even have an official name, let alone any regularity of measurement. It can be referred to as the U.S. Customary System, or the inch/pound system, and it includes more than 300 different units to measure various physical quantities. Frightfully complicated, yes, but not when it is our frame of reference, as ingrained into brain automaticity as is counting or telling time. Given our degree of attachment, it's hard to imagine "a gram of prevention" becoming worth "a kilo of cure" in one's lifetime.

On the subject of what America does differently than most of the world, there are a few more aspects of ordinary life we might consider:

* * *

In the Miami airport, before boarding a charter flight for Cuba in the spring of 2015, we all had to fill out a form for the Cuban government that instructed the order for birth date to be written in the order of day/month/year. In other words, an American born on January 7, 1962 would customarily write 1/7/62, but outside of the United States it's usually written 7/1/62. Despite our guide's warning, one member of the group went on auto-pilot and wrote 1/7/62. Although she neatly crossed it out and rewrote the requested birth date order, she was charged $100 for the mental blip and a new blank form. No excuses, no discussion. Although we experienced two weeks of uniformly welcoming generosity from the Cuban people, I suspected this particular act of punitive policy to be a bit of embargo revenge. After all, who else but an American would write month/day/year?

* * *

On the subject of airports, a colleague showed up to teach classes on a Monday morning, though I was sure she'd said that on Friday she was off to Bali or some such exotic, faraway place. With great and sheepish embarrassment, she told me she had misread the itinerary and arrived at the international terminal for what she thought was an 11:00 p.m. flight that had already departed at 11:00 that morning. Why aren't we using the 24-hour clock—at least for public transportation—like most of the rest of the world? It is used in American hospitals and in the military because lives depend on synchronization. Patients must receive their doses of medications at the right time, and squadrons need to know precisely when to move into strategic position. So why aren't the rest of us using it in time-sensitive contexts? The answer is that we just don't think of afternoon/evening hours as 13:00 to 24:00; we have to stop and count on our fingers, and even then, we're never fully convinced that 19:00 hours is really 7:00 p.m.

* * *

Here is another sneaky pitfall with numbers that awaits the innocent American in Foreigndom. You are quite certain that the only way to write your bank balance is $3,400 (perhaps while envying your brother's at $3,400,000). At the time of this writing, the exchange rate for the euro is now—hallelujah!—1.18 per dollar. (I know, I know, it may not be good for our export economy, but the travel group going to Italy this fall is ecstatic.)

I admit to shock in discovering that most parts of the world put commas in numbers where we put periods, and periods where we put commas. It looks like this: Your bank balance is $3.400 and your brother's is $3.400.000 (but Mom always liked him best). The exchange rate for the euro is 1,18; and clock time is even written 7,30. I know it just seems *wrong,* but that shows how attached we are to the particular meanings we give to a dot and a squiggle when used with numbers.

* * *

Another oddity that sets the United States apart is that our currency bills are all green and the same size. Though we think this is perfectly normal, workable, and logical, in most countries bills are different colors, and their size also often varies depending on denomination. Colorful bills in varying sizes can be pretty to look at, but it really is more about practicality than esthetics. Have you ever had to say to a clerk, "But I gave you a 20 and you only gave me change for a 10"? In our twilight years, with eyesight failing, will we struggle to tell the difference between a five-dollar bill and a one?

* * *

When trying to locate an office or return to your hotel room in a foreign country, you might wander around for a long time on the wrong floor before realizing you've taken one set of stairs too many. In the U.S., the ground floor is numbered as the first floor, but in most other countries it's not numbered at all. Spanish speaking countries will serve as a typical example: You enter on the ground floor, *la planta baja*, and ascend to the first floor. Americans think they're on the second floor by then, and spend half their valuable vacation time negotiating elevators and stairwells.

* * *

There is also the matter of wielding knife and fork at the dinner table. Watch carefully in slow motion the right-handed version of how Americans eat: Using the right hand, we transport food from plate to mouth with the fork tines *up*. Then we switch that fork over to the left hand (tines *down* for stabbing), take the knife into the right hand, and cut our steak. Then we set the knife down, and transfer the fork back to the right hand (tines *up*) to make its way to the mouth. Quite a production! Most foreign knife/fork wielders look on this as inefficient and clumsy (read: "inelegant"), and might even liken it to the way toddlers handle the utensil before they've learned to eat properly.

I remember sitting in a café in Antwerp with my Belgian cousin, marveling at how she cut the meat, retained the fork (tines *down*) in her left hand, deftly used the knife with her right hand to assemble a neat packet of meat and accompaniments onto the *back* of her fork, and flawlessly guided it into her mouth. This is called Continental or European style, and it is obviously more economical and practical; that is, *if* you can master the successful docking of fork plus contents in mouth. I daresay it is also more graceful, and am glad to see it is gaining in popularity, although many Americans still regard this style of eating as a lack of good table manners, somewhere between questionable and uncouth.

* * *

As any world traveler has experienced, countries that use 220 volts vastly outnumber the United States and others that use 120. I made my first trip to Italy at just about the time the travel industry was putting dual-voltage personal appliances on the market. Even though I was armed with my first such gadget, I still packed my voltage converter, just in case. My hotel in Siena was a former convent staffed by nuns with the stern and intimidating Mother Superior herself doing front-desk duty.

On our first morning, I recall my long mental debate over what to do about the hairdryer, the converter, and the 220-volt wall socket. I finally decided that the best strategy was to plug the dual-voltage appliance into the converter *just to make sure* it got enough electricity. That well-thought-out act blew the electricity on the whole second floor. (There is a reason I am a linguist and not a scientist or an engineer.) I slunk downstairs to the front desk and confessed in jumbled Italian. Mother Superior was so furious with me I could see the steam coming out from under her wimple. Suffice to say, it took a lot of penance to get back in good standing as a tourist at the "convent."

* * *

Based on my experience of traveling to 20 or so countries on several continents, I can assert that *no one* does bathrooms like we do in America. For us, a bathroom is a sacred place, and it must be built, outfitted, and appointed as such. More than once, when out dining with friends, one comes back to the table and says, "Oh, you've just *got* to see their bathroom!" Design and decor of bathrooms are treated like curated art installations, and plumbing has developed into a fine American art form of its own. The toilet always flushes, and there's always water in the shower—hot on demand, and with enough power to rinse the shampoo out of the thickest head of hair. We take this completely for granted—that is, until we travel to a foreign country.

I used to have a Lady Godiva-length mane, and hair washing was always at the top of my list of travel concerns. On family visits to Europe, I was stymied by trickling showers and tiny water heaters that barely put out enough to wash a teacup in the sink. Electricity and gas were hugely expensive, and people were very frugal with resources and supplies of just about everything. This may be hard to believe, but my Dutch grandmother only washed her hair every five to six weeks, even when she came to live in the United States after WWII. Between visits to the salon, she used powders that she combed through to absorb the excess oil. She also burned candles in the evening to save on electricity; even in the land of plenty, she adhered to a culture of economization.

While visiting a friend in Spain, I realized from the start there was no hope of washing my hair in her trickle of a shower with a miniature on-demand water heater of lukewarm output, so I parted with many euros as a regular customer at the nearby salon.

During a study/travel program to Cuernavaca, Mexico, I stayed with a family who was proud to offer me the apartment they had added to their suburban home. The so-called shower consisted of a lead pipe, with no showerhead, protruding from a hole 3" below the ceiling, with a nice, strong jet of water that was aimed uselessly and irremediably at the side wall, 6" above my right shoulder. One of my fellow travelers to Cuba swore she would pack a toilet seat into her luggage if she ever returned to the island. Bathroom facilities have been the source of some of my greatest travel frustrations, and I'm not alone because hilarious illustrated books, websites, and even a wall calendar have been created by traumatized Americans subjected to interesting but bewildering foreign facilities.

* * *

Another thing observable in bathrooms worldwide is that water going down the drain swirls counterclockwise in the Northern Hemisphere and clockwise in the Southern Hemisphere. I remember jokingly asking my geologist colleague, "So what happens at the equator—the water goes straight down?" He said, "Actually, yes, it does." I have since observed these phenomena numerous times in demonstrations at the Inti Nan Museum on the true equatorial line near Quito, Ecuador. Storms in the atmosphere also swirl counterclockwise in the northern skies and clockwise in the South.

* * *

How differently we all experience the world! Enjoying barbecues late into our balmy summer evenings, I'm reminded that friends in Uruguay and cousins in South Africa are stoking furnaces and wearing woolens through their winter. I look up at the Big Dipper and, while it's one of only three constellations I can reliably identify in our Northern Hemisphere sky, the whole starry expanse looks familiar to me. My mind reaches into the future for the next time I'll be far enough south to search unfamiliar heavens for *their* stellar icon, the Southern Cross.

For now, though, I'm trying to embrace the metric system before my paella-cooking class in Valencia, Spain by measuring out 600 grams of rice, 300 grams of prawns, a liter of broth, 100 milliliters of white wine . . . and it will all be ready to serve between 21,15 and 22,00—the window of time that much of the rest of the world regards as the most civilized hour to dine.

Vive la différence!

Minding the Metaphor, Part I

We were talking about metaphor while keeping an eye on the tango dancers circling the floor. He said, "Whenever I want to express an idea in metaphor, my mind is in a *haze* and nothing comes up." Then as we both admired a particularly graceful dancer, he said, "She's a *doll*, but when I dance with her, I have *two left feet.*" Sure, these are simple examples, but he proved to be adept at metaphors after all.

Whether we can define the term or not, we likely demonstrate some mastery of metaphor all the time. I yearn to understand it at a deeper level, and what better way than to write about it! Best to start with something we all have experience with and have a lot to say about, so let's take *life*. We can describe it with adjectives: Life is *hard/exciting/challenging/fun.* However, if we want to spice it up, communicate with more impact, and fire the imagination and the senses, we can opt for a metaphor: Life is *a bowl of cherries/a rocky road/a rat race/a bed of roses/a beach/"but a dream, sweetheart."*

Of course, metaphors can be original instead of the familiar old *workhorses* that easily come to mind. A friend recently said, "My life is one barrel ride over Niagara Falls after another." In a flash (then and now), my imagination creates the roar of the Falls, the cold spray in my face, and the horrifying sight of my friend's barrel launching into free-fall. My senses are fully engaged, and my heart rate probably spikes as well. That is precisely why we express ourselves in metaphor—to create image and impact by appealing to the imagination through the five senses.

Imagine you are working on a project. It's easy or hard, rewarding or dull, difficult or smooth. You report to friends that this latest challenge is *a bear/Mount Everest/a walk in the park/the icing on the cake*. In this way, you describe what *is* (A: your project) with what it *is not* (B: a bear)—but B works well as a descriptor because of the image it creates. When clouds *sail* across the autumn sky or tornados *barrel* through the Midwest, the brain has something far more interesting to work with than "move fast."

There is movement in most metaphors, if not overt, as in, "Their marriage was a *roller coaster*," then perhaps more suggested: "Monday morning, and it's back to the *salt mines*." I get a motion picture of hard labor with bent backs and sweaty arms wielding heavy metal mallets. If *there's an elephant in the room*, its tail swishes while everyone in the overstuffed chairs nervously averts eyes to floor and ceiling, pretending not to see, hear, or smell what's really going on. Dad, on a strict diet, says his beloved afternoon ice cream bar is *forbidden fruit*, and the metaphor itself intimates the movement of that hand reaching into the tree to pick that of which he should not partake. When the government's response to an intractable social problem is temporary and inadequate, we can virtually see that *Band-Aid* being slapped over a wound that begs for deeper treatment. All those loans secured by plastic add up to *a house of cards*, and we already picture the impending collapse from a puff of air or the placement of one more card.

Metaphors from literature, history, visual media, and song weave their way into the woof and warp of culture and become such familiar fabric that we might even forget from whence they came. Here is a six-point quiz to identify the source of these famous metaphors:

1. "The fog comes/on little cat feet./It sits looking/over harbor and city/on silent haunches/and then moves on."
2. "Out, out, brief candle! Life's but a walking shadow, a

poor player that struts and frets his hour upon the stage and is heard no more. It is a tale told by an idiot, full of sound and fury, signifying nothing."

3. She finally met her Waterloo.
4. "He's a boil on the butt of humanity." (Double points if you get this one! Hint: in the film, these words are spoken by an older woman about her neighbor.)
5. "My mama always said life is like a box of chocolates. You never know what you're gonna get."
6. "When the moon hits your eye like a big pizza pie, that's amore."

That's the end of the quiz,‡ but consider this: if mama said life is *like* a box of chocolates, and if the moon hits your eye *like* a big pizza pie, it's a simile and not a metaphor, right? With all due respect to our middle-school teachers, it turns out that *metaphor* is an umbrella term, and *simile* is one of the several literary devices in its shelter. *Simile*, in other words, is the type of metaphor that uses the words "like" or "as."

Jane Hirshfield, renowned poet, essayist, and translator, created an engaging animated TED-Ed Original called, "The Art of Metaphor." In it, she states, "A simile is a metaphor that makes you *think* it's making a comparison." The *Oxford Companion to*

---

‡ Answers to the quiz:

1. Carl Sandburg's poem "Fog."
2. Shakespeare, of course, but whence? Ah, therein lies the rub! (*Macbeth*: Act 5, Scene 5)
3. Napoleon Bonaparte was finally defeated at the battle of Waterloo, Belgium in 1815; also the 1974 megahit from ABBA.
4. One of many memorable lines uttered by character Ouiser Boudreaux, played by Shirley MacLaine, in *Steel Magnolias.*
5. Forrest, on the park bench at the beginning of *Forrest Gump*.
6. "That's Amore," the hit song from 1953, sung by Dean Martin and composed by Harry Warren and Jack Brooks; theme song of the 1987 movie *Moonstruck*.

the English Language defines metaphor as "all figures of speech that achieve their effect through association, comparison, and resemblance. Figures like antithesis, hyperbole, metonymy, and simile are all species of metaphor." Okay, I'll accept that, but rest assured, we are not going to touch those first three with a metaphoric 10-foot pole between these covers of *Wordstruck!*

Now, back to that "pie in the eye"—a perfect note to end on because it's a double metaphor (or metaphor plus simile, if Sister Josita of freshman English insists). It is action-packed, though questionably romantic: "Love is the *moon* hitting your eye like a big *pizza pie.*" Ah, love! What fertile *field* for metaphor!

On the very next page, I promise you metaphors of love never to be forgotten; metaphors for the soul from my poet/Scorpio friend Nancy Harris McLelland; a true confession of my life as the Golden Gate Bridge; and some rib-tickling *mixed metaphors.* It won't be long! I can already see the *light at the end of the rainbow.*

Minding the Metaphor, Part II

Welcome back to the Land of Metaphoric Make-Believe, where nothing is *really* as stated. Rather, somehow, in this fantasy world, the linguistic act of comparison creates a more palpable reality through word and image. Just hearing the metaphors "a light at the end of the tunnel" or "a pot of gold at the end of the rainbow" might deliver a dose of optimism with the promise of cheer and the hope of good fortune. Before we assume we're all on the same metaphoric *page,* let's consider how one person's metaphor can be another person's mystery.

A metaphor often represents or symbolizes an abstraction. Maybe in your family, some object, person, or activity morphed in meaning over time to become a metaphor, and if so, maybe no one outside your genetic nucleus was in on the secret. I'll let you in on two from the Janssens: When we say "V Street," we don't necessarily mean the physical street we kids grew up on. We mean those idyllic childhood years of playing Robinson Crusoe in the orchard (in the blazing summer sun of Bakersfield, California, a "loaf" of mud would bake solid in two hours); riding bikes with our kiddy pals; plying the sidewalks on metal skates; and watching Ed Sullivan's "really big shoe" on Saturday nights.

My second example is an abrupt pop of that bucolic bubble. Everyone who experienced a childhood knows or can imagine what a "spanking stick" is. Mom's was the flat, back slat of a kitchen chair, 6" wide and 2' long, as I recall, but probably more like 3" x 14" in reality. The sides were curvy, so she could grip it tight and wield it fast and hard. That stick was such a presence in our childhood years that it became a metaphor for everything we kids shouldn't have done/said, or failed to do/say (similar to the word "confessional," if you grew up Catholic). Just hearing Mom intone "spanking stick," as in, "Don't make me get my . . ." or "Stay right where you are; I'm coming back with my . . ." (It lived on top of the refrigerator ever within her reach) conjured up a whirlwind of distressing images but always meant one thing: *You're in trouble.*[§]

It's also worth mentioning that one culture's metaphors will likely not be easily grasped by another. This is so obvious it needs no illustration, but it's kind of fun to think about a foreigner's confusion when he's told by his American friend that learning English is not a "walk in the park," or if another friend offers to "show him the ropes."

I was delighted to hear from Barbara, a reader of my newspaper column, who told me that in Norway, the word "Texas" has become a slang metaphor for something "really out there/completely crazy." Sure enough, there's a photo online of an enormous swordfish leaping from the waters off the coast of Norway with the caption, *Det var helt Texas*. Best translation: "It was totally bonkers." I wonder whether that new metaphor makes Texans polish their stars with pride or snort into their 10-gallon hats[¶] with disdain.

---

§ It never occurred to me to engage in defensive maneuvers, but my little brother was smarter, more agile, and less fearful than I. One day, as the legendary stick was slicing through the air toward his standing backside, he deftly dodged sideways. It missed its target and instead crashed down upon a nearby chair with enough force to split it lengthwise down the middle. Now Mom had two sticks, and while there were other generations of spanking sticks after that, none was ever as spring-loaded and atomic-powered as the original.

¶ There are two possible origins for the name of this famous cowboy hat, but both originated from the Spanish, and the hat itself was imported from south of the border. The first explanation offers that the Spanish phrase *tan galán*, was applied to a sombrero that was "so fine," easily anglicized by American cowboys to "ten-gallon." The second and more likely comes from the Spanish word "galón," which was a thin strip of braided trim around the crown of a hat. On the preferred high-crowned *vaquero*-cowboy style, not just one galón but 10 might adorn it.

In the richly metaphoric realm of love, here are some unforgettable ones: "Happiness is the china shop; love is the bull" (H.L. Mencken, *A Little Book in C Major*, 1916); "They say love is a two-way street. But I don't believe it, because the one I've been on for the last two years was a dirt road" (Terry McMillan, *Waiting to Exhale*, 1992); "Love is an exploding cigar we willingly smoke" (Lynda Barry, cartoonist); "Love must be as much a light as a flame" (Henry David Thoreau, letter, 1852).

My poet/Scorpio friend Nancy Harris McLelland wrote, "I would like a love IV: a slow and steady flow of affection." Nancy writes and speaks in metaphors that fill me with wonder, inspiration, amusement, and sometimes longing, even sorrow. Here is another of her gems: "I could no longer swallow my resentments whole. The heartburn was overwhelming"; and another: "I feel like a Red Cross volunteer, likely to get shot by either side."

Long ago, Nancy told of a paradigm shift she experienced at her ironing board: "I was always bothered by my ironing basket filled with ironing to be done, until the morning I changed my POV and told myself, 'That's the way an ironing basket is *supposed* to look!'" In addition to appreciating her change in *point of view* toward the task, I took on the image of that ever-full basket as a metaphor for how we tick off life's chores, only for more to pile on, stressing ourselves to the breaking point with the misguided belief that the goal of life is to keep the basket empty.

Like Nancy's ironing basket, my most enduring and bracing metaphor for life as I live it is the job of painting the Golden Gate Bridge, San Francisco's most iconic symbol. The GG Bridge Highway and Transportation District confirms that the structure is painted continuously: International Orange, 52 weeks a year. That quite perfectly describes my eternal project of dealing with the clutter in my life. I'm immune to self-reminders that "flat surfaces are not storage areas" and that I don't need to clip more recipes, save those articles, or take notes on every available scrap of paper about book titles, good movies, interesting words, and secrets to enlightenment. In order to manage, I keep "painting the Golden Gate Bridge" year after year. Once the full-house decluttering and reorganization project is complete, I gleefully pop a champagne cork . . . and then begin again, continually reminding myself to stop grousing and celebrate instead that there is still a bridge to paint, and that I'm still able to wield that brush every day.

In his article, "Why Metaphors Beat the Snot out of Facts When it Comes to Motivating Action," a title that practically says it all, Douglas Van Praet asserts that metaphors motivate us to buy because they "evoke feelings that bypass critical thinking." When you see that sweet family and their little house safely nestled in the "good hands" of Allstate, you just get a warm, fuzzy feeling that everything is going to be all right. Tropicana's irresistible orange juice metaphor, "your daily ray of sunshine," speaks of warmth, health, and vibrancy. "Show 'em you're a tiger" is a powerful promise that keeps the kids clamoring for Frosted Flakes. If you run out and buy yourself a new Lexus, you will "unleash the beast!" and become powerfully unstoppable.

Wishful thinking and hype aside, let's now top off the tank with a few mixed metaphors: "Button your seatbelts" (Rush Limbaugh) because "the dirty laundry is coming home to roost" (Ray Romano). "A leopard can't change his stripes" (Al Gore); "Can you read the handwriting in the wind?" (Major Frank Burns, in M.A.S.H.); "These hateful few who have no conscience, who kill at the whim of a hat." (George W. Bush); "She's a sharp cookie" (oops, Yours Truly).

Amidst this inviting potential for enlivened thought, enriched expression, and ignited imagination, I say embrace the metaphor!

Be it slang, cliché, commercial, mismatched, or as provocatively original as Nancy Harris McLelland's, metaphor is a window into the mind and soul, and an invitation to gaze into the milieu in which we perceive, think, and speak.

Let's Play the Dictionary Game

I love this game! That's saying a lot, because I don't play cards and am easily bored by board games. In fact, just a few pages ago, you learned of my abysmal performance at Scrabble with Mom. I just acted out my first-*ever* charade last Thanksgiving and, back when Pictionary was all the rage, I failed due to insurmountable artistic challenges. But Dictionary (also called Fictionary) is a game I can really sink my teeth into and wrap my mind around.

Lest you think it's played by a table of stuffed shirts with Coke-bottle eyeglasses beneath haughtily raised eyebrows, let me emphasize that playing this game with family and friends has provided some of my life's greatest moments of suspense and hilarity, to say nothing of gloating victory and ignominious defeat.

Before I describe the simple rules and play a round with you, I must digress a moment. What about dictionaries anyway? Are they becoming dinosaurs? I occasionally look up words online if I'm already on the computer, simply because it's so convenient, but it feels very cold and unsatisfying. Sure, it provides what I need at the moment, but that pales in comparison to the visual, tactile, and intellectual stimulation of opening a beloved dictionary. It's like eating three-day-old leftover rice versus glorying in a whole plate of delectable paella from Dora's Gourmet Café in Ukiah. (Uncontrollable flights of culinary fancy are a peril of writing while hungry.)

Frequent use of a behemoth dictionary also affords fitness advantages, especially in the prevention of osteoporosis. My *American Heritage* weighs in at over five pounds, and getting it down from the bookshelf surely qualifies as a weight-bearing exercise. Physical fitness aside, let's get down to the details of the game, and have a little fun.

To play Dictionary, you need five to 10 players, paper, pencils (or pens of the same color ink), several small pieces of paper for each player, and a good-sized dictionary which all agree to use as the reference. Do not, under any circumstances, use your Scrabble dictionary for, as I alluded to in "The Tower of Scrabble Babel," it comes from a different lexical solar system and contains words only known to my mother and impossibly distant or long-extinguished ancient civilizations.

When it is your turn, the challenge is to choose a word from the dictionary, from your vast vocabulary, or from your secret list. Select a word you hope none of the other players will know. Say it aloud, and spell it for your opponents. *You* write the correct definition on a small piece of paper in erudite, zany, minimalist, or primitive language. The choice is yours, but the definition has to be the correct one. The other players will each invent a definition, and even if some know the real definition of your word, they will still write a contrived one in the most believable fashion possible. Then you collect all the papers, shuffle them, number them, and read them aloud in no particular order, as impartially as possible.

This is usually when the hilarity starts and sometimes progresses into pig-snorts and the loss of control over bodily functions. The other players vote on the definition they believe to be the true one. A correct guess earns two points, and players earn one point every time someone votes for their phony definition. You only score during your turn if you stump all the players and none of them votes for the correct definition. Then, the turn to present a new word passes to the next player.

Here are some tips on choosing great words to play in the

Dictionary Game. The most challenging and entertaining ones have a meaning that is comical, strange, or unbelievable. Steer clear of chemical compounds or arcane botanical references because, though they are weird, they are no fun. No foreign words are allowed. Try to design your definition to fit the part of speech: noun, verb, adjective, and so on. It's best to avoid words with multiple and divergent meanings like "conjugate," which has several definitions, including a) to inflect a verb, as in the Spanish *hablo, hablas, habla* ("I speak, you speak, he/she speaks"), or b) to have sex. With all that in mind, let the game begin!

There are seven of us at play around the dining table: Ross, Pattie, Candie, Ricardo, Tom, Barbara, and me. It's my turn, and my word is "orotund." I write the true definition while the other six players invent phony ones. Then I collect, shuffle, and number the definitions. Making sure no one can see the author's handwriting, I read each definition aloud a couple times:

"Orotund":

1. a kind of permafrost that gives off a warm glow
2. bullion formed in a round shape during the Spanish conquest of the Americas
3. referring to anything pear-shaped; wider and heavier on the bottom than at the top
4. the technical name for airport bathrooms with different entry and exit doors
5. said of a pompous person who loves the sound of his or her own voice
6. the type of tuna most commonly used in commercial canning
7. a word that describes large, round mountains

After thirty seconds, the laughter and derision dies down, and tension runs high.

For the sake of my illustration, the number in front of the name below indicates which false definition each player wrote, and after the name you see which definition each voted for:

1. Ross: voted for #2
2. Pattie: voted for #7
3. Candie: voted for #5
4. Ricardo: voted for #3
5. Susanna: no vote (my word)
6. Tom: voted for #5
7. Barbara: voted for #6

Here's the scoring:

1. Ross: 0: No one voted for his definition (#1).
2. Pattie: 1: Ross voted for her definition (#2).
3. Candie: 1 + 2 = 3: Ricardo voted for her definition (#3); and she voted for the correct definition (#5).
4. Ricardo: 0: No one voted for his definition (#4).
5. Susanna: 0: Both Candie and Tom voted for my correct definition (#5).
6. Tom: 1 + 2 = 3: Barbara voted for his definition (#6); and he voted for my correct definition (#5).
7. Barbara: 1: Pattie voted for her definition (#7).

Play goes on until all seven of us have presented at least one word, and it can continue for more rounds after that.

There you have it—a game that guarantees a provocative and delightful evening. I can't claim that Dictionary will increase your vocabulary, make you a more persuasive speaker/writer, or win you a contestant slot on *Jeopardy*, but your brain neurons will push out miles of dendrites, and your gray matter might just be more vibrant and lit up by the end of the game, even if you come in last.

I cast my vote for activities where people actually sit in the same room looking at each other and not at the screen of an electronic device. Dictionary is free and loaded with benefits for body and mind. You only need to haul that big book off the shelf (a weight-bearing, anti-osteoporosis activity), open a bottle of red wine (great for cardiovascular health), assemble the players (ensuring greater longevity through social contact), and try to fool every one of them (brain-strengthening through firing neurons and dendrite growth). And in the course of play, you just might engage in laughter, and that, as we all know, is one of life's best elixirs for mind, body, and spirit.

I keep a top-secret list of words stored up for my next round of *Dictionary* play. Are you game? I'll bring the wine!

Pants on Fire

Big and fat or teeny and white, researchers say that a lie comes at us as often as 200 times a day. That might seem impossible, but consider a few possible sources: online dating profiles (reports say 90% contain at least one lie), job resumes (estimated at 40% containing lies), family and friends (averaging 75%), product hype to make our wrinkles disappear and grow back our hair (this author estimates 99.9%), and presidential candidate debates (your turn).

According to a study by the University of Massachusetts, in 10 minutes of conversation 60% of adults lied an average of three times. I'm sure all of *us* are among the perfectly honest 40%, right? Actually, the 60% who lied thought they were the honest ones too; they didn't believe the outcome until they listened to a playback of their conversation.

It goes without saying that the great majority of lies are not damaging. Rather, they are the fibs we tell to come off as smarter, wittier, more "with it," or more worthy in the eternal game of comparison to others. Most of us want to fit in and be liked, gracefully back out of social obligations, and avoid hurting another's feelings.

Lying is a skill that most of us discovered around age four, honed throughout childhood, and practiced avidly in our teen years. By the time we reached adulthood, our patterns were pretty well set in stone. When my grandmother left post-WWII Europe to come to America, her new life included major plot alterations of the one she'd left behind. These became such a part of her new identity that I am convinced she died actually believing her father really *was* a surgeon and that she really *did* study music at the Sorbonne.

The Italians have a wonderful expression to articulate their prime cultural commandment: *fare la bella figura*, literally, "to make the beautiful figure," meaning to create the best possible impression in every situation while looking and sounding great throughout. It comes down to impeccable fashion sense, good manners, and a flair for producing just the right words and actions to fit the moment. One can't help but wonder how many *piccole bugie bianche* (little white lies) it takes to keep all that glued together.

It would be fun to go on in an anecdotal vein, especially since I was on the verge of confessing a *bugia* or two of my own, but I'll save those for later and turn now to the "lexicon of lying," the real motive for this piece. I became interested in the subject years ago when my ex was a detective for the state police and I used to read his training manuals on lie detection. Everyone knows at least a few of the what-to-look-fors in terms of gestures and body movements that might indicate a person is lying: no eye contact, touching the mouth or throat, shuffling feet, excessive fidgeting, and so on. However, what follows is the Dirty (Baker's) Dozen of *verbal* clues that might indicate an untruth is being fired your way:

1. If you ask, "Did you eat the cookies I made for the potluck?" some stalling tactics might include "Huh?" or "What?" to get you to repeat the question, or "Well . . ." All three are designed to buy time to figure out how to construct a believable but less-than-straightforward answer.
2. Repetition of the question is another way of buying time. Your question, "Did you go to Taylor's Tavern after work today?" may be repeated right back to you: "Did I go to Taylor's Tavern after work today?"

3. Another form of repetition occurs when all the words of your question are included in the answer: "No, I did not go to Taylor's Tavern after work today."
4. Assertions of truth like "To be perfectly honest . . . To tell the truth . . . You listen to me . . ." and "I swear to . . ." might indicate dishonesty.
5. A very common red flag is not using contractions. Notice "did not" instead of "didn't" in #3. This is also a way of asserting truth (#4) or showing indignation.
6. Retort question: To the teacher's "Did you lift that term paper from an online source?" the trapped student might respond, "What do you mean?" The tone may be aggressive, innocent, or confused, as the speaker is hoping to throw you off and, again, stall for time.
7. Common is the use of nonspecific words and generalizations. You texted: "What happened to our lunch date today?" Texted reply: "We got hung up in a bunch of crazy stuff." Neither "hung up" nor "a bunch of crazy stuff" tells you anything about what actually happened.
8. In that same texted reply, notice the subject, "We." A liar often unconsciously tries to create distance by avoiding individually incriminating pronouns such as "I" and "me" and using the plurals "we" and "us," as well as "the" instead of "my." Saying "that" instead of "this" also creates distance: "I have no idea how that jewelry got into the purse."
9. Be wary of a very short answer with no detail: Jiltee asks, "Why don't you ever call me anymore?" Jilter replies: "It's complicated."
10. The opposite can also be a danger sign: long, rambling blah-blah-blah that doesn't answer the question. Here is Confession #1, for the sake of illustration: I told

my parents I was going to see a classic movie with my boyfriend (The African Queen starring Katherine Hepburn and Humphrey Bogart), though we were really going to a party. The next morning, in answer to, "How was the movie?" I blabbed on for a good 10 minutes about how romantic and exciting it was and how cool it would be to go on an African safari someday.

11. Statements made in uncharacteristic monotone (example coming right up)
12. Overemphasis of words (ditto)
13. The speaker abruptly ends the communication (ditto).

The most effective form of illustration would be to embed a video into this page, but you will have to use memory and imagination, or just google "Bill Clinton lied about Monica Lewinsky." The intent is not to rehash the incident or to bash William Jefferson, but rather to study this classic and powerful example of lying from January of 1998. Watch for the clues:

> "But I want to say one thing to the American people. I want you to listen to me. I'm going to say this again: I—did—not—have—sexual—relations—with—that—woman, Miss Lewinsky. I never told anybody to lie, not a single time, never. These allegations are false, and I need to go back to work for the American people." (He then stands up and leaves the press conference.)

Here is it again, cued to our list of verbal clues:

> "I want you to listen to me (4). I'm going to say this again (12): I—did—not (5)—have—sexual—relations—with—that (8)—woman (11, 12), Miss Lewinsky. I never told anybody to lie, not a single time, never (4, 12). These

allegations are false (4), and I need to go back to work for the American people (13)."

* * *

The Pulitzer Prize-winning fact-checking project, PolitiFact, bestowed on Donald Trump its infamous "Liar of the Year" award for 2015. The fact-checkers determined that 76% of his official statements fell into one of the categories: *Mostly False, False*, or *Pants on Fire*. In June of 2016, PolitiFact revealed that only 23% of his claims made during the first half of the campaign year were *True, Mostly True* or *Half-True;* 58% were *False* or *Mostly False;* and a whopping 18% were *Pants on Fire!*

According to PolitiFact, Hillary Clinton's pants went up in flames seven times during the campaign due to false claims, while Donald Trump's sartorial conflagrations reached 70. PolitiFact continues its scrutiny and, along with the Washington Post and other respected sources, will publish its statistical analysis of untruths during Mr. Trump's presidential years and beyond.

Maybe you'll agree that most people are well intentioned and basically honest, but it can be useful to know what to listen for when we suspect that someone might be lying. I was overly optimistic in wagering that the University of Massachusetts researchers' finding of 200 lies per day would decrease dramatically in a non-election year. Truth is not an absolute, but in an era of "fake news" and blatant lies, how will it fare as a societal and cultural value?

* * *

Confession #2: Susie Janssen, age six, repeatedly and righteously asserted that it was not she who stuck a bobby pin in the bathroom wall socket of the big house on V Street. She experienced "pants on fire" (and her parents thanked heaven it was not "house on fire") for a good 24 hours after that spanking, and actually had something worth confessing to the priest before Sunday Mass.

How Are You Fixed for Time and Money?

I got to thinking about how we take for absolute truth values that are unique to our culture, going so far as to assume all people on Earth believe, think, and react as we do in regard to the essential aspects of their lives. "Culture" can be defined in simple terms as "everything people learn to think and do from those who raise them and the environment they live in."

The iceberg analogy is a wonderful and very illustrative model that helps us think more clearly about culture. The part of the iceberg we can see above water is massively obvious and identifiable, but that's only a fraction of the whole. What's below the visible surface is huge, and hard to detect or anticipate. The protruding iceberg of culture includes things like foods, music, traditional dress, and holiday customs. Below the surface lurk deep familial and social conditioning such as gender roles, attitudes toward social status and the treatment of women, romance and relationships, religion and spirituality, and basically everything that is so ingrained that we might say, "That's just the way it is."

Let's consider cultural conditioning around time and money, since most of us perceive these as dominant, if not controlling, factors in our lives. Our attitudes about time and money are deeply and subconsciously ingrained into our thoughts, feelings, language, and actions. This conditioning is created and reinforced from birth to death by parents, teachers, government, film and television, advertising, and the lyrics of popular songs. Our basic cultural assumption about them is that there is never enough of either.

To one degree or another, we all struggle throughout life with issues of time and money, continually trying to do exactly what Einstein told us is, at best, utterly impossible and, at worst, the road to insanity: We cannot solve a problem with the same thinking that created it in the first place, because this leads us to do the same thing over and over again while expecting different results. We strive to create abundance from a deep sense of scarcity, and from that launching pad the rocket always goes down in flames.

This scarcity of time and money is a slippery slope, almost like a love-hate relationship. Our perception of time is a cultural value, not an absolute. We actually promote, admire, and highly prize the scarcity of time in others, yet we spend endless energy trying to find more time for ourselves, all the while boosting our personal sense of worth by staying busy and advertising how we haven't even time to take a breath. In America, we equate being busy and having no time with being important and even *worthy*. Those whose overstuffed calendars do not allow for one moment of time to themselves are thought of as successful and valuable; hence the saying, "If you want something done, ask a busy person." On the other hand, we may cast a suspicious eye or be prone to a negative value judgment toward the person who saunters the office halls with a relaxed gait and stops for casual conversation, even if he always does get the job done.

We are totally accepting and sympathetic, even admiring, when acquaintances comment about the scarcity of money, be it their personal funds, an aging parent's bank account, or government spending. However, when a colleague said in a faculty meeting, "I don't really need this raise because I feel I have enough money," eyebrows shot up, emails started flying, and her sanity came into question. If you have bought into and live by the law of scarcity, we totally get you and resonate with your dilemmas. However, if you are floating on some cloud of temporal or fiscal abundance, you are suspect, and we might wonder what you're sprinkling on your breakfast cereal.

Let's look at the language we commonly employ to speak about our two favorite purgatories, time and money. What about the verbs we use in relation to money? We earn, make, spend, save, and hoard money. We lose it, but rarely find it. We bleed money, but far less often transfuse it.

When it comes to time, the terms take a turn toward the violent. Yes, we can spend it, borrow it, and save it, but too often time runs out, or is against us. It flies by, but only stands still for an emotionally overwhelming moment. We buy it, waste it, steal it, cheat it, and kill it. We long to save time in a bottle, but it is always running through our hands. We can feel in our viscera how Ben Franklin's claim, "Nothing is certain but death and taxes," plays on our fear of having the time and money we so long to control snatched from our grasp by an invisible hand of fate.

It's said that we get exactly as much in life as we think we deserve. It is also said that whatever we focus our attention on, we get more of. Our attention might be totally glued on money because there's not enough coming in. Does that mean we'll get more of it? Not until we stop fighting what is, and practice shifting our cultural default from scarcity to abundance—from "There's not enough, and I'm running out" all the way to "There's an unlimited supply, and I am able to tap into it."

It's true we lead busy lives in the 21st century, especially with all of our "time-saving" devices. Time, however, is not an absolute. That's why it is known to both "drag" and "fly." What might happen if we were to befriend time and invite it over to our side? What if we started each day *knowing* there is ample time for work, rest, and play? This will definitely take some practice and cultural retooling, but it could result in getting more of what we *say* we really want and need.

This could be taken by some as impossibility, or as cultural heresy. It's a provocative conundrum to live in a culture that simultaneously admires and decries an insufficiency of time and money. Choice is always an option; we can step outside of considerations of fate, one's lot in life, who does and doesn't get a hit of g.l.a.d. (good luck angel dust), and "that's just the way it is," to actively cultivate a consciousness of abundance. Culture is created, and so are the abundance and the scarcity of time and money.

CHAPTER TWO

Whence These Words?

The Herd Mentality

Why just a "flock" of flamingoes when you can visually create a "flamboyance" of them? Why say "herd" when you can describe what's coming at you as a "crash of rhinos" (with a "tower of giraffes" in the background)? *Terms of venery*—their origin is captivating and, as you will see, the possibilities for continued creation are endless.

Shakespeare: The Legacy in His Lines, Part I

The Bard forever changed the English language with creative word mash-ups, and what would become proverbs and expressions that seem to have been with us for all time.

Shakespeare: The Legacy in His Lines, Part II

Here we take a look at Shakespearean idioms and insults as we attempt to convey and grasp his legacy and genius. There's a delightful surprise at the end that I think the Bard himself would have endorsed.

On the Trail of Word Origins, Part I

Words feel richer on the tongue and to the ear when we know their origins. Here we look into the etymology of words derived from place names (denim, jeans, dollar), people's names (derrick, raglan, tantalize), and some very violent and bloody acts (assassin, berserk, amok).

On the Trail of Word Origins, Part II

More etymology—this time of innocent words gone bad *(idiot);* words so close to, yet unrecognizable from, their foreign source *(alligator);* words that are delightfully much more than meets the eye *(muscle);* and words we forget are really acronyms *(snafu).*

On the Trail of Word Origins, Part III

This final section on the endless subject of etymology scoops up words born from misconception *(lunatic, hysteria),* and words that are exactly what they say they are but with great stories to tell *(toady, infantry, whipping-boy, white elephant).*

The Familiarity of Foreign

English is a sponge for foreign words, and the circumstance of their acquisition is the stuff of history and comedy. Here you'll discover a sampling of words that were lifted from other languages, but are now so easy on the American tongue and ear.

The Scholar's Ink and the Martyr's Blood

We barely acknowledge the Arabic influence on the English language, but it is significant and enriching when we understand and can identify it. Hint: there is one simple characteristic that tips us off to a large percentage of the Arabic words in English. Revealed herein!

The Herd Mentality

It was a sleepless night. In addition to the spotlight of a full moon shining through my bedroom window, I was subjected to the successive and sometimes simultaneous operas of a *kennel of dogs,* a *clowder of cats,* and a *chorus of frogs.* Sunrise came, and with it the cacophony of a *scold of jays.* I looked out the window and was horrified to witness a *murder of crows* in my own backyard! Well, there goes the neighborhood. Even the *exaltation of larks* that followed couldn't lift my spirits. What's next—a *plague of locusts?*

If there's a group of something, we might casually call it a *lot,* a *bunch,* a *pile,* a *mess,* a *crowd,* a *hoard,* or a *ton.* When it comes to animals, if they have hooves, we'll probably call them a *herd,* and if they have wings, a *flock.* Ah, but this is English, so it can never be that simple—or, thankfully, that boring. If a collection of graceful white water fowl shows up in my yard, I could shout to the neighbors to come see the *bank, team, bevy, ballet,* or—my favorite—*lamentation of swans.*

I would bet my bank account that no other language on Earth offers so many different and specific words for groups of animals. There's drama in an *ambush of tigers,* poetry in a *bouquet of pheasants,* rhapsody in a *flamboyance of flamingoes,* hilarity in a *lounge of lizards,* rhythm in a *rhumba of rattlesnakes,* and endless possibilities for political commentary in a *congress of baboons.* When you come back from your photo safari in Africa, your mesmerized friends will clamor for yet another thousand or so photos of a *tower of giraffes,* an *implausibility of gnus,* a *bloat of hippos,* a *zeal of zebras,* a *crash of rhinos,* a *memory of elephants,* a *cartload of chimps,* a *congregation of crocodiles,* a *pride of lions,* and a *leap of leopards.*

There's something menacing about a *descent of woodpeckers*, a *sneak of weasels,* and a *shiver of sharks,* yet I'm strangely comforted at the prospect of encountering a *parliament of owls,* a *coterie of prairie dogs,* or a *gaze of raccoons* on future nature walks. These colorful collective nouns for animals are called *terms of venery,* and they originated with the gentleman's sport of hunting in England and France in the 15th, 16th, and 17th centuries.

Many of these terms were recorded in the *Book of Saint Albans,* published in 1486 to itemize and describe the topics and interests a gentleman of that era might allow to occupy his time. There are articles on hawking, hunting, heraldry, and fishing ("angling"). Interestingly, authorship is attributed—though perhaps only the sections on hawking and hunting—to the Benedictine prioress (Mother Superior) of the Priory of St. Mary of Sopwell, near St. Albans in Hertfordshire, where the St. Albans Press—only the third printing press in England—was established in 1479. Wealthy lords entertained and competed with each other, inventing creative and descriptive collective terms for animals such as a *clutch of chickens* and a *school of fish,* which then became accepted terms of venery.

What about collective nouns for groups of people? A *bevy of girls* followed by a *gaggle of onlookers* sounds pretty commonplace. Terms for lawyers in the collective might depend on the recent experience of the client, but the official ones are: an *argument,* a *disputation,* an *eloquence,* an *escheat,* a *greed,* a *huddle,* or a *quarrel.* Doctors clump together as a *dose,* a *doctrine,* a *scope,* or a *field*. In addition to the predictable *cast of actors, den of thieves,* and *team of athletes,* modern terms include the following collective nouns for people: a *tabernacle of bakers,* a *babble of barbers,* a *promise of barmen,* a *shuffling of bureaucrats,* a *goring of butchers,* a *sneer of butlers,* a *shrivel of critics,* a *conjunction of grammarians,* a *herd of harlots,* an *illusion of magicians,* an *unction of undertakers,* and an *ambush of widows.* (I set aside considerations of political correctness for another day.)

One clever contributor to my newspaper column proposed a *mandible of dentists,* and I'll toss off a few inventions of my own: a *couch of psychiatrists,* a *toil of teachers,* and a *wrench of plumbers.* Other readers offered: a *combo of safecrackers,* a *magnificence of models,* a *sash of seamstresses,* a *brace of orthopedists;* and, returning to the four-legged subjects: a *racket of raccoons,* a *dollop of Dalmatians,* and a *mixed bag of labradoodles.*

In closing, I give you my best wishes with a warning attached: I hope you soar with a *convocation of eagles,* and find delight in a *charm of hummingbirds*—but be wary when approaching a *business of ferrets,* and stay on the safe side when crossing paths with a *wake of buzzards* or a *prickle of hedgehogs.*

Shakespeare: The Legacy in His Lines, Part I

Having recently celebrated the 400th anniversary of the death of William Shakespeare (1564–1616), it seems most fitting and fun to celebrate how English has been deeply enriched and forever changed by the way the Bard of Avon invented, combined, and repurposed words in wholly new and unique ways. Let us begin not with biographical detail but with a look at how many words are in the average verbal domain, beginning with our own.

Our "receptive vocabulary"—all the words we recognize—falls somewhere in the vicinity of 12,000 to 27,000 words. Yours is on the high side, I'd wager, because the fact that you're reading this book suggests you have an affinity for words. Our "productive vocabulary"—the words we actually use in speech and writing—comprises a smaller number, hugely variable due to age and reading habits. Homer used a total of 9,000 different words in the *Iliad* and the *Odyssey.* That may seem rather paltry, but we must cut him some slack; without Facebook, global warming, the *Huffington Post,* and the millions of distractions that drag our attention hither and yon from moment to moment, life in the late eighth century BC may have required fewer terms than it does today. Furthermore, maybe a lot of the colloquial, everyday words Homer knew and used in the bathroom, the bedroom, or the kitchen didn't find their way into his ancient classic writings that have survived and thrived as the oldest known works in Western literature.*

* Despite the recent surge in popularity of the Odyssey, do not name your child or your dog "Odysseus," as that means trouble—literally so in ancient Greek.

We could also bat about stats on the productive literary vocabulary of John Milton (in *Paradise Lost* and dozens of works of poetry and prose), Miguel de Cervantes (in *Don Quixote* (Spanish: *Don Quijote*) and thousands more pages of poetry, novels, and short stories), and Sidney Sheldon (in 18 novels, *The Patty Duke Show,* and *I Dream of Jeannie),* but no one holds a candle to the Bard. The number of different words counted in the totality of William Shakespeare's work is over 30,000, and statistical estimates as to Shakespeare's total productive vocabulary go as high as 60,000 words. Again, those are the words he employed to create literature, not necessarily the ones he might have used to trade gibes at the pub or scare up dinner in the kitchen.[†]

We will not attempt to do the Bard literary justice in a few paragraphs, but rather to set a simple stage and populate it with words, idioms, and adages from his plays to illustrate the vast expressive impact his works have had on modern English. Shakespeare inducted over 2,000 words into the language that had never before been seen in print. He did not invent most of these from whole cloth, but rather by tweaking existing words into another part of speech; for example, from the noun "swagger" he launched the verb "to swagger"; and from the verb "to manage" he is credited with coining the noun "manager."

He liberally attached the prefixes "un-/in-/dis-" to existing words to create theretofore unheard-of opposites: unclog, undress, uncomfortable, uneducated, unreal, inaudible, indistinguishable, inauspicious, dishearten, and dislocate. He was also a wordsmith

† I finished graduate school with an ample literary vocabulary in Spanish, and could hold my own in a discussion about Don Quixote or the poetry of Pablo Neruda—but I was a babe in the woods and completely out of my lexical element when it came to the kitchen (I'd never even heard the word for "frying pan") or the bathroom ("flush the toilet" wasn't in textbooks), and as for the bedroom—well, we won't go there.

with suffixes like "–able/-ful/-less," as in "fashionable/eventful/dauntless/remorseless." Perhaps his most *zany* (another of his words) inventions are the many compounds in which he married two or even three simple words into a whole new concept. To name just a few: bold-faced, hot-/cold-blooded, fainthearted, lackluster, newfangled, fancy-free, bedroom, eyeball, eyesore, fortune-teller, laughingstock, birthplace, moonbeam, puppy-dog, shooting star, star-crossed lovers, madcap, outbreak, full circle, primrose path, and wild goose chase.

The popular proverbs and expressions that come to us from Shakespeare's plays are legion. A few years back, I watched a local production of *Hamlet*, and this is just a sampling of what I heard from the stage: "Neither a borrower nor a lender be"; "To thine own self be true"; "Though this be madness, yet there is method in't"; "The lady doth protest too much, methinks"; "A little more than kin, and less than kind"; "Brevity is the soul of wit"; "Conscience does make cowards of us all." In the most famous soliloquy of all time, there is much to recognize and perhaps resonate with in Hamlet's heartache and existential crisis. Here are the first 13 of his 35 agonized lines:

> To be, or not to be—that is the question:
> Whether 'tis nobler in the mind to suffer
> The slings and arrows of outrageous fortune
> Or to take arms against a sea of troubles
> And by opposing end them—to die, to sleep
> No more—and by a sleep to say we end
> The heartache, and the thousand natural shocks
> That flesh is heir to? 'Tis a consummation
> Devoutly to be wished. To die, to sleep—
> To sleep, perchance to dream—ay, there's the rub,

For in that sleep of death what dreams may come,
When we have shuffled off this mortal coil,
Must give us pause.

Alas! Parting is such sweet sorrow, but let us do take a pause to shake off that dire contemplation and meet again at the turn of a page, whence we will continue the staging on a lighter note with Shakespearean proverbs and expressions in popular use today—along with a few insults thrown in for good measure.

Shakespeare: The Legacy in His Lines, Part II

"Knock, knock."

"Who's there?"

It's the Bard, once again. Yes, that entrance to silly jokes is attributed to Shakespeare in *Macbeth.* Sayings, oft repeated, can become proverbs, but though they express widely held truths, someone has to be the first to tack together that particular sequence of words. The King James Bible ("in the twinkling of an eye," "the writing on the wall") and William Shakespeare are the two most prolific sources of English expressions and proverbs.

Part I of this 400th anniversary celebration of the Bard of Avon ended with some of the many proverbs that came to us from *Hamlet* ("Neither a borrower nor a lender be"), and with a cliff-hanger as the tortured protagonist asks himself whether he should continue "to suffer the slings and arrows of outrageous fortune" or to end his life with a "bare bodkin" (sharp dagger). We all know the tragic outcome of that existential debate.

From Shakespeare's numerous other plays come a trove of adages: "The truth will out"; "What's done is done"; "The better part of valor is discretion"; "A rose by any other name would smell as sweet"; "Parting is such sweet sorrow"; "The world's my oyster"; and "All that glitters is not gold." A couple of my favorites aren't as widely known yet, but I present them here as candidates for your adoption: from *The Comedy of Errors,* "There's many a man has more hair than wit"; and from *The Twelfth Night*, "Many a good hanging prevents a bad marriage."

Many Shakespearean idioms seem as if they've been with us forever, rather than a mere 400 years: "in my mind's eye"; "as luck would have it"; "to break the ice"; "be-all and end-all"; "forever and a day"; "in my heart of hearts"; "in a pickle"; "brave new world"; "dead as a doornail"; "seen better days"; "eaten me out of house and home"; "Greek to me"; "kill with kindness"; "into thin air"; "neither rhyme nor reason"; "one fell swoop"; "play fast and loose"; "pomp and circumstance"; "set my teeth on edge"; "make short shrift"; "wear my heart upon my sleeve"—and countless others. It's a thrill to recognize and to experience this exquisite bond of words and concepts that create a bridge over four centuries between Shakespeare and English speakers of the modern day.

The immensity of this legacy of words, wit, and wisdom is awe-inspiring to the mortal mind, and ever more so as we deepen our investigation. What intelligence! What creativity! What a sense of pathos and humor! What a deep well of understanding and compassion for the human condition! It is incredible that such exalted literary, lexical, and humanistic creation flowed from the soul and into the pen of this 16th-century man of humble origins with no documented educational background. Hence, there have long been "anti-Stratfordian" theories that claim a different author or multiple authors, though most scholars had credited William Shakespeare of Stratford-on-Avon as being the single mind and hand of the entire body of work: 37 plays (comedy, history, and tragedy) and many works of poetry, including 154 sonnets.

Until now, that is. In October 2016, after years of research, the Oxford University Press took center stage in media and academia, announcing that, in the new edition of the complete works of William Shakespeare, Christopher Marlowe would share credit as the co-author of the three *Henry VI* plays. This is an earth-shaking development and, of course, not all scholars agree with the researchers' conclusion. One thing is for sure: controversy and theories will continue to abound, seasoned with scholarship, speculation, scandal, and the obsession to discover the "truth" about William Shakespeare that, despite wondrous technology in the 21st century, can never be completely known.[†]

Returning to Shakespeare's use of words, let us recall that his insults are legion and legendary, a far cry from "Shall I compare thee to a summer's day?" *(Sonnet 18).* Some insults might seem almost courteous in their subtlety: "I do desire we may be better strangers" (*As You Like It*, Act 3, Scene 2); and "Go to Hell for an eternal moment or so" (*The Merry Wives of Windsor,* Act 1, Scene 1).

More often than not, Shakespeare's insults are double-barreled and fully loaded: "Thou art a boil, a plague sore, an embossed carbuncle in my corrupted blood" (*King Lear,* Act 2, Scene 4); and "You bawling, blasphemous, uncharitable dog" (*The Tempest,* Act 1, Scene 1). Withering? Yes, but so pungently creative that if such verbal volleys were fired today, the intended targets might pass several moments in awe of the linguistic acrobatics before they would even think to take offense. If "You lunatic, lean-witted fool" (*Richard II*, Act 2, Scene 1) and the like hold a certain appeal, you can download any number of handy Shakespearean Insult Generators that will guide you to recombine the Bard's own words to your own unique taste and needs.[§]

---

† Editor Mary Buckley's theory about Shakespeare authorship, based partly on her many years in theater—but she's never heard this idea expressed before, amidst various theories about Francis Bacon, etc.—is that "Shakespeare's" plays are most likely the result of William's decades of performing and developing the same repertory of stories with a colorful, creative company of actors who must have been continually adding, subtracting, refining, and improving sections of scripts over many years of testing them out on live audiences—so that even though the scripts all ended up with his name on them, the author we call "Shakespeare" may really just be a collective term for William himself plus a *folio of playwrights!*

§ See References for my own favorite.

Since 1993, the *Washington Post* has held its weekly "Style Invitational," challenging readers' knowledge of politics, history, and current affairs. Most of all, this contest seeks their cleverness in manipulating words to humorous effect. For example, a favorite challenge asks readers to change one letter in a word and give it a new meaning (e.g., "Reintarnation": coming back to life as a hillbilly; "Foreploy": any misrepresentation about yourself for the purpose of obtaining sex; and "Sarchasm": the gulf between the author of sarcastic wit and the person who doesn't get it).

In one *WP* Style Invitational, readers were invited to submit instructions for any activity, written in the style of a famous person. Winner Jeff Brechlin gave to readers the "Hokey-Pokey" as it might have been written by William Shakespeare:

O proud left foot, that ventures quick within,
Then soon upon a backward journey lithe,
Anon, once more the gesture, then begin:
Command sinistral pedestal to writhe.
Commence thou then the fervid Hokey-Poke,
A mad gyration, hips in wanton swirl.
To spin! A wilde release from Heaven's yoke.
Blessed dervish! Surely canst go, girl!
The Hoke, the Poke—banish now thy doubt.
Verily, I say, 'tis what it's all about.

I think, somewhere-on-Avon, the Bard is "shakin' it all about" with a smile.

On the Trail of Word Origins, Part I

My sources tell me that you enjoy delving into word derivations, or *etymologies,* and since this is one of my fondest pursuits, I have been looking forward to sharing some of my favorites in these pages.

Let's start with a few English words derived from the names of places. Aside from Mom and apple pie, is there anything more American than denim jeans, or the dollars it takes to buy them? Let's have a look:

- ***Denim:*** This iconic fabric started out as a coarse cotton originally imported from Nîmes, a city in central France that was a prominent textile manufacturing center before the French Revolution. *De Nîmes,* of course, means "from Nîmes."
- ***Jeans*****:** A similar coarse material was woven in Genoa, an Italian city called *Gênes* in Old French. It is said that this fabric first came to America as the sails on Columbus's ships.
- ***Dollar:*** West of Prague, in what was then Bohemia, there was a rich silver mine near the town of Joachimsthal. In 1519, a large silver coin was minted there called a *Joachimsthaler,* or *thaler* for short. This coin was used as currency in Denmark and Sweden as well as in the German states, and American colonists used the same word to refer to Spanish coins. In the Continental Congress of July 6, 1785, the word "dollar," derived from *thaler,* was adopted as the name of US currency because the term was widely understood and—more importantly—was *not* British.

- ***Siamese*** twins: The first of these twins to be publicly exhibited were born in Siam (now Thailand) in 1814. They eventually moved to the States, married two sisters, and settled down as farmers in North Carolina. Chang and his wife had six children; Eng's wife bore him five. Chang and Eng lived their 60 years of life joined at the waist—a challenge for the imagination.
- ***Canter:*** This describes the easy pace at which pilgrims rode their horses to Canterbury, England in the Middle Ages to pay homage at the shrine of the martyr St. Thomas à Becket.

* * *

Words derived from the name of a person or group of people are constantly added to our vocabulary. Here are some notable ones:

- ***Derrick:*** This comes from the last name of a 17th-century English hangman in the Tyburn gallows of London. Since his job was to execute people by hauling them up by means of a rope on a stationary arm, a crane came to be known as a *derrick.*
- ***Clerk:*** In the Middle Ages, when only the clergymen knew how to read and write, any person with this ability was assumed to be a cleric, shortened to *clerk,* a title extended to anyone who performed these literate duties.
- ***Boycott:*** Captain Charles C. Boycott demanded unreasonably high rent from his tenants in 19th-century Ireland, who finally revolted and refused to pay. His neighbors shunned him, his own servants deserted him, and no one would sell him food. The Irish Land League Organization adopted similar disciplinary measures for

other unscrupulous land agents, along with the phrase "Let's boycott him," meaning, "Let's give him what Mr. Boycott deservedly got."

- ***Hocus-pocus:*** This is a good example of a word whose origin is uncertain. It's possibly a variation on the name of a wizard in Scandinavian mythology, *Ochus Bochus.* However, some sources provocatively claim it's a corruption of the Latin *Hoc est corpus,* the phrase said in the Catholic Mass at the moment the bread becomes the body of Christ. Scholars of etymology love to argue this stuff.
- ***Raglan:*** This is a type of sleeve that starts at the collar, with no shoulder seam. It was a favored style of British Field Marshal Lord Raglan, who lost his right arm in the 1815 defeat of Napoleon at Waterloo. Do you think it ever crossed his mind that losing his arm in battle would affix his name to a style that has lasted two centuries?
- ***Crapper:*** Oh, we do wish this colorful etymological legend were true, but I include it because it's *not.* Yes, there was a London plumber named Thomas Crapper (1837–1910) who may have contributed to the development of the modern toilet (although Arab peoples had been flushing for around 500 years by then). However, his unfortunate name was purely coincidence. In Middle English, *crappe* meant "residue," "rubbish," or grain left on the barn floor that was trodden underfoot. As writer and word master Willard Espy concludes: "Though 'to crap' may have antedated Mr. Crapper, he undoubtedly nailed the word to the mast," or, I might humbly offer, to the outhouse door.
- ***Tantalize:*** As punishment for offering humans the food and drink of the gods from Mt. Olympus, Tantalus, son of Zeus, was condemned to spend eternity in the nether

world, standing in water up to his chin. The water receded when he tried to drink it, and the clusters of grapes hanging over his head remained forever out of his reach. In the world of mythology, there are seldom second chances. It seems the human foibles committed by gods, goddesses, and their offspring receive the harshest, swiftest, and most irrevocable punishment.

- ***Mosey:*** Whenever the dictionary says "origin uncertain," it's likely there will be something fun to dig for. *Vamoose* was early cowboy slang in the 19th century, corrupted from the Spanish *vamos* ("let's go"). One of my favorite etymology sources, Professor Emeritus Jordan Almond, suggests that "mosey" in turn derives from "vamoose," but I opt for Willard Espy's theory. He maintains that Jewish vendors in olden days were so weighted by their wares that they made slow progress along the road. Many were named "Moses"—or called that by non-Jewish observers—leading to his conclusion.

* * *

This next category of derivations I call "Not a Pretty Sight," and you shall see why:

- ***Amok/amuck:*** The phrase "to run amok," first noted in the 1670s, referred to some people of Malaya who, when under the influence of opium or stimulants, ran wild through the streets attacking unfortunate passersby with daggers while yelling, *"Amoq! Amoq!"* ("Kill! Kill!").
- ***Assassin:*** In another murderous, drug-related etymology, a fanatical Mohammedan sect in eleventh-century Persia (now Iran) murdered Christians during the Crusades

while high on hashish. They were known as *hash-hashin,* "hashish-eaters."

- ***Havoc:*** A word of early Germanic origin, *"Havoc!"* was a signal yelled out by the chief to his invading horde that they were now free to pillage and plunder the village at will. To "wreak havoc" in this day is so very tame by comparison.
- ***Vandal/vandalism:*** The Germanic tribe known as the Vandals sacked Rome in 455 AD. Although this is not historically verified, some accounts claim they gratuitously mutilated works of art and public monuments; hence our modern meaning of careless and intentional destruction.
- ***Amazon:*** The most popular derivation comes from Greek mythology, in reference to a race of female warriors who were so fearlessly dedicated to warfare that they cut or burned off one breast so that it would not interfere with the drawing back of the bowstring in battle: *a* ("without") + *mazo* ("breast").
- ***Berserk:*** A *berserker* was a "warrior clothed in bearskin." These were Norse warriors of superhuman strength and ability who fought like wild animals in battle, foaming at the mouth and attacking with enormous strength and fearless aggression.

Now that we're through with the blood and gore, we'll take a short break from violent images of berserk assassins running amok with the promise of more etymological excitement to come.

On the Trail of Word Origins, Part II

We ended our first foray into word origins on a violent, bloody note with the derivations of the words "assassin," "havoc," "berserk," "vandal," and "Amazon" (not the .com variety). Our next exploration will be gentler but I hope equally riveting.

The words in this first category started out innocently enough, but you'll soon see where they ended up:

- ***Marooned:*** In Spanish, *marron* means dark brown or chestnut-colored. In the 17th century, a (generally dark-skinned) *maron* was a fugitive slave in the jungles of the West Indies. From this, our English verb "maroon" came to mean "to be abandoned on a desolate island or coast."
- ***Fiasco:*** No one disputes that *un fiasco* in Italian is simply a glass flask, but how this word came to mean "a failure or a disastrous outcome" remains a matter of debate. Some say that the famed Venetian glassblowers tossed aside defective art pieces to later be made into simple flasks. Another more colorful theory relies on the Italian expression *fare il fiasco,* meaning "to play a game so that the loser buys the *fiasco,*" that is, pays for the bottle of wine. Imagine what a "fiasco" the cost if you lost three times in a row!
- ***Cheat:*** This word derives from the legal term *escheat* whereby, under English feudal law, if a vassal died without legal heirs, his land would become the property of the lord. This was not looked on as fair play by the deceased vassal's family—hence a shortening of the word into a verb meaning "to swindle or defraud."

- ***Idiot:*** Innocently enough, the Greek word *idiotes* referred to one who did not hold a public office, or who lacked a professional skill. By the 12th century, however, the term referred to "an uneducated or ignorant person," and by the 14th century it meant "one so mentally deficient as to be incapable of ordinary reasoning." That's evolution for you!
- ***Villain:*** Going back again to feudal times, a villain was simply a peasant or servant who worked at a villa (manor house). Etymology wizard Willard Espy suggests that "the notion of wickedness grew out of the assumption on the part of the lord that all servants were knaves."
- ***Alimony:*** From the Latin for "food or nourishment," in the mid-17th century, the word came to mean "allowance to a wife from a husband's estate." As an aside, the variation *palimony (*pal + alimony*)*, meaning "financial support after the termination of a live-in relationship out of wedlock," is said to have been coined by a divorce attorney during an unsuccessful lawsuit in 1977 against movie actor Lee Marvin by his long-term companion, Michelle Triola.

* * *

Here are several fascinating words, so close to their foreign source, and yet . . .

- ***Gargoyle:*** This derives from the Old French *gargouille,* meaning "throat" (hence our verb "gargle"). These fantastical stone figures, most often found on roof corners, were downspouts to channel off rainwater, which then spurted out the mouth of the sculptures. Usually grotesque in appearance, they did double duty by frightening away evil spirits.

- ***Alphabet:*** This is a simple one—a combination of the first two letters of the Greek alphabet, *alpha* and *beta.*
- ***Point-blank:*** To fire a weapon "point-blank" is literally to aim at the white spot in the center of the target. This derives from the French *point* ("aim") and *blanc* ("white"). It has come to mean a way of firing at close range for maximum impact, whether with firearms or words.
- ***Tycoon*****:** From the Japanese *tai* ("great") and *kun* ("lord"), this came to refer to a wealthy and powerful businessman after WWI.
- ***Alligator*****:** This word comes from the Spanish *el lagarto,* "the lizard," but to American ears, it sounded like one word, and was scooped into our language as such.
- ***Arena:*** From Spanish *arena,* this simply means "sand."
- ***Dandelion:*** The French *dent de lion*, "tooth of lion" (describing the pointed leaves of the flower) was anglicized into our dandy word for this edible flower—though maybe not so edible if you have dogs in the yard!

* * *

And now, three words that are delightfully much more than meet the eye:

- ***Inaugurate:*** Every new president and grandiose project is initiated this way, right? Interestingly enough, the Latin verb *inaugurare* means "to take omens from the flight of birds." Before any ancient Roman was installed into office, there was the requisite interpreting of signs and omens by an *augur*, or soothsayer. Do you think our political polls and pundits (from Hindi *pandit*, "a learned man") predict the future of our government and its elected officials with greater accuracy than the reading of tea leaves, animal entrails, or birds in flight?

- ***Muscle:*** The Latin word *musculus* means "little mouse" and gives us our word because the shape and movement of some muscles was thought to resemble a little mouse moving to and fro. Try flexing your biceps in the mirror, and you'll see what the Romans saw.
- ***Pupil:*** This comes from the Latin *pupilla*, "little-girl doll," for the tiny image seen of oneself reflected in another's eyes. As Plato wrote: "Self-knowledge can be obtained only by looking into the mind and virtue of the soul, which is the diviner part of a man, just as we see our own image in another's eye."

* * *

Acronyms are just abbreviations, but some become so common that we forget to wonder when and how they came into everyday use:

- ***GI:*** The U.S. Army stamped "GI" on all goods, supplies, uniforms, and so on that were used by soldiers, to identify these as "Government Issue." With this ubiquitous monogram on every cap and canteen, it's no wonder the enlistees themselves soon became known as GIs.
- ***Jeep:*** In the early 1940s, this was American military slang for the sturdy car that had "GP" painted on the side to identify it as a "General Purpose" vehicle.
- ***OK:*** This comes off as downright silly, but here goes: In Boston and New York of the late 1830s, it was all the rage to misspell and abbreviate colloquial sayings, for example: *K.Y.* for "know yuse" (no use) and *N.C.* for "nuff ced." *Oll*

> *Korrect*, the humorous form of "all correct," was shortened to "OK" during the re-election campaign of President Van Buren (1840) who was nicknamed "Old Kinderhook" after his place of birth. "OK" captured imaginations and tongues across the nation and, thankfully, is the only survivor of this fad.

Here's a research assignment for you lovers of the lexicon and enthusiasts of etymological trivia:

> Your mission, should you choose to accept, is to investigate how and when the term "snafu" came to be. You may have heard this one before and thought it was a joke—but no, it's the real deal, and if I printed it this section might self-destruct. Have fun with that!

On the Trail of Word Origins, Part III

How rich the flavor of a word on our tongue when it evokes not only meaning but something of its birthing and history!

We begin with two interesting words, born mostly from misconception:

- ***Lunatic:*** The other night, with the full moon shining in my east window, I was feeling a little crazy under the spell of *la luna.* Ancient Romans blamed madness on the moon, and "lunacy" is sometimes still attributed to lunar cycles.¶
- ***Hysteria:*** From Latin *(hystericus)* and Greek *(husterikós)* words meaning "of the womb," this was believed to be a women's neurotic condition induced by uterine dysfunction. There you have it, dear female readers. It's etymology, and we're stuck with it!

* * *

This next group has origins that are quite literal, but not totally obvious. The first few are deeply medieval, so don't be surprised if you hear echoes of the clanging chaos of battle and smell the smoke from fireplaces in great stone halls.

- ***Freelance:*** Coined by Sir Walter Scott in his historical novel *Ivanhoe* (1820), this refers to a medieval mercenary soldier without loyalty to any particular leader or

¶ The Italian *lunatico* and the French *lunatique* both mean "moody."

kingdom. He and his "free lance" were hired to fight wherever needed.

- ***Infantry:*** While not referencing "infants" as we know the word in modern English, this part of the army was made up of the knights' page boys, the youths who assisted the master and were in training to become knights themselves—if they survived battles in the front lines.
- ***Mantelpiece:*** A ledge over the fireplace, this was originally where you hung your *mantel* or loose, sleeveless cloak to dry, ready to return to your shoulders the next morning—perhaps singed and smoky, but totally serviceable. In modern English, the spelling for that cloak has changed just slightly to *mantle.*
- ***Whipping-boy:*** The king's son, being of royal blood, was exempt from whippings, so it was the custom to keep handy in the court another boy (of lower status, of course) who could take the punishment in the naughty prince's stead. I would have begged, borrowed, stolen, and thrown in my dollar-a-week allowance to have had such a one in the wings of my childhood home and on the (ouch!) receiving end of the spanking stick.
- ***Toady:*** This word denotes a "sponger" or a "flatterer." Originally, in the mid-1700s, a magician's assistant had the unfortunate but obligatory job of eating the toad during the show—since toads were considered poisonous, the master used the spectacle to demonstrate his magical healing powers and "save" the young man from certain death.
- ***Tumbler:*** From the mid-1600s, a drinking glass with a pointed or curved base would literally tumble over if you tried to set it down before you drained the brew. Bottoms up!

- ***Trump:*** In card games, this is a variation of *triumph.* Another more common use of the word (as in "trumped-up" charges) derives from the Old French *trompe,* meaning "to deceive" or "to mock," and is tied to the musical instrument "trumpet," alluding to charlatans who blew a horn to attract a village audience, only to cheat them into buying some worthless product. As for American politics, I leave it to you, my reader, to choose the derivation.
- ***Windfall:*** In the mid-1500s, when all timber was reserved for the exclusive use of the English Royal Navy, land dwellers were only allowed to take the trees that were blown down by wind. With this unexpected stroke of good luck, Mother Nature provided them with building materials plus warm hands and a fire to cook by.
- ***Scapegoat:*** This means "one who is blamed for the mistakes or sins of others." According to the Book of Leviticus in the Old Testament (English translation from Hebrew), during the celebration of the Day of Atonement, the sins of the people were ceremonially transferred onto a goat, which was cast—or made to *escape*—into the wilderness, thus releasing the sinners from their guilt and God's punishment, leaving them spiritually spruced up and with a clean slate ready to sully with sin once again.
- ***White elephant:*** The story goes that the King of Siam devised the strategy of presenting his enemies with the gift of an albino elephant. Since the animal was sacred, it could not be put to work, and because its upkeep was an enormous expense, the enemy of said king would go bankrupt from its care and feeding. It was and still is the ultimate in passive-aggressive gift-giving!
- ***Earmark:*** English farmers cut a notch in the ear of their

cattle and sheep as an identifying mark—a practice also inflicted on some criminals. As an aside, during recent disastrous wildfires in Norther California, I heard of horse owners marking their animals' hooves with a permanent marker to identify them in case they became displaced—an effective low-tech method, faster and more humane than notching or branding.

- ***Undertaker:*** Previously called a "grave-digger" (now simply a "mortician" who does not actually dig the graves), "undertaker" was a euphemism for one who undertook the onerous (but profitable) task of preparing and burying corpses. One of my most colorfully memorable times during travels in Ecuador was hanging out with a ragged but cheerful crew of grave-diggers on the early morning shift in a rural cemetery who were passing around the bottle while waiting for the cadaver to arrive. As we chatted, they passed me the bottle, and of course I took a gulp because they were kindly offering to share what little they had, and refusal would have been insulting. With *aguardiente* (firewater) that raw, one needn't worry about exposure to germs!
- ***Alarm:*** This came into English from Old Italian *all'arme!*—"To arms!" Now, of course, it's a warning of impending trouble—or a call to hit the snooze button on the bedside clock.
- ***Minutes*** (of a meeting): Rather than from the minutes of the hour, this term derives from the adjective *minute* ("tiny") because, before shorthand was invented, notes were taken in small handwriting to save ink and parchment.
- ***Companion:*** From the Latin *com-* ("together") and *panis* ("bread"), a companion is one you share bread with. Here

in the wine country of Northern California, I'm lucky to have wonderful companions and *comvinions*** with whom to break bread and enjoy a glass of great local wine.

- ***Quarantine:*** This comes from the Italian *quaranta,* meaning "40." In the 1500s, the word developed because a widow was allowed to remain in her husband's house for 40 days after his death. In the 1600s, a ship was held out of port for 40 days if it was suspected that the vessel or its crew might be carrying a contagious disease. This use of the number was meant quite literally, but its use by the ancient Jews and in the Bible simply meant "a really long time." For example, when it's recorded in the New Testament that Jesus fasted in the desert for 40 days and 40 nights, the number is a metaphor for a long, difficult task over time.
- ***Real estate:*** Here we must take the Spanish meaning of *real*—"royal," as in *El Camino Real* (The Royal Road/The King's Highway/Highway 101) that connects California's 21 missions from Misión San Diego de Alcalá in the South to Misión San Francisco de Solano in Sonoma County. A *royal estate* was a land grant, and since all land belonged to the Spanish king, being rewarded by him with a small patch of dirt (or the entire valley of Oaxaca, México, as was granted to Hernán Cortés after he overthrew the Aztec Empire in 1521) was the only way to become a legal landowner. Of course, the concept of "owning" land was a European import to the "New" World. Native peoples, though often territorial, could not grasp it fast enough to

---

** Every linguist has the right and perhaps the obligation to coin at least one new word a year, similar to a botanist looking for an undiscovered plant, or a biologist in search of a new bacteria.

gain a clue as to what the planting of the banner in the sand and the accompanying proclamation, "I claim all of this for the King of Spain," would mean in their lifetimes—which were not likely to last much longer after that momentous pronouncement—as well as for all time.

* * *

I haven't yet run out of fascinating word origins, nor do I expect I ever will. I accumulate new ones every day, and I love to share them with fellow word-lovers. For now, I shall save them for another volume as we move to other topics in this bountiful smorgasbord of words.

The Familiarity of Foreign

We Americans are endlessly creative with the pronunciation, spelling, and usage of words from other languages. Whether on our own soil or another land, we hear some foreign word or expression that serves the moment well, so we mimic the sounds—guttering up the vowels from the back of our throats and twirling the consonants around our American tongues. Then, faster than you can say *voilà* or *chop-chop,* it becomes firmly planted, if not yet in the dictionary, at least into the lexicon of popular usage.

All languages tend to absorb the foreign words they're exposed to, but English (the American variety in particular) seems to vacuum them up from all corners of the world, even though the language is already over a million words strong. In the acquisition process, pronunciation is radically Americanized, and often spelling as well.

Picture American soldiers in France during World War II hearing the locals bid each other a breezy, or perhaps hopeful, "See you soon," spelled à tout à l'*heure* and sounding to the Americans like *"too-tah-lure."* The GIs got the general gist of the phrase, and at some pregnant moment of linguistic critical mass, one of them cut loose with his own attempt to let the *mademoiselle* know he might drop by the *patisserie* again a bit later. The new word spread throughout the battalion and beyond, and in no time everyone back stateside was calling out "Toodle-oo!" as they drove off in their Ford Deluxe Tudor sedans. If they were really in a hurry, "Toodles!" would suffice.

If French speakers want to call for help, they say *"M'aidez!"*

("Aid me!"). In 1924, the senior radio officer at the airport in London needed to come up with a word that could be easily recalled and widely understood in an emergency. Since most of the air traffic was between London and Paris, he chose *m'aidez* but wisely simplified the spelling while retaining the basic pronunciation. Thus, English acquired our "mayday" as an international radio-code distress signal.

Now, let's return to the WWII era, this time in England, and listen in on another conversation. Dodging Nazi fire, the Allied soldiers consoled themselves by talking about a favorite subject that happily used the same word in both American and British English. However, something just sounded odd with the Americans talking about "girls" and the English going on about the same subject but calling them *gehls*—roughly halfway between "gales" and "gulls." "Gal" had been used in some parts of Britain since the late 18th century as slang for "girl," and had already made its way into American English. The song "(the bells are ringing) For Me and My Gal" was written in 1917, but a Hollywood movie of the same name came out in 1942 starring Judy Garland and Gene Kelly, leaving no doubt that "gals" was as firmly established in Americana as hotdogs and apple pie.

You'd have to be from another era to express your consternation, disagreement, or ridicule by saying, "That's just balderdash/ rubbish/claptrap/blather/poppycock!" In the 21st century, these terms sound so quaint! These days, you might still call it "garbage," but in casual speech, many would say, "That's bullshit/BS/bull/a crock," all referring to excrement—its source, the container, or the stuff itself. Of those erstwhile terms, the cutest-sounding is "poppycock." Given my 50% Dutch heritage, I think I'll adopt that one because it combines my father's native tongue and the same substance, preferred in today's disparaging remark but somehow less brown and stinky-sounding. It's the Dutch word *pappekak*—*pappe* ("soft food") + *kak* ("dung") = soft (edible?) shit. Being aware of that derivation does detract from its seeming innocence, but only you will know the depth of your disgust at your neighbor's explanation of those tire tracks on your front lawn when you adjust your monocle and firmly announce, "That's poppycock!"††

In the spring, we clean up the patio, fit the canvas umbrella into its concrete doughnut, start making piña coladas, fire up the grill, and invite friends over to dine *al fresco*, an Italian term literally meaning "in the fresh air." In Italy, not just eating and drinking but most of life takes place out of doors, in open air, and *bella figura*, of course! I was brimming with confidence as we approached *un ristorante* just off the Piazza del Campo in Siena. I had mastered a few present-tense verbs and learned some basic vocabulary at the Dante Alighieri language school just up the *strada*.

I mashed up one verb, one noun, and that seductive Italian term from our English repertoire: "C'è una tavola *al fresco?*" The waiter looked wearily amused, as if he'd just been asked if there were a leaning tower in town, or whether the Coliseum was within walking distance. While leading us to a lovely outdoor table, he combined words and mime until I finally understood that it sounded as if I had asked for a table in prison—*al fresco* to Italians is colloquial for to be "in the cooler," that is, "in jail."

Who would have thought? Now I think twice before assuming that a word or phrase must mean the exact same thing just because we've absorbed it, intact or mostly unchanged, into our English language. I don't think I'll be trying out, "Oh, poppycock!" on my Dutch aunties any time soon!

---

†† Perhaps Orville Redenbacher didn't do his homework before naming his caramel corn "Poppycock: clusters of almonds, pecans and popcorn covered in our amazing glaze."

The Scholar's Ink and the Martyr's Blood

There's something different about Spain. It's difficult to pinpoint, but this peninsular country is just *different* than most of the rest of Western Europe. Yes, it's geographically unique, situated on a huge peninsula that juts out and away from the Mediterranean and into the North Atlantic, so close to kissing North Africa that even those 8.9 miles seem to disappear on a clear day, but there's more.

After the fall of the Roman Empire, the rest of Europe endured the chaotic, violent Dark Ages until the 10th century, followed by the turbulent Middle Ages that lasted until the 15th century while, despite the Crusades and local wars, the Iberian Peninsula (Spain and Portugal today) enjoyed the early flowering of philosophy, sciences, literature, education, and the arts.

By the time of his death in 632 AD, the prophet Muhammed had united Arabia into a single Muslim regime. The second massive expansion of the Arab empire from 632 to 661 scooped in everything as far as Central Asia in the east, the Caucasus in the north, and North Africa from Egypt to present-day Tunisia in the west, forming the largest land empire in history up until that point. It is the third Arab campaign, however—the one that took place from 661 to 750—that occasions this lexical investigation, because it is the reason why a few hundred Arabic words have found their way into the English language. The Arabs conquered the Iberian Peninsula in 711 during that expansion and, although the peninsular lords (it was too early in history to call them Spaniards or Portuguese) immediately initiated the *Reconquista*

(Reconquest) to take back their lands, the Arabs were not finally vanquished until 1492.

In that year, King Ferdinand and Queen Isabella (Spanish names: Fernando and Isabel) were already up to their royal earlobes with getting Columbus and his three ships launched for a New World; solidifying the union of the five principal kingdoms of Iberia and their jealous rulers into a single country; and ramping up the infamous Spanish Inquisition targeting Muslims and Jews, with tragic consequences ricocheting into the present day. Nevertheless, they successfully laid relentless siege to the last Moorish kingdom, and Granada fell to the Christians in that unbelievably eventful year.

Before we examine some of the Arabic words found in the English language, I would like to share a few clarifying notes:

- The Arab occupation of the Iberian Peninsula is usually referred to as the Moorish occupation, and the invaders as Moors, because they advanced toward the peninsula from the Moroccan coast. Many were Berber Northwest Africans, however, the bulk of the armies hailed from other parts of Arabia.
- Although the Reconquest consisted of a series of military campaigns in which Christian armies pushed back the Arabs over centuries from the Iberian Peninsula, it is essential to realize that Arabs, Christians, and Jews mostly coexisted peacefully and even intermarried, sharing culture and knowledge over the same pot of stew during those 781 years.
- Ultimately, the Moorish occupation had a profound cultural and scientific influence on all of Western Europe because of advancements in arts and sciences on the Iberian Peninsula.

Most English words that derive from Arabic actually entered via Spanish, and many of those via Mexico, after its colonization by Spain. While English includes some 300 such words, Spanish boasts around 4,000, comprising 8% of the Spanish dictionary and making Arabic its second-largest lexical source after Latin. You will immediately see what these words have in common: albatross (*al-ghattās*: "the diver"); algebra (*al-jabr*: "the restoring of broken parts"—a method of equation-solving that first appeared in a ninth-century book by mathematician Muhammed Ibn Musa al-Khwarizmi); algorithm (from a corruption of al-Khwarizmi's name); and alchemy *(al-kimiya,* "the art of transforming metals").

Hundreds of three- and four-syllable Spanish words begin with *al-*. The peninsular speakers of Celtic, Latin, Hebrew, and so on simply mimicked the Arabic sounds to create new words, unaware that *al-* (meaning "the") was not actually part of the word. Let's analyze multilingually for a moment: saying "the artichoke" or, in Spanish, *la alcachofa* (from Arabic *al-kharshuf)* is like saying "the the-artichoke." This is a common phenomenon when a foreign word is adopted into a language. Witness the creation of our word "alligator" from the Spanish *el lagarto* ("the lizard"), and "lariat" from *la reata* ("the noose").

In that era of Muslim history, learning, and scholarship were revered and promoted, even mandated. Muhammed taught that "the scholar's ink is holier than the martyr's blood," and that "seeking knowledge is required of every Muslim." Under Arab tutelage, mathematics and science flourished on the Iberian Peninsula. From them, English has "zenith," "nadir," and "chemistry." From the Arabic-derived *cipher* comes not only our word "zero" but the actual concept of this digit that originated earlier in the Orient, reached Europe via Moorish Spain, and was to have such tremendous consequences in future science, mathematics, and even philosophy.

English has absorbed many Arabic words for foods, products, animals, and plants: apricot, alfalfa, jasmine, julep *(julāb:* "rosewater"), lemon, orange, lime, spinach, sugar, candy *(qandī:* "sugared"), coffee, syrup, sherbet, safflower, saffron, tamarind, tarragon, tuna, ambergris, alkali, cotton, benzene, borax, gazelle, gerbil, and giraffe—several of which were brought to Sicily from Cairo in the 1400s. For the home and furnishings, we've adopted alcove, adobe, mattress, and sofa. In fashion, we use gauze *(qazz:* "silk"), sequin *(sikki:* "coins"), crimson, and carmine. Here are some words one might easily relate to Arabic culture: henna, hummus, hookah, hashish, harem, lute, mecca, monsoon, mummy, safari, and typhoon. However, with "ghoul/loco/serendipity/Swahili," who would ever guess?

In his excellent article, "What Did the Moors Do for Us?" Nick Snelling describes Córdoba, Spain in the 10th century as "one of the most important cities in the world, rivaling Baghdad and Constantinople. It boasted a population of 500,000 and had street lighting, 50 hospitals (with running water!), 300 public baths, 500 mosques, and 70 libraries. All of this at a time when London had a largely illiterate population of around 20,000 and had forgotten the technical advances of the Romans some 600 years beforehand."

It may be difficult to envision such a flowering of science and humanistic culture from the perspective of this age of ISIS and Boko Haram, but perhaps even such imagining opens a door to greater hope for peace and understanding. May it be so.

CHAPTER THREE

Grammar Grievances, Malaprop Muddles, and Pronunciation Pickles

Inconstant Consonants and Sudden Vowel Movements

If you're not already in awe of those who have learned English as a second language and can use it at least passably well, you might be after reading this. I thank my linguistic stars that English is my native language.

Grammurder in the First Degree

Fun grammar: Is that an oxymoron, like "pretty ugly," "jumbo shrimp," or "act naturally"? You'll be the judge—but even grammar is palatable with a little humor and a light hand.

Grammurder in the Second Degree

There are two possible rewards awaiting the reader of this section. One is the resolution of any remaining doubt about "him and me" vs. "he and I." The other is the revelation of what Sir Francis Drake was really doing out there on the high seas—at least according to a certain seventh-grader.

The Law of Schwa

You know the vowels in English: A, E, I, O, U, and . . . schwa? Yes, it's the most common of all vowel sounds, contributing to challenges for us native speakers, and untold headaches for those trying to learn to spell and pronounce accurately.

The Abdominal Snowman on the Cal-Can Highway

What planet are you on if you "plummet to the top," where Spaniards dance the "flamingo," where our opinions are "diabolically" opposed, and where we all mope around and "commensurate" about this sad state of affairs? Why, the Planet Malaprop, of course!

Into the Prepositional Fray

This piece is dedicated to my Chilean friend Mónica who, for all her enthusiastic diligence in learning American slang, never quite mastered the not-so-subtle differences between *screw up, screw over,* and *screw off.*

Inconstant Consonants and Sudden Vowel Movements

Is it possible to get through primary education without being subjected to a spelling bee? Not in American or British schools! But what if you grew up in Mexico, Munich, or Moscow? There wouldn't be much point in staging a bee in Spanish, German, or Russian because, unlike English, these and most languages are phonetic: they say it as they see it. Thus, if it's a word never encountered before, they hear it and know how to write it with minimal margin for error.

Do you see that little word "it's" in the previous sentence? That's what flunked me out of the first round in my fourth-grade spelling bee. I can still hear the nun's voice as she gave me my word. I can still hear myself thinking, "Oh, three letters—sooo easy!" Sister Mary Spelling Bee then gave me the sample sentence: "The cow rubbed its horns," and I gave back, "i-t-apostrophe-s." Ouch! Just like that I was out of the running, red-faced, and sitting back down at my little wooden desk. It was so belatedly obvious to me! Am I the only one who still mentally slaps my forehead in shame a half-century after the regrettable event?

There are legions of world languages considered harder to learn than English: Greek, Hebrew, Arabic, Russian, Polish, Vietnamese, and Japanese, to name just a few. But I am gratefully certain that I would *not* want to have to learn English as a second language for all the tea in China, or half the kimonos in Japan. Nonetheless, compared to other languages, there are some aspects of our tongue that make it relatively easy to learn, and if you've ever been a foreign language student, you'll appreciate these four:

1. There aren't two ways (formal and informal) of addressing a person. Good old "you" will suffice for anyone—and even for more than one "you," giving rise out of necessity to the charmless "you guys."
2. English verb conjugations are stunningly simple: I honk, you honk, he/she/it honks, we honk, you guys honk, they honk. In past tense, it's even easier: everybody—including I, you, he, she, it, we, y'all, and they—honked. Most verbs just throw "–ed" on the end to create past tense: "opened/cooked/winked/dressed." There are some pesky irregulars including "went/saw/met/brought/lost" and so on; but the –ed is so dominant that those in the learning stage, children in particular, almost always pattern with it: "He hitted me first"; "It goed away"; "They bringed it"; "I losed it."
3. English nouns aren't masculine or feminine, and our adjectives don't have to adjust to what and how many they are describing. The adjectives "long" and "delicious" can apply to a nap as well as, unchanged, a Cuban cigar, a handful of red vines, or Sunday suppers at Grandma's.
4. English has no subjunctive case, except for a few vestiges such as, "If I were you." We won't even go into what "subjunctive" means (or the sound of fingernails scraping on chalkboard when you hear, "If I was you . . ."), but suffice to say that it causes volumes of grief for English-speaking learners of most foreign languages.

There are now more second-language speakers of English in the world than there are native speakers,* and that is cause for awe when we consider these five factors that make our language truly daunting to learn:

1. We use prepositions to change the meaning of a verb, for example, "carry over/carry through/carry forward/carry off/carry on/carry out." My Chilean friend Mónica (see "Into the Prepositional Fray"), never did internalize the difference between "screw off" and "screw over," and continued to screw up her prepositions throughout grad school.
2. Our neat little tricks with contractions: "You're coming, aren't you?"; "They left, didn't they?"; "He couldn't have known"; "It isn't the end." If you listen to the speech of English learners, you'll notice they rarely master this major feature of English—but that doesn't mean they can't get their point across.
3. We have that crazy way of using "do/does/did" to ask and answer questions ("Did you see that?"; "No, I didn't."), when every other language in the world other than Celtic says something more direct along the lines of, "Saw you that?"
4. Our inconsistent pronunciation must feel like a game of roulette to non-native speakers. To illustrate, here are several words containing "-ough." Dictate this sentence to an English learner, and they'll run screaming from the room: "Though I thought it through, the bough I bought and wrought was too rough, and made me cough." Also, let's consider words in which a shift in the stressed syllable changes the meaning (usually from noun

* In his delightful book *The Mother Tongue,* Bill Bryson informs us, "There are more students of English in China than there are people in the United States."

to verb): "PRO-duce/pro-DUCE; AD-dict/ad-DICT; CON-flict/con-FLICT; IN-sult/in-SULT; PRES-ent/pre-SENT; REC-ord/re-CORD; OB-ject/ob-JECT, DI-gest/di-GEST; EN-velope/en-VEL-ope." To further flummox English learners, we have pairs of words that keep the same spelling but add a syllable to the pronunciation of the verb to create an adjective: "blessed/bles-sed"; "supposed/suppos-ed." And take care, in setting up your will, that you ask the chosen one to be your ex-EC-utor, and not your exe-CU-tor.

5. We must cope with some downright impossible spelling. Why is English so hard to spell? Mainly because it's a mash-up of Germanic (Anglo-Saxon) and Latin (Old French). In 1066, when William the Conqueror of Normandy crossed the channel, charged into England, and defeated Anglo-Saxon King Harold, English was already a complex tongue created by Celts, Angles, Saxons, Jutes, Frisians, and Vikings. With the Normans ruling England, Old French was added to the pot, creating an even richer but very inconsistent linguistic stew. Willy tried to be a sporting chap and learn the local Anglo-Saxon-based language, but eventually dismissed it as indecipherable and unpronounceable. Angles and Normans intermarried, of course, but all government and church affairs were conducted in French while English remained the language of the common folk—though increasingly altered by French influence. Modern word pairs illustrate this cultural-linguistic divide, with Latin-based words from Old French usually being less common and sounding more "cultured" than the Germanic: "brotherhood (G)/

fraternity (Fr); weakness (G)/debility (Fr); begin (G)/ commence (Fr); brainy (G)/cerebral (Fr)."

The English alphabet has only 40 sounds, but 500 different ways to spell them. It was George Bernard Shaw who jokingly suggested that "fish" could be spelled "ghoti":

gh = "f" as in "enough"
o = "i" as in "women"
ti = "sh" as in "nation."

Shaw's suggestion is perfectly logical when the language is English, but orthographically it's a nightmare. Imagine trying to learn a language that seduces you with repetitive sounds but crucifies you with indefensible spellings.

Vowels are the worst offenders, and here are a dozen examples to entertain us native speakers and horrify our English-learning friends:

1. I zoom to the flume with my groom to exhume the rheum in the tomb. Va-voom!
2. If it's true Hugh threw the shoe at the yew near the slough with a view of the loo, we'll sue you too!
3. The reign in Spain was on the wane with Elaine, who was so vain, and Jayne, who was insane but sure could feign a brain and entertain in a plain but gainly vein! Arraign the twain!
4. On all this Earth the "surf and turf" grilled by his serf was worth the dearth of girth.
5. The nerd in the herd stirred the curd while he purred and lured a bird he heard say the word "absurd!"
6. I sigh "Hi" to my guide for, aye, it's quite a lie that the guy made me cry from mine eye.

7. Ah! I'm in awe that I saw a flaw in Pa after a pause.
8. The moose signed a truce with a boost from the juice he drank with Zeus and Toulouse.
9. The town crier was a liar who sang in the choir. As a flyer, he went higher but landed in a pyre.
10. It was not for naught I sought and bought the plot.
11. Will Joe know he must go low to throw a faux crow at that beau, his foe, who won't sew or mow?
12. In the end, we ate the bait at eight after a great wait and gained a heinous freight of weight out of hate that the tortures of English spelling will never abate!

By now, I've probably driven even native English-speaking readers around the bend.† En*ou*gh of this st*u*ff!

† In my younger life, I made the mistake of trying to pronounce the following words before I had the benefit of hearing them: *anemone, heinous, halcyon, ubiquitous, massacre, Worcestershire, Yosemite, apocryphal, egregious*, and, more recently, *equanimous.* (Even spellcheck doesn't like that last word.)

Grammurder in the First Degree

When a friend showed me a cartoon that gave me a wonderful belly laugh, I took it as a sign that it was time to write about grammar. Picture this in cartoon style: Very large family dog sniffs at a sheet of binder paper on the floor. He sits down dejectedly and says, "Grammar errors, spelling mistakes . . . no, I cannot eat this homework!" I hope it's not just my decades of teaching that cause me to find that hilarious. Yes, the time has come to explore grammar errors. If you don't think grammar can ever be glamorous[‡] and exciting, just hang in for another paragraph.

Over 80% of Americans regularly make one or more common English errors. "Oh, but not me!" you say. Oops, that was the first mistake, and perhaps it will be the last, but the odds are against English speakers—including you and I. Uh-oh. That was number two. Neither of these errors are considered egregious, and they will go unnoticed by the majority of people—as will the third at the beginning of this very sentence. We'll return to analyze all three in a bit, but first, let's have fun with grammar!

It used to be considered incorrect English to end a sentence with a preposition. We were instructed to say and write, "I don't know about what you are talking" instead of "I don't know what you are talking about" (and if you are under 30, maybe you don't!); "For whom did you buy the chocolates?" and not, "Whom did you buy the chocolates for?" With a sigh of relief, we note that the Grammar Powers-That-Be in America (the GPTBiA: self-coined with tongue-in-cheek because I can't figure out who adjudicates

‡ The word "glamour" evolved from "grammar" because learning was associated with magic and enchantment.

these things) capitulated a while back, and we can now say with impunity, "What did you do that for?"

It's hard to imagine asking your neighbor, who has just cleaned up very large family dog's messes and thrown them into your yard, "For what did you do that?" I'm glad Ernest Hemingway borrowed a phrase from a poem by John Donne and titled his masterpiece *For Whom the Bell Tolls*, but I'm also glad to be relieved of the pedantic pressure to say, "To whom do I need to speak of these charges to my account about which I have no knowledge?" The old preposition rule is famously parodied in the phrase, "This is the type of arrant pedantry up with which I will not put," apocryphally attributed to Winston Churchill.

Thankfully, we are cleared to dangle our prepositions at the end of our sentences, but the GPTBiA hold firm on "who" vs. "whom," to much general dismay across the nation. If it is the subject of a sentence or clause, we should use "who": "I told you *who* is coming to my party." In this sentence, "who" is the subject (the doer) of the verb "is coming." In reference to an object in a sentence, use "whom": "I already told you *whom* I invited." "Whom" here is the object (receiver) of the verb "invited." Hemingway had to write about *For Whom the Bell Tolls* because "whom" is the object of the preposition "for."

Depending on to whom you are applying for a job, misuse "who/whom" and that bell might be tolling for thee. That's unlikely, though, and you needn't worry excessively over who vs. whom unless you are aspiring to teach English at a university, address the United Nations, or become a copy editor. It seems that rather than fretting with confusion over "who" and "whom," most Americans have given up on analyzing the distinction and instead adopted the attitude of "Who/Whom gives a hoot?"—sometimes articulated as a resounding, "Whatever!"

Now let's revisit those three errors from the second paragraph.

1. "Oh, but not me!" should be "Oh, but not I!" because "I" is the subject, as in "I don't make errors." That said, I'm sure the first thing to come into my own mind and out of my mouth will be, "Oh, but not me." I know it's incorrect, but I'll say it for the same reason I don't answer the phone thusly:

   Caller: "Hello, may I speak with Susanna Janssen?"

   SJ *(option 1): (!@#$%! marketing calls!)* "This is she." *(OK, maybe.)*

   SJ *(option 2):* "It is I." *(Never, unless I am acting in a play set in the time before telephones.)*

2. "The odds are against English speakers, including you and I" should be ". . . including you and me." Let's split the pronouns you and I, and try it both ways: "including you" may sound fine, but we would never say, "including I." Unlike the need for "I" as the subject in error #1, now we are dealing with an object and must use "me." If this makes your eyes cross, hang tight, for it will be clarified in just a moment.
3. "Neither of these errors are considered egregious." To say this correctly, we'll have to change "are" to "is." Errors are considered egregious, but "Neither is considered egregious." "Neither" cannot be plural, only singular.

I bet you can hardly wait to check out more grammar errors, so on to some really glaring ones—the kind that make you cringe like the sound of fingernails scraping on a chalkboard. Spot the problems:

1. "I could of went there."
2. "Me and him went with Noah and her."
3. "She came shopping with him and I."
4. "I seen cousins I didn't seen for years." (It hurts my ears as much as it hurts your eyes, but this was uttered by a high-school graduate with a decent GPA, and that's the only reason I'm including it.)
5. "Her and me don't talk no more." (Said by a well-known TV personality during a talk show interview.)
6. "We're hoping you can come with me and him."

The most common errors we hear or read revolve around confusion of subject pronouns (I, she, he, we, they) vs. object pronouns (me, her, him, us, them). (The pronouns "you" and "it" are the same for both, so they don't cause problems.) As a refresher, a pronoun is a word that takes the place of a noun. If the noun is "Mom," the pronoun is "she" or "her," depending on whether "Mom" is a subject (doer of the action: "She [Mom] beats me at Scrabble") or an object (receiver of the action: "I have yet to beat her").

Whew! We'll get to the resolution of #1 through #6 on the next page, and there is even more investigative intrigue to come in "Grammurder in the Second Degree." First, though, it's time to take a short break, and very large family dog has done just that; he still will not eat the homework, and has gone off to do his business in the neighbor's yard again.

Grammurder in the Second Degree

Here we go with more grammurder, and another guaranteed good time. The "First Degree" ended with a cliffhanger: the sound of fingernails scraping down a chalkboard (I know, they've all been replaced by slick whiteboards), and very large family dog standing over a sheet of paper full of grammar errors and spelling *misteaks,* still refusing to eat that homework. We shall now pick up where we left off, fortified with the knowledge that there will most definitely not be a "Third Degree."

Let's go for the resolution of examples 1 through 6 from "Grammurder in the First Degree":

1. "I could of went there." We often hear "could of/should of/would of" instead of "could have/should have/would have"—perhaps influenced by the colloquially wistful "coulda/shoulda/woulda." Then there's "went," which should be "gone." Let's hear it for the correct "I could have gone there."
2. "Me and him went with Noah and her" should be, "He and I went with Noah and her." "He" and "I" are the subjects; "Noah" and "her" are the objects of the preposition "with." Splitting the pronouns and trying them out separately always resolves the doubt: "Him went?" "Me went?" Oops, no: "He went"; "I went."[§]
3. "She came shopping with him and I." "She came shopping

§ It is standard in English to put oneself last in a series. Hence, we say "He and I" rather than "I and he." Interestingly, the same goes for Spanish—but Italian speakers put themselves first: *Io e lui.*

with him and me." Self-explanatory, no? It's sad to say, but if you construct that sentence correctly, many people who pride themselves on "proper" grammar will overcorrect and mistakenly tell you it should be, "She came shopping with he and I." Now you can demonstrate to them that it just isn't so, by splitting the pronouns right before their eyes and ears: ". . . shopping with he? . . . shopping with I? Sorry, smarty."

4. "I seen cousins I didn't seen for years." For the record: "I saw cousins I hadn't seen for years."
5. "Her and me don't talk no more." "Her don't talk?" "Me don't talk?" Of course not. "She and I don't talk anymore." I don't think the GPTBiA will loosen up on double negatives (don't . . . no more), not even in our combined lifetimes.
6. Look at this one carefully and split the pronouns: "We're hoping you can come with him and me." Yes, and bravo! It's correct as is. (I agree that "us" sounds more graceful.)

People often overcompensate because they've been corrected on "me" and "him/her" so often (wrongly, I suspect, much of the time) that they're afraid to use these object pronouns together and sometimes even altogether. In a restaurant, I overheard a young man order for his date, and then his own meal saying: "And for I . . ." An acquaintance said of her longtime friend, "I feel the same way about he." Another said, "I saw John and she at the play." Yet another spoke, "This is between he and I." The speakers were trying to be correct in their choice of pronouns, but were as far off the mark as, "Me and him are going to the park." You might see an eyebrow dart up when you say, "I'm doing this for him and her" or "Mom bought it for me and them," but the proof of correctness is in the pudding of separation, and it will be obvious every time. Pull the two pronouns apart and try them on separately:

- "I'm doing this for *him*" + "I'm doing this for *her*" = "I'm doing this for *him* and *her*." Yay!
- "Mom bought it for *me*" + "Mom bought it for *them*" = "Mom bought it for *me* and *them*. Hooray!
- "*Me* is going to the park" + "*Him* is going to the park" = Oops!
- "I saw John at the play," yes, but "I saw *she* at the play"? No-no!

It all goes back to subject vs. object. "*He* and *I* are going to the park." "Him" and "me" can never be "doers" (subjects), only "receivers" (objects). "She named *him* and *me* in the lawsuit." "The scandal involved *her* and *us*." After a preposition *(by, with, for, to, in, of, about, between,* etc.), there is always an object: "She likes to gossip about *him* and *them*." "This is between *her* and *me*."

Now let's get a bit more sophisticated. Can you identify the problem in these statements?

1. "Each of the yoga postures have several variations."
2. "None of my friends were at the party."
3. "Neither of them have money for a ticket."

All three scare up the same common error: using a plural verb with a singular subject. This is very slippery because the plural words "postures/friends/them" trick us into thinking they are the subjects. If we examine the sentences more closely we see that the real subjects are "Each/None/Neither"—and all of those words are singular. So to correct these sentences we change the verbs to singular form:

1. "Each of the yoga postures has several variations."
2. "None of my friends was at the party." (Even an editor commented, "I know this is right, but it sounds so wrong.")
3. "Neither of them has money for a ticket."
4. Here is a bonus quiz for you to complete: "Both of them ___ coming, but neither of them ___ dressing up." ¶

Kudos to you for having come this far! Realizing that grammar errors do not constitute the juiciest of topics, I thought about attaching a five-dollar bill to this page as a reward for the persistent reader, but that didn't seem too practical when I thought it through. I recall when one of my ingenious colleagues, wondering if anyone ever really read our yearly *Program Review* reports, slipped into Page 15 of her report a one-time offer of five dollars to anyone on the academic committee who read that far; one committee member actually did claim the cash. Even better than a cash prize, I reward you with these recently minted, spliced, and/or mutilated five-dollar words that have not yet qualified for inclusion in the "youth-friendly" *Merriam-Webster* or any other standard dictionary:

- "Clumbersome": favorite descriptive adjective of a former college administrator who, mashing up "clumsy" and "cumbersome," used it with innocence and certainty.
- "Flustrated": a zany blend of "fluster" and "frustrated."
- "To conversate": an unnecessary but increasingly popular invented verb. Thankfully, most people still prefer to "converse."
- To "pronunciate" and its variation, to "pronounciate": Is this a fancy way to "pronounce"?

¶ Bonus-quiz answer: "Both of them *are* coming, but neither of them is dressing up. ("Both" is plural; "neither" is singular.)

What will be next? To reservate? To cancelate? To vacationate? To insultate? It makes me chuckle as I think fondly of my student assistant who complained about having to type on "carbonated" forms. That gaffe would be called a "malapropism," and in "The Abdominal Snowman on the Cal-Can Highway," we visit those in rib-tickling depth. A malapropism is defined as "the act or habit of ridiculously misusing words, especially by confusing words that are similar in sound." That definition explains how, according to one middle-school student who shall remain anonymous, "In 1580, Sir Francis Drake circumcised the world with a very large clipper named The Gold Hand."

Whew! Now that the worst of the grammar errors have been cleaned up, very large family dog has just enthusiastically eaten the homework.

The Law of Schwa

Do you want to be a better speller, or at least acquire more evidence of why English spelling is such a minefield and why your spellchecker has to work overtime? Let's launch this topic, and you can decide.

How many vowels are in the English alphabet? This is not a trick question, so go ahead and shout it out. Yes, right answer! There are five vowels: *a-e-i-o-u*, and I agree—that was too easy. Try this one: How many sounds do these five vowels make? Yes, this is a hard one, but if you guessed any number over ten, good for you! Amazingly, our five written vowels produce 15–20 sounds (depending on the dialect and not including vowel combinations). For example, the vowel A sounds very different in these three words: "hat," "ate," and "father."

Here's your next question: What's the most common vowel sound in English? We'll ponder this one for a moment: "Uhhh . . ." Yes, that's it—"uh"! It's the favorite, or at least most frequent, vowel sound in our language, and we almost never spell it with the letter U. Face it, U is not a lovable vowel when it sounds like the "uh" in "slug/dung/ugh/underdog/ugly" and so on. (Sorry, Humbert and Sunny.) We like it better when it sounds like "you," as in "unity/university/usual/Hugh."

That ubiquitous sound "uh" is called the "schwa," and appears in pronunciation guides as an upside-down, backward letter E: ə. Say the name "Kevin" out loud: "Ke-" gets the emphasis, and on the second syllable, "–vin," the voice goes soft and low. Do we say "Ke-VIN" as in the VIN (vehicle identification number) of our car? No, we say, "Ke-*vuhn*" ("Ke-vən"). Whether we spell his name as Kevan, Keven, Kevin, Kevon, or Kevun, it is pronounced the same. Some of our words have different pronunciations between the true vowel sound and the schwa: "today" can sound like *"too-day,"* but usually leaves the mouth as *"tuh-day."* In my neck of the woods, we hear "Mendocino" as "Men-*doh*-cino," but locals more frequently say, "Men-*duh*-cino," leading to much speculation about what folks are smoking.

The schwa is one of the reasons English is a difficult language to spell. Even we native speakers think so—just imagine how hard it is for foreigners! Friends text to meet for Friday happy hour at a nearby winery, and everyone has their own favorite spelling of the name: "Ravino/Revino/Rivino/Rovino/Ruvino"—which is it?—because they all sound the same! We'll choose Door Number Three with certainty only if we've seen the name in print.

In a radio show, the astronomer Milutin Milankovic was mentioned. I googled him as "Malankovic," knowing it could just as well be spelled as Melan-, Milan-, Molan-, or Mulan-. You get the idea.

Now, it's your turn again. Find the schwa in these common words:

- compose
- freedom
- communication
- tropical

I'll write the schwa sound as "uh" instead of ə, for the sake of illustration:

- c*uh*m-pose
- free-d*uh*m
- c*uh*m-mu-ni-ca-sh*uh*n
- tro-pi-c*uh*l

Good work!

Now here's a two-part question for you: How long are words that contain a schwa, and in which syllable does it appear? First, the word has to be more than one syllable (one syllable: "beast"; two syllables: "beastly"), and the schwa is always on an *unstressed* syllable. If the syllable carries emphasis (as the "-li-" in "de*li*cious"), we're going to pronounce that vowel in its unique way, but the unstressed vowels get muttered into the gray slush of schwa more often than not; in this case, we get de-li-sh*uh*s, or even d*uh*-li-sh*uh*s.

In English spelling, as explored in the earlier "Inconstant Consonants and Sudden Vowel Movements" section, what you see is often not even close to what you hear. The schwa seems to make pronunciation easier, allowing the mouth to get lazier, but it's curtains if you're trying to win a spelling bee!

There will be more ado about crazy English spelling, but for now, thank you for your ətenshən and *particəpashən.*

The Abdominal Snowman on the Cal-Can Highway**

I admit to being a tad judgmental when it comes to vocabulary errors in English. In truth, I am judgmental about spelling errors, too—although I remind myself every time I write the word "judgmental" that I discovered only recently that the E in "judge" isn't part of the accepted American spelling of the word. Until then, I thought it was a word the spellchecker just hadn't learned yet.

I also confess I was brought to my lexical knees when corrected, while speaking of Dutch and Italian ancestors, for calling them my "forebear*ers*." Ever linguistically self-assured, I contradicted smarty-pants when he insisted it is "forebears." Then I humored him, thinking, "Ha!—*bears?* That's ridiculous!" And I let it go, certain that my trusty *American Heritage Dictionary* would vindicate me. Upon discovering that it didn't, I humbly ate those two letters of crow, and never made that mistake again.

It's a given that the more we read, the bigger our vocabulary and the more accurate our spelling. For some people, their grip on their native language is more tenuous than firm, creating occasional confusion and frequent comedy.

** A friend and I were tossing around the idea of a road trip through Alaska and Canada via the Alcan Highway. One of us mispronounced it (our recollection of the guilty party conflicts), perhaps having seen too many dog-food commercials on TV. From there, conjuring up an *abdominal* snowman was only a half-hop/skip/jump, and the rest was side-splitting laughter and every malapropism we could splutter in that state of hilarious unravel.

Exhibit A: A friend of mine in law enforcement quoted to me from reports written by officers:

- "We petitioned off the area as soon as we arrived." *(partitioned)*
- "Her husband had died, so the claim was a mute point." *(moot point)*
- "In lieu of the hour, we had to postpone the investigation." *(In view of)*
- "Before the stakeout, we simonized our watches at 9:00 p.m." *(synchronized)*
- "He went off on a tyrant as soon as I started to question him." *(tirade)*
- "To calm the crowd, we had to nip it in the butt." *(bud)*
- "The whole scene reeked of havoc." *(from "to wreak havoc")*
- "The suspect appeared to be blind and was accompanied by a sight-seeing dog." *(seeing-eye dog)*

During several decades in education, I recorded some memorable mistakes and malapropisms. An English teacher reported that her editor had ruthlessly "dessicated" the first pages of her book proposal. An administrator was preoccupied with paying faculty "stifends" for special projects. One student's greatest desire was to become "fluential" in Spanish. Another's major challenge was "pronounciating" correctly. The student assistant who hated typing on "carbonated" forms wrote a message informing me that she would be out the following week for a "tubal litigation."

A quiz in English on cultural topics in a beginning Spanish class produced the following errors, mostly mix-ups of some of those pesky English homophones—words with different meanings but the same pronunciation:

- "It has a *fare* (fair) trade system for the workers.
- "And they get to work in *there* (their) own language."
- "Gabriel García Márquez is a Colombian *arthur*." (author)
- "He *one* (won) the Noble *Piece* (Peace) Prize."
- "Francisco Franco was a *dicktater* (dictator) of Spain."

It was around that time that I began seriously planning my retirement.

An acquaintance in the retail business lamented that there is such a "stigmata" about buying used clothing. A family member maintained that it was just a "plutonic" relationship. And who needs a comedy writer when you can listen to politicians' pronouncements? To wit: the former U.S. Senator from Nevada, Chic Hetch, is immortalized for opposing the waste repository at Yucca Mountain by refusing to have his state become a "nuclear suppository."

The verbal gaffes of George W. Bush could fill a presidential library:

- "Too many OB-GYNs aren't able to practice their love with women all across this country."
- ". . . so when the history of this administration is written, at least there's an authoritarian voice saying exactly what happened."
- "Our enemies are innovative and resourceful, and so are we. They never stop thinking about new ways to harm our country and our people, and neither do we."

Dan Quayle, Vice President of George Bush, Sr.'s administration, infamously stated, "I was recently on a tour of Latin America, and the only regret I have was that I didn't study Latin harder in school so I could converse with those people." On another occasion he stated, "Republicans understand the importance of bondage between a mother and child." And finally, "I believe we are on an irreversible trend toward more freedom and democracy, but that could change."

Several years ago, when I became the legal guardian of an elderly friend, I met with her lawyer to discuss her welfare. What he said shocked me into taking notes, and here they are verbatim: "The last time I saw her she was still *livid* and active"; "It *vacillates* whether she eats or not"; and "There's no point sitting around *commensurating* about it." That is what might be (gently) called a tenuous grasp of the native language.

Now we'll hear from 16-year-olds answering questions on the General Education Development (GED) test to obtain a high school diploma:

Q. "What guarantees may a mortgage company insist on?"
A. "To buy a house, you have to be well-endowed."

Q. "What happens to a boy when he reaches puberty?"
A. "He says goodbye to his boyhood and looks forward to his adultery."

Q. "What is the fibula?"
A. "A small lie."

Q. "Give the meaning of the term Caesarean section."
A. "A district in Rome."

In a paper attempting to describe the interconnectedness of all things, a high-school student wrote, "The universe is a giant orgasm," inadvertently omitting two crucial letters ("-ni-") in the middle of the key word. The teacher couldn't resist writing at the end of the essay, "Your answer gives new meaning to the Big Bang Theory."

I humbly admit that I make mistakes, too; but proofreading, lots of research, and a crack copy editor keep them in check. All that, and I'm never far from my well-worn copy of *Roger's Catharsis*—you know, that dictionary of synonyms that helps you find just the right word to get out what you need to say.

Into the Prepositional Fray

If just the sight of that P-word in the title made you think, *Oh, maybe I'll skip this section,* I assure you this is not another grammar lesson. I promise to be gentle, and I encourage you to read on. If you're not sure what a preposition is, not to worry—you're in friendly and ample company. By the time you get *into* and *out of* this prepositional fray (alive and smiling, I promise), not only will you be on friendly terms with these mostly two- and three-letter words but you'll also have great respect for them because communication, especially in English, cannot survive without them.

One of my best friends in college, the beautiful and exotic Mónica from Chile, spoke English with the most beguiling lilt and charming accent. It was her third language, and she was dedicated to mastering as much slang and colloquial speech as possible during our graduate school years. Alas, there were three expressions she never got right no matter how much we coached and corrected her. When the car mechanic didn't actually fix the problem but overcharged her for it anyway, she complained, "I really feel like he screwed me off." When we walked out of Dr. Castillo's Modernism poetry exam, she moaned, "I really screwed that one over." About the unfaithful boyfriend, she reported, "It felt good to tell him to *just screw up!*"

Of course, a native speaker would never confuse two or more expressions created with the same basic verb and different prepositions, but can you imagine how this challenges someone learning English as a second language? There are so many idiosyncrasies and complications in our language that I admire anyone who can learn it even passably well. The point is that what seems so obvious and unmistakable to the nimble native speaker can be a serious minefield to the brave learner of any second language, and English is a wickedly rough one to learn.

Sticking with prepositions, let's take the common English verb "to take" and change its meaning by tacking different little words (prepositions) on the end. In no particular order, here's an even dozen for you to imagine how you would use in a sentence: *take on, take after, take off, take over, take out, take in, take down, take back, take upon, take to, take up, take up on.* (Will you *take me up on* that?)

As a native speaker of English, you had no trouble making up examples for each of those, and you probably even noticed that there is sometimes more than one obvious meaning, such as "take off" shoes or "take off" in a plane. If you were a foreigner learning English, could you accurately manage that prepositional dozen? Or might you slip up occasionally and, gazing at a photo, tell your friend, "I can see that you take to your mother"?[††] We native speakers should pause to admire the linguistic leaps of meaning we achieve with something as tiny as a change of preposition. If English is *not* your native language, and you can manage these dozen "takes," plus combinations like "take away/take apart/taken aback," I bow at your feet and kiss the linguistic ground you talk on!

I can't speak *in* or speak *for* all the world's languages, but in the Latin-based Romance languages (Spanish, Italian, French, Portuguese, Rumanian, and over 30 lesser languages and dialects) there are not 12 variations on the single verb "to take" but 12

†† I used the wrong preposition while trying to tell a Spanish-speaking friend that I took after my father. Instead of saying *Salí al padre* with the preposition a, I said *Salí del padre* with the preposition de, basically stating that I had come from my father's womb.

totally different verbs. If you have any Romance language bilingual dictionary, look up "take," and then peruse the expressions following the basic definitions. You'll see that each is elegantly rendered by one or more verbs (e.g., "take away" = *quitar* in Spanish), not a train wreck of two- to five-letter add-ons. For a foreign-language student, that is infinitely easier to learn and simpler to remember than having to internalize the difference between "tell on" and "tell off."

Imagine the poor young man, after a class in English for non-native speakers, trying to be cool but struggling to remember if he wants to ask a girl to *hang in, hang out, hang on,* or *hang over* with him. Does he long for her to *fall in, fall out, fall for*, or *fall off* him? Is he hoping she will *give up, give over, give out,* or *give in?* In his heart, does he pray things will *work over, work up, work in, work with, work at, work on, work for,* or *work out* for them? Does he promise not to *let her down* or *let her out?* After their first crisis, do they *make for, make up, make over*, or *make out?* Ultimately, will they *break in, break out, break up, break down, break off*, or *break through*?

A preposition is just a handy little word that usually tells us the relationship between what precedes it and what follows it. "The wart *on* his nose" tells us how the wart and the nose are related. "The wind *beneath* your wings" gives a certain understanding of wind relative to wings, and "The wind *from* your wings" creates a different image altogether. Dictionaries do manage to give definitions for prepositions, but they are the hardest little things to pin down when it comes to meaning. How would you define *out?* Does your definition cover the expressions *get out, pass out, make out, find out, give out,* and *work out?*

Romance languages do have prepositions (a wart on the nose in Spanish is *una verruga* en *la nariz*), but it's a relatively rare verb that alters its meaning when a preposition is added. So, instead of doing mental backflips trying to remember if you need to *come to, come in, come off, come for, come on, come out,* or *come by,* you only need to learn seven verbs, each with its own clear meaning. Trust me: The only reason that doesn't sound easier is because we're lucky enough to have those pesky prepositions hardwired into our English-speaking brains, so that they come out right every time. You're not caught in even a split-second debate about whether that toy airplane just *cracked down* or *cracked up.*

Imagine sitting in an office meeting and wondering whether you should suggest that a new hiring practice be *carried over, carried through, carried forward, carried off, carried on, carried out,* or *carried away.* Next, you wonder if you will be *passed out, passed up, passed on, passed by,* or *passed over* for a promotion. The verb "get" takes up over two pages in the English-Spanish dictionary, and it is one of the most essential but hard-to-master verbs in our language. By now, I'll bet at least a half-dozen combos of "get" + preposition are rolling off your mental tongue.

The first group trip I ever organized was to Costa Rica in 1996, with eight intrepid eco-tourists and a great local guide whose English was perfect—well, almost. One night, we were in our minibus, creeping through the jungle in search of nocturnal animals. Intense darkness, complete silence, total concentration. Abruptly, the driver stopped the bus and our guide, Beto, hissed, "Get down!" We looked at each other, hoping for some sign of what was going on and what we should do. While we were still hesitating, mentally debating what might be about to happen, he repeated more insistently, "Get down!"

At this, the lawyer in our group flattened onto the floor of the bus, and the rest of us were in crouch position ready to hit the floorboards as well. I remember my heart pounding at the thought of some machine gun-wielding or machete-slashing maniac boarding our bus. Finally, after several tense seconds and fearful scenarios rolling through our heads, the driver flipped on the interior lights, and there stood Beto in the doorway of the bus, pointing outside and saying in total exasperation, "Get down!!" We all *cracked up* laughing in relief and disbelief, helped the lawyer off the floor, and then *cracked down* on Beto with a lesson in prepositions I'm sure he's never forgotten.

This is Susanna of Lexiconland, signing over, off, out, up, and away!

CHAPTER FOUR

Windows on the World

It's All Bubble and Squeak to Me

Once you get the 'ang of Cockney slang, you'll be chewin' the fat in a whole different tongue, intelligible only to you and your mates. If you really get it down, you might try it out on the blokes in London, but don't expect applause.

Lost (But Not Forgotten) in Translation

This is about what happens when well-meaning people try to translate linguistic items into a foreign language where they have no credentials to operate. I'm at a loss as to what more to say. You simply must read it and weep—then laugh, and know that I couldn't possibly make this stuff up.

We Don't Have a Word for It, Part I

Sunil Bali writes that there is no word in the Tibetan language for "guilty," and that the closest translation would be "intelligent regret that decides to do things differently." In this section we look at terms from other languages that not only speak volumes, but also require a good phrase or two to get their meaning across in English.

We Don't Have a Word for It, Part II

I'm back on my home territory with common Spanish words whose English translation must occupy from several words to a whole paragraph to convey the same meaning. One of the first is the Spanish word for a citizen of the United States, and *we* don't have a word for it. Imagine that!

News from the World of Words

If you love words and language, tune in to news items like these: Foreign Accent Syndrome, where one awakens from a brain trauma speaking with a foreign accent or, in rare cases, speaking a foreign language; languages "winking out" all over the world; and the uplifting story of a seventh-grader who invented an affordable Braille printer.

Speaking of Tongues

This is a personal tale of tacos and tongues—the ones we speak, and the anatomical organ with which we speak. It ends with a lovely Afro-Cuban legend that plays beautifully between the two meanings.

Pigments of Our Imagination

Color is language. It speaks of mood, emotion, event, and expectation. However, be aware of cultural differences: while Americans are green with envy, the French are green with fear, the Italians are green with rage, and a Spanish-speaker might be green with dirty thoughts.

Between the Sword and the Wall

While we are "between a rock and a hard place," the Spanish speaker is "between the sword and the wall." Here we explore the parallels and deviations of bicultural folk wisdom, and usually find ourselves saying the same thing, only with different words and images.

Stereotypes in Stereo

Exploring stereotypes is an excellent activity in foreign-language classrooms to get students enthused about using adjectives (friendly, rude, formal, welcoming, etc.), and interested in examining the what and why of our ideas about other groups of people. I had always been on the teaching end of this exercise until I became a student of Italian in Siena. To hear my fellow students of various nationalities deliver their list of stereotypes about Americans was an experience both unforgettable and hair-raising.

The Language Police

130 language academies in the world hold the reins on 110 different languages in an attempt to keep them pure and regulated. English not only influences other languages more than any other in the world, but also absorbs vocabulary from foreign sources like a global sponge, all without any oversight or regulation. Is this anarchy, creativity, linguistic explosivity, or what?

Rum and Revolution, Part I

The perfect moment to visit Cuba is fast receding as "normalization" of Cuban-American relations is stalled, yet ever-larger numbers of U.S. visitors flood the island. Do not dismay for, before Cuba becomes "just another Caribbean island," you can share a vivid experience of revolution and transition in these pages.

Rum and Revolution, Part II

Now that we've met the Revolution, Cuban cigars, the Soviets, "Guantanamera," the Castro brothers, and Che Guevara, we'll talk about Cuban Spanish, architecture, the embargo, and a $4,000 lobster dinner.

It's All Bubble and Squeak* to Me

Back in the good old Sacramento days, when we were neither "good" nor "old," my pals and I never tired of Mr. Daugherty's funny little rhymes that rolled off his tongue in oddly accented English that sounded like Eliza Doolittle's father in *My Fair Lady:* "Your *rattles and jar,* that's your car. Your *trouble and strife,* that's your wife. *A hit and a miss,* that's a piss. *Dog's meat,* that's your feet." Between chuckles and curiosity, I soon found out he wasn't making this stuff up, but simply carrying on the tradition of rhyming Cockney slang that's now almost 200 years old.

The word "Cockney" has evolved in meaning over time from a reference to all city-dwellers to a label for the residents and their speech in the Cheapside neighborhood of London. These days, it refers to the dialect and accent of working-class Londoners in general. It's precisely the speech that Henry Higgins, played by Rex Harrison in the legendary musical *My Fair Lady,* proposes to train out of Eliza, played by Audrey Hepburn, in order to win a bet with his linguist friend that he can coach a Cockney into speaking like a duchess.

The musical is based on the 1913 play *Pygmalion* by George Bernard Shaw, who commented on English accents in the preface: "It is impossible for an Englishman to open his mouth without making some other Englishman hate or despise him." Cockney will never be spoken by the British royal family, but it has acquired status on the isle as a valid English dialect, and gained popularity among Americans (who always love a "foreign" accent), thanks to

* To decipher the title, apply the rule of rhyme, and imagine what word rhymes with "squeak" and fits this context: "It's all _____ to me."

the fame and now-familiar speech of celebrities like Phil Collins, David Beckham, Michael Caine and—the voice we can't get enough of whether speaking or singing—Adele.

A very outstanding feature of the Cockney accent is the absence of the *h* sound: "Ow, me 'ead 'urts!" Yes, they really do say "me" instead of "my." You won't catch a Cockney saying, "*My* girlfriend broke *my* heart," but he might say, "The cheese broke *me* 'eart." "The cheese"? Sure, you know—that rhyming thing again: *cheese and kisses,* that's your "missus" (wife or girlfriend). With a little practice, you too can learn to speak Cockney! Just check out the online tutorial, "Learn the Cockney Accent with Jason Statham." Jason gets right in your face with his demonstration of the dialect, and that essential insouciance that goes along with it, for a spellbinding 7.27 minutes. At the end of the crash course, you could give it a try, but be forewarned. The British, and Londoners in particular, think we Americans sound "ridiculous, bordering on pathetic" when we try to imitate any of the accents of the kingdom.

That said, why not spice up our speech with a few rhymes borrowed from Cockney slang? Some have already become so ingrained in American English that we have long forgotten that they originated on the other shore of the "puddle." The Cockney rhyme for *money* is "bread and honey," but I'd always assumed it was the hippies who had creatively coined that usage for *bread* back in the sixties! To understand what's behind our expression, "getting down to brass tacks," we must think like a Cockney and understand their rhyme of *tacks* with *facts. Chew the fat* is Cockney for "have a chat." A life coach might urge us to "blow a raspberry" at negative self-talk, and knowing this to originate with the Cockney slang *raspberry tart* (the rhyming stand-in for "fart"), that imaginary gesture suddenly takes on promising power.

What that "raspberry" demonstrates is that the slang starts out as a rhyme, but the rhyming word is often lost through familiarity. Hence, every Cockney gets that your *china*, short for *china plate*, is your "mate" (pal or friend). "I still 'aven't got a *Scooby*" leaves off the "Doo" of "Scooby Doo" but, since the missing word rhymes with "clue," everyone knows you're still in the dark. "Use yer *loaf!*" shortens "loaf of bread," which rhymes with "head." Your *tom* is your "jewelry," from *tom-foolery*. *Titfer* is slang for "hat," from Cockney *tit-for-tat*.

Indulge me through a few more classics: *dog* is the "phone," from *dog and bone; mincers* are "eyes," from *mince pies*. Picture yourself as a fly on someone's wall in Tottenham (Adele's home turf): "I couldn't believe me mincers! The cheese showed up with all that new tom, and I 'aven't even got the bread to keep me rattles on the Kermit. It'll be me Scotches carryin' me tomorrow." (Note: *frog* and *toad* = "road," and it's just a short leap from there to *Kermit; Scotch eggs* = "legs.")

As with all slang, there is constant coinage of fresh phrases that can be admired for their creativity. *Watch and chain* is Cockney-clever for "brain": "*Is yer watch a bit slow today?*"; *thick and thin* is "skin"; *field of wheat* is a "street"; and *Spanish onion* is a "bunion."

The word "Cockney" itself is traceable to *cockeney*, meaning a misshapen egg, first used a few centuries earlier to refer derogatorily to city folk ignorant of real life. (Ironic, isn't it?) Oddly enough, it remains unknown how all this rhyming slang got started. Was it a linguistic Big Bang of spontaneous generation? Perhaps it was a game of wit that captured imaginations and tongues, like terms of venery (see "The Herd Mentality" section in Chapter 2). Or was it the conscious invention of a secret code meant to keep outsiders out of Cockney business, akin to the invented *Boontling* language of the Anderson Valley in Northern California; the original

Lunfardo of the Buenos Aires underworld; or Bolivian *Machaj Juyai*, used to secretly pass medicinal knowledge from healer father to apprentice son? Some researchers suggest Cockney was originally the code language of thieves in London.

However it came about, we can be sure that standing on a busy *field* in Eastside London, listening to the Cockney world go by, we won't have a *scooby* what they're saying.

Lost (But Not Forgotten) in Translation

While working as a volunteer translator at a clinic in Mexico, my assignment in surgery was to give post-op patients their discharge instructions in Spanish. This should have been a straightforward matter of handing them the page with boxes checked by the surgeon and adding a few verbal clarifications, but when I looked at the forms more closely I found myself somewhere between horror and hilarity at the translation of the English directives into Spanish. It was hopelessly misbegotten, accidentally rhapsodic, and blastedly unintelligible, especially for the many folks with limited reading skills.

I give you in English a snippet of what the Spanish translations actually instructed the patient to do: "The look into your incision wounds you every day. Of that which you see more redness, swelling, pus, drainage, or sangria, or if you make that a fever, turn around to see the doctor." To make matters murkier, the patient's wife consults the instructions for changing the bandage on her husband's hernia incision and discovers she is to "wash the hands well before putting the new preparation ablaze." In the section about when to remove the surgical dressing, here is a real head-scratcher: "You can take off the overcoat to dress in three days."

Among the dietary guidelines, the patient was instructed to avoid *bebidas suaves,* which to a Spanish speaker means "mild, gentle drinks." It would never occur to him that the injunction was against what we call "soft drinks" and, suffering the pain of that recent hernia surgery, he might just opt for a double whiskey. Nothing mild or gentle about that—just following doctor's orders! The surgical nurse was gratefully willing for me to rework the form, and admitted it had been tacked together by a mish-mash of electronic translation and dictionary digging, with a few high-school Spanish opinions thrown in, for better or worse.

You might guess in what regard I hold electronic translators (e.t.s), and you are correct; but, truth be told, I do often use one to send Mariann a greeting in Swedish, or wish Ludovica a happy weekend in Catalan. I also use online dictionaries to resolve arcane words and regional colloquialisms in Spanish. When it comes to whole sentences, let alone paragraphs, the e.t. falters despite huge improvements in recent years.

An e.t. can be a useful tool but, if you need to deliver a clear message, hire a human who gets paid for doing this very challenging job for which they have had years of training and experience. (Written translation was one of my former professions and, frankly, I came to the conclusion that it was just too hard.) Language is so deeply personal, cultural, and nuanced that we won't be saying farewell to real, live translators anytime soon, even if e.t. does keep "learning" from its mistakes. In 2012, the U.S. Department of Labor Statistics predicted that jobs for translators will expand by 46% by 2022 due to increasing globalization in all major sectors. Hence, translator/interpreter will become the fifth-fastest-growing occupation in the United States, serving commerce, government, law, education, and especially health care.

Translation missteps have been entertaining us for years. Surely you've seen the supposed gaffes of American corporate advertising abroad that have been circulating on the Internet for decades: the Chevy Nova flopped in Latin America because in Spanish *no va* means "it doesn't go"; Parker Pens translated the slogan "It won't leak in your pocket and embarrass you" with the Spanish verb *embarazar* (to make pregnant); in Taiwan, "Come alive! Join the

Pepsi generation!" was rendered, "Pepsi will bring your ancestors back from the dead."

Yes, these and so many other favorites are the stuff of legend—spurious and oh-so-entertaining *urban* legends. In fact, Chevrolet sold a lot of Novas south of our border, and sales even surpassed expectations in Venezuela. Now, before you label me a killjoy, let me add that yes, Mazda did name a new 1999 model *Laputa* ("the prostitute" in Spanish). Nissan gave us more to hoot about with the 2011 release of a mini-car they called the *Moco,* Spanish for "booger," and the American Dairy Association translated "Got milk?" as ¿Tienes *leche?* which can mean, "Are you lactating?"

Let's see how English translation shows up abroad in our foreign hosts' attempts to keep us well-behaved, safe, and likely to choose enjoyable menu selections. A sign in English near the entrance of a church in Spain reads: "We thank him to discover their head before entering this enclosure. This is a place of cult." (How it went south: *descubrir* means "to discover" as well as "to uncover"; *culto* = worship.) A sign in Spanish at a road closure that reads, *"Peligro! No pasar!"* ("Danger! Do not pass!") was translated for the safety of the foreigner as, "I am in danger! Not to happen!"—and then perhaps interpreted by the English-speaking passersby as existential roadside agony. Ah, those pesky words with multiple meanings!

In China, the translations into "Chinglish" are earnest, compelling, surreal, and often captured on camera. At a vista point we read the warning: "Beware of missing foot!"—then look down just to check, and lose our footing on the steep hillside. At construction sites, it is stated: "Execution in Progress," "Erection in Progress," and "Beware of Safety!" The fire extinguisher in a high-rise office building is labeled "Hand Grenade." Nokia's inviting slogan, which promised to connect people across the globe, was translated from elegant Chinese characters into an ignominious message: "Connocting Poopie."

When it comes to restaurant menu translations from Chinese into English, the lexicon takes a turn toward the psychedelic. Consider these irresistible offerings: "The Palace Oil explodes the duck/Potato the crap/Six-roasted husband/The fragrant spring onion explodes the cow/Meat muscle stupid bean sprouts/Wang had to burn/Fries pulls out the rotten child/Chicken rude and unreasonable/F*** the duck until exploded," and . . . hmmm, let me think it over while I nibble on my last protein bar. Indeed, we all have plenty on our to-do list, but would someone please fix that glitch in Chinese-to-English translators that persists in rendering the culinary term "dry-seasoned" (among others) as "f***ed"?

Here are a few choice Chinglish memories from editor Mary Buckley's travels in China: a restaurant menu featuring "Fry hair-tail . . . with green moss"—yum!; a sign on steps saying, "Do not stampede"; signs in parks reading, "Don't relieve yourself everywhere" and "Don't strip to the waist and lie at discretion"; a sign on a boat dock saying, "The safety-conscious slips carefully"; and businesses named "Aftertaste Classical Furnishings" and "Aroma Meat Packing." She is sure her attempts at Mandarin sounded much worse to her Chinese hosts—but there's no "better" or "worse" here, just comical errors!

Despite all the Spanish-language resources available in early 21st-century America, the "Exit Only" sign in Starbucks was translated for the convenience of Spanish-speaking customers as Éxito Aquí ("Success Here"). In 2010, coming back from a trip abroad, I felt I was surely hallucinating in front of a sign in Spanish pointing to "Customs" in the San Francisco Airport that spelled out not *Aduana* but *Costumbres,* as in "cultural practices."

Finally, two words of advice: Do *not* drop your Spanish class, and under no circumstances should you put your faith in an electronic translator, then walk into a salon in Argentina, Mexico, or Spain to request a wash and a blow dry. You'll get the wash—but it might be followed by a "dry" blow to the head, delivered by a very puzzled but compliant beautician.

We Don't Have a Word for It, Part I

Our topic now is fascinating foreign words that have no equivalent in English, so let's dig right into some of my favorite untranslatable terms from around the world. As you shall see, in each case we can string together enough words to create a passable definition, but though English speakers may have a concept of what the foreign term expresses, our language just doesn't have a word for it.

- ***Schadenfreude*** (German): Taking pleasure in another's misfortune. This is perhaps the most well known and oft-quoted of the untranslatables, for the obvious reason that the English language really could use a word for something we do all the time. "When the cop pulled the guy over who passed me going 85 mph, I was glad it was him and not me. He had it coming!" In a word, *schadenfreude.*
- ***Age-otori*** (Japanese): To look worse after getting a haircut. Who hasn't suffered this ignominy, albeit temporarily? Thank goodness and the gods of grooming that hair does, after all, grow back.
- ***Forelsket*** (Norwegian): The euphoria of first falling in love. Love songs since time immemorial have tried to describe this feeling, but it apparently never occurred to us in English simply to invent a word for it. It's easy to see why the Eskimos have a number of words for snow and the Fijians have but one, in keeping with their respective experiences with the substance; but wouldn't you think

that the universal experience of love would demand the generation of words for *all* its stages?

- ***L'esprit de l'escalier*** (French): This is usually translated as "staircase wit," but that doesn't nearly convey the frustration of coming up with the perfect comeback *after* an encounter is over and you're already headed upstairs to bed for the night.
- ***Meraki*** (Greek): This is what is generated when you put heart and soul, creativity, and love into what you are doing. It's what is created when a group of dedicated folks put on a fundraiser to benefit the Boys and Girls Club; it's my niece, Lauren, writing a song to reach out across continents to a little girl from Northern Africa headed for to Colombia to be fitted with a prosthetic foot; and it's the spirit of all those who raised the money to make that miracle possible.
- ***Wabi-sabi*** (Japanese): This is the celebration of the impermanent, the imperfect, and the incomplete as essential elements of art and life. This Japanese concept of beauty is sweeping the nation just as *feng shui* did in the nineties. Not only is *wabi-sabi* a bed and breakfast in Maine, an art center in New York, the name of numerous restaurants (some featuring incomplete dishes of flawed food), and a popular name for pairs of kittens and goldfish but, according to author Arielle Ford in her book *Wabi-Sabi Love,* it's the way to find perfect love in an imperfect relationship. It could also characterize my style of gardening and housekeeping, as well as my computer skills, my understanding of finances, and the last soufflé I attempted.
- ***Hygge*** (Danish): Practicing the pronunciation of this word with Ida, my Danish exchange student, I knew that, even if

we can't name it with a single word in English, I want more of it. It's a state of mind marked by cozy, warm togetherness. Think of sitting by a crackling fire in snuggly slippers with glowing cheeks alongside your favorite companions, enjoying a wonderful vintage of your favorite beverage at the start of an endless weekend. Maybe someone has found a way to bottle the stuff because, although Scandinavian winter days are long, dark, and cold, Denmark dependably comes up as one of the happiest countries in the world.

- ***Shinrin-yoku*** (Japanese): Literally "forest-bathing," it means improving one's health by spending time in nature amidst trees. There's plenty of science to back this up, and the practice is free and abundantly available to us all.
- ***Gökotta*** (Swedish): To go out early in the morning to hear the birds and appreciate nature. My Swedish friend Mariann confirms, "Yes, that is correct. *Gök* means cuckoo and *otta* means early morning." Isn't that adorable?
- ***Toska*** (Russian): One cannot improve on Vladimir Nabokov's description: "No single word in English renders all the shades of *toska.* At its deepest and most painful, it is a sensation of great spiritual anguish, often without any specific cause. At less morbid levels, it is a dull ache of the soul, a longing with nothing to long for, a sick pining, a vague restlessness, mental throes, yearning. In particular cases, it may be the desire for somebody or something specific, nostalgia, lovesickness. At the lowest level, it grades into ennui, boredom." That's a lot of mileage for a five-letter word, and it rings of the truth that he knows of what he speaks.
- ***Tartle*** (Scottish): This means hesitating while introducing someone, because you've forgotten his or her name. "He

tartled for more than a few seconds while introducing his wife to his boss." Funny how some of our most universal and tenderly human foibles embarrass us the most. Kudos to the Scots for giving this one a name.

- ***Torschlusspanik*** (German): "Gate-closing panic" is the fear of diminishing opportunities with advancing age. German is a language where you can tack several nouns together to create a new concept in a single word, thus opening new gates to endless possibilities even while *torschlusspanik* reminds us that old ones are clanging shut.
- ***Ya'aburnee*** (Arabic): Literally "You bury me," meaning, "I hope I die before you because I love you so much I couldn't stand the pain of living without you." Sweet? Selfish? Maybe both.
- ***Yoko meshi*** (Japanese): *Yoko* means "horizontal" and *meshi* is "boiled rice." You're going to love this one! It's the Japanese term for the stress of communicating in a foreign language, and could be roughly tacked together in English as "a meal eaten sideways." This term holds clever wordplay in the fact that Japanese is written vertically while most other languages are written horizontally. Even so, don't you think all languages, especially English, should have a word for that particular discomfort?
- ***Korinthenkacker*** (German): This rollicking word translates literally as "raisin-pooper" and refers to someone who is too absorbed in nitpicky details and busy with petty trivia to be of any use. It makes me think of a restaurant manager who, in the chaos of the lunch rush, could be found in his office perfecting the peeling of an apple in a single, unbroken strip, or, better said, "He sat at his desk pooping raisins."

- **Fortnight** (British English): Oddly, this is a word we know, but simply don't use on our side of the Atlantic. American English has survived without a word meaning "a period of two weeks," but it sure would come in handy to resolve the confusion around the meanings of "biweekly" and "semi-monthly."
- ***Retrouvailles*** (French): The joy of being back together with someone after a long absence.

Now, dear reader, when you turn the page, we shall have a rush of *retrouvailles* as we reunite to delve into some Spanish words that have no direct translation into English: some are deliciously enchanting, others are downright practical, and a few border on wicked.

We Don't Have a Word for It, Part II

"We were sitting around the patio table after the meal, talking with my kids' godmothers and my son-in-law's parents about how people in the United States worry so much about what other people will say about what they do. Lorna, who always loves to be pampered and fussed over, was wearing her new Coach tennis shoes for the first time. Her husband, Louie, who has no hair on his head or face and is cross-eyed, announced it was time to go because he had to get up very early in the morning."

Now, in Spanish:

"Estábamos de ***sobremesa*** *en el patio, platicando con* ***comadres*** *y* ***consuegros*** *de cómo los* ***estadounidenses*** *se preocupan tanto del* ***qué dirán.*** *Lorna, siempre* ***mimosa, estrenaba*** *nuevos tenis Coach. Su marido, Louie,* ***lampiño*** *y* ***bizco,*** *anunció que era hora de irse porque tenía que* ***madrugar.****"*

English is considered economical with words when it comes to the number it takes to get your meaning across, but in this case it took almost twice as many as in the Spanish version. Of course, I planned it that way, since our focus here is on things that there are simply no English words for:

- ***Sobremesa:*** This is a lovely word for the time spent sitting at the table to chat after a meal. We do this with friends at a dinner party, but it has become an almost extinct custom among families in the United States because it requires that the household members first sit down to a meal together.
- ***Comadre, compadre:*** In Spanish-speaking countries,

children have multiple godfathers and godmothers *(padrinos y madrinas)* for all major life events: baptisms, first communions, and confirmations in the Catholic Church; graduations, *quinceañeras,*[†] weddings, and so on.[‡] Thus, Spanish has a name for the relationship between the child's parents and the godparents: *comadres* ("co-mothers") and *compadres* ("co-fathers"). These two words are also used to refer to lifelong family friends.

- ***Consuegros:*** This is the word for your relationship with your married son's or daughter's parents-in-law. You might have to diagram that one.
- ***Estadounidenses:*** Life would be easier if English had an unambiguous name for our nationality, such as "Unitedstateser." I know, too cumbersome—but what to do? Spanish has an official and unambiguous name for our nationality, although it is used mostly in official or formal contexts. Confusion ensues. We call ourselves Americans, and we can go to Spain or Italy as *americanos,* but in Mexico, they insist on calling us *norteamericanos.* (There's no capitalization of nationalities in Spanish.) However, technically, they too are North Americans,

† *Quinceañera* is the celebration of a Latina girl's 15th birthday to mark her passage into womanhood. Traditionally, it begins with a Catholic Mass and is followed by a grand party. As in a wedding ceremony, the girl wears a long, elaborate gown and is surrounded by her *chambelanes* (maids of honor and groomsmen).

‡ Hispanic celebrations include many godparents because all the extended family and close friends must be involved, and also because those *padrinos* and *madrinas* pay for the various aspects of the event. In a wedding, for example, there are godparents for the church, the reception hall, the flowers, the food, the music, the decorations, and many other features. For my student Cristóbal's wedding, I was asked to be *la madrina de la Biblia en español,* the godmother of the Spanish-language Bible. ¡Un honor! When my student Jaime graduated from Mendocino College with highest honors, he asked me to be a *madrina* for that important milestone in his life. Again, I was honored.

as are Guatemalans, Hondurans, Costa Ricans, and so on, down to the end of the Isthmus of Panama since, in geographical terms, there is only North America and South America; "Central America" may be a useful demographic and political designation but it is technically part of North America. North America also includes Canada and Greenland, and extends to the border of Panama with Colombia. In South America as well, it is unacceptable to call ourselves *americanos* because they are too—*sudamericanos* (South Americans). Yes, we are *norteamericanos* but, more accurately, we are *estadounidenses.*

- ***El qué dirán:*** Literally, "What they will say." This signifies the worry over what others will think and say about what you do. It shows up less these days in literature and media because, frankly, things are loosening up and folks are caring less about how the flies on their wall might react to their bad habits and peccadilloes. That said, if I'm visiting Mom in Bakersfield and a friend is dropping me off after an evening out, I'd better be in the front door within five minutes, or she will be deeply worried about the *qué dirán* of her neighbors—even though I'm old enough to be a grandmother myself!
- ***Mimoso:*** This is a person who loves to be pampered and fussed over. We might say "high maintenance," but there's a sweetness about *mimoso/mimosa* that would be lost in that translation.
- ***Estrenar:*** You could say "to debut," but we wouldn't "debut a pair of shoes." In Spanish, it means to show off something for the first time: a jacket, a dress, a car, a sassy attitude; also, to premiere a play.
- ***Lampiño:*** "Beardless and bald." Luckily for the

follicle-challenged, this is a trendy masculine look in the early 21st century.

- ***Bizco:*** Surprisingly, Spanish has single words for some physical differences (I'm trying to be PC here) that English must describe with a modifier to the body part. This one means "cross-eyed." And there are several more:
- ***Tuerto:*** "one-eyed"
- ***Manco:*** "one-armed"
- ***Zurdo:*** "left-handed"
- ***Madrugar:*** As illuminated in our opening story, this means "to get up early in the morning."

Here are a few more, including some that budding bilinguals will recognize:

- ***Entrecejo:*** This is the space "between the eyebrows." Actually, there is a very arcane word in English for this area between *(entre)* the brows *(cejas),* and in this age of Botox, someone should invent a better name for it than "glabella."
- ***Chapuza:*** "Shoddy work" or a "botched job." I think I stayed in a hotel of this name in Paraguay.
- ***Anteayer:*** This is so handy! A single word to say, "The day before yesterday." And Spanish also has ***pasado mañana*** for "the day after tomorrow."
- ***Lustro:*** "A period of five years." Let's see . . . what would your age be in *lustros*?
- ***Tardar:*** This is a verb meaning "to be late" or "to take a long time." Although the syllable count is almost the same, there is an economical elegance to *tardaron mucho en llegar,* as compared to, "It took them a long time to get here."

I've saved two of my favorites for last:

- ***Tertulia:*** This is a meeting of like-minded individuals to engage in learned discussion of a particular topic at a regular time and place, usually a bar or café. Ernest Hemingway was a well-known participant in literary *tertulias* when he lived in Spain as a reporter on the Spanish Civil War in the late 1930s. We sometimes have *tertulias* of Spanish-speakers at my house, and while we definitely think alike (particularly in our love of food, wine, books, and travel), our discussions are often more lively than learned. *Tertulia* is a word that reflects a cultural aspect of Spain and some parts of South America but isn't widely known in Mexico. It's similar to a *salon,* but usually held in a public place rather than in a private home.
- ***Duende:*** A *duende* is a magical creature such as an elf or goblin, but I include the word here because it's most often a kind of magic or charm, an ineffable and enchanting quality present in some people and in certain works of art and literature. *Tener duende* is to have "it." Wikipedia has this to say about *duende* in reference to flamenco and art in general: "*El duende* is the spirit of evocation. It comes from inside as a physical/emotional response to art. It is what gives you chills, and makes you smile or cry as a bodily reaction to an artistic performance that is particularly expressive."

May the spirit of *duende* reside in your heart and mind and dwell with you always.

News from the World of Words

How would you like to undergo a medical procedure (brief, painless, no side effects) and wake up speaking the foreign language of your choice as fluently as a native speaker? That would make for a great sci-fi linguistic thriller, but for now, it seems ridiculously impossible (though some of us long-term students of languages are already putting our names on the advance-waiting list). It's just a wishful fantasy. Or so I thought until a news item about foreign language syndrome gave me hope. Pimsleur, one of the world's top foreign language-teaching companies, describes these cases:

> In April 2012, a 17-year-old Malaysian student involved in a motorbike accident emerged from unconsciousness speaking four new languages: Chinese, Japanese, Korean, and Indonesian. In what was considered to be an extreme form of this syndrome, the language changed on a daily basis, lasting for several hours at a time.
>
> In a bizarre twist on the theme of foreign language syndrome, a Croatian girl woke up from a coma speaking fluent German. As this was her second language, it was not a particular surprise. Most intriguing was the fact that she could no longer speak Croatian, Her ability to speak the native language had somehow been inhibited by the accident. (2010)
>
> In a third example, a Czech speedway driver who had just begun learning to speak English came back to consciousness after a motorbike crash, speaking fluent English to

> the astonishment of his friends, especially as there was no trace of an accent. Later, he could speak to an English reporter only through an interpreter. (2007)
>
> Other examples specifically related to the syndrome include a British woman who began speaking with a French accent after a stroke. An American woman who was put under anesthesia for dental treatment woke up speaking with a curious combination of English, Irish, and other European accents. In one of the most extreme cases, a Norwegian woman injured by shrapnel during World War II began speaking with a German accent. She was subsequently ostracized by her local community.

The rare phenomenon of foreign language syndrome, or foreign accent syndrome, was first reported in 1907 and has since manifested in over 100 recorded cases. These most often resulted from damage to the brain, usually on the left side where language is processed, caused by stroke or other types of trauma, as in the cases quoted above.

As of this writing, the most recent case of foreign language/accent syndrome was reported in early 2016. It involved a woman in Texas who had surgery on her jaw to correct an overbite, and woke up speaking with a heavy British accent. All the cases of this disorder are inexplicable, but hers is particularly rare because it was not precipitated by a blow to the head, but anesthesia is a form of brain trauma. The online video featuring her case (see References) is compelling. We hear her say that her only trip out of the United States was to Mexico, while we listen not only to her British-accented speech but her British *choice of words.* Despite all the scientific advances of the early 21st century, there is still no official explanation for the phenomenon of foreign language/

accent syndrome. The brain continues to be a mysterious and many-splendored thing.

* * *

Continuing now with other news from the world of words:

In 2013, a Tennessee judge handed down a ruling (since overturned) that a mother could not name her baby "Messiah." In early 2015, a judge in France ruled that the parents could not name their baby "Nutella," the trade name for a popular chocolate-hazelnut spread, on the grounds that it was against the child's interest. Where do we draw the line, and who should decide what is in a child's best interest?

I know of a woman who named her son "Blyth," and I feel for him. Facebook indicates that there are many unfortunate males in the world named "Jay Walker," and another legion of them named "Pete Moss." Would Mrs. Butts end up before a judge defending herself if she chose to name her son "Seymour"? My dear friend Pattie really wanted to christen her baby boy "Johan," but decided to name him just "J" and let the boy later decide for himself, since Johan di Maggio sounded like a bratwurst pizza.

* * *

Also in the news, languages are going extinct all over the globe. This is a phenomenon that has been occurring since the dawn of speech, but linguists note that it is accelerating now because of globalization, the loss of rainforests, the movement of people out of rural areas into cities, and of course technology and the worldwide dominance of English. Renowned linguist John McWhorter (The Power of Babel) and many of his colleagues estimate that, 100 years from now, only about 600 of the world's 6,000 or so languages will remain.

To learn that the Sumerian language died out in Mesopotamia before the birth of Christ, that the last speakers of Punic expired in North Africa in the early fifth century, or even that Latin became extinct in the 700s (but has achieved immortality as a dead language) does not really bring sadness. But what poignant loss is felt to know that Klallam was forever silenced in the state of Washington with the death of Hazel Sampson on February 4, 2014; that there was no one left to speak Yurok in California after Archie Thompson died on March 26, 2013; and that the 2011 passing of Brownie Doolan Perrurle signaled the end of Lower Arrernte in the Northern Territory of Australia.

Over 50 languages died out with their last speaker in the first decade and a half of the 21st century. Compared to the 170 that disappeared during the entirety of the 20th century, we can see the process is snowballing. If the trend continues with increasing speed throughout the 21st century, those linguists' prediction for a century hence will surely become reality.

* * *

In other worldwide lexical news, Rome's city council recently approved a regulation to phase out and ultimately eliminate Roman numerals on street signs, official documents, bills, and identity cards and replace them with written-out numbers. Many Italianos are understandably upset by the elimination of the numerical symbols that have named sites and ordered lives in the Eternal City for about 30 centuries. For example, Corso Vittorio Emanuele II, the boulevard that runs east–west through central Rome and is named after the first king of united Italy (1861–78), will now be Corso Vittorio Emanuele Secondo.

Mario Ajello, a commentator for *Il Messaggero,* voiced the sentiment of many of his countrymen: "Is it easier and simpler to have no link to the past? Maybe, yes, but it is cultural suicide." Fortunately, all the "MDCLXVIII"-style dates chiseled into stone will remain. Fueling the backlash, the city's new branding slogan is in English: "Rome and You," replacing the elegantly straightforward *"Roma Capitale."* Meanwhile, the Marina Militare has adopted the English slogan, "Be cool and join the Navy," in the hopes of attracting more young recruits via English than in their native Italian.

* * *

There is major linguistic upheaval on the continent of Africa. Ghana, Tanzania, and Zimbabwe are "casting off the language of the colonizer," in the words of Charles Mubita in *New Era,* and installing plans to discard English as the principal language of instruction and replace it with native languages.

* * *

In the arena of language politics during the 2016 presidential campaign, Donald Trump called it "stupid" for Jeb Bush, his fellow Republican presidential contender, to speak Spanish, and claimed he should "set the example by speaking English while in the United States." Carly Fiorina agreed, asserting that English is the official language of the United States—which it isn't. And Sarah Palin, who could always be counted on for quotable contributions to any discussion, said we should all just "speak American."

* * *

Here is a thrillingly upbeat lexical item that fuels the "love" side of my love-hate relationship with the game of Scrabble: New Zealander Nigel Richards won the French-language Scrabble World Championship in July of 2015, not because he is well versed in French (he doesn't even speak the language) but because he memorized the words in the French dictionary. At least one expert on the game has called him "the greatest Scrabble player of all time, hands down." It's nothing short of amazing, and you don't even have to be a word geek to be jaw-droppingly awestruck.

* * *

To close this lexical news report on another uplifting note, here's an item to gladden all hearts. In January of 2014, a seventh-grader from Santa Clara, California invented Braigo, a Braille printer, from a Lego robotics kit, printer parts, and a computer chip. How did it all come about? He saw a flier soliciting donations for the blind and, his curiosity aroused, asked his parents, "How do blind people read?" They told him to google it, and he dove in. After finding out that a simple Braille printer cost around $2,000, Shubham Banerjee combined tech savvy, Lego-love, and philanthropy to create a product that can be marketed for about $350. Intel provided funding for the young entrepreneur to take his seventh-grade science project to the next level, and he became a worldwide phenom. (Does the Nobel Prize have a junior division?)

Shubham was born in Belgium, and his family moved to the United States when he was four. I'd bet he speaks at least two languages: English, obviously; plus he may have learned Hindi from his family, and Belgium is a bilingual country inhabited by Flemish and Walloons who speak dialects, respectively, of Dutch and French. Research proves overwhelmingly that children who are bilingual from their earliest years show higher development of problem-solving skills, multitasking, and logic, as well as more cognitive flexibility. That news alone should revolutionize American education.

Speaking of Tongues

In my early years at Mendocino College, Dean of Instruction Susan Bell and her husband Neill were enthusiastic students in my beginning Spanish classes. The Bells threw great parties on Black Bart Ridge. Susan was a fabulous cook, the guest list was eclectic, and the conversation was always lively. The couple and I became fast friends, and having them in my classes was a delight. Susan took on Spanish with the same joyful enthusiasm that seemed to motivate her overall approach to life. Gregarious and uninhibited, she sought to practice Spanish with Neill and other students, with bilingual college employees, and in the community every chance she got.

One day before class, she recounted what happened when she engaged the owner of a local Mexican restaurant in conversation after finishing her lunch. First, she introduced herself and warned him that she knew *poquito español.* Fair enough. Then she began to tell him how much she was enjoying her *clase de español.* So far so good; he even complimented her pronunciation and her dedication. Susan loved conversation, and she was just warming up into this one—in a foreign language at that!

The pesky trouble with all lexicons is that a single word often harbors multiple meanings. As Susan was going on about how much she loved the language, and *el señor* heard her say for the third time, "*Me gusta mucho la lengua,*" he responded with, "*Un momento.*" He disappeared into the kitchen, and returned minutes later with *un taco muy especial para la señora,* and placed before her with a flourish a very special taco of beef tongue made especially for the lady.

As she chewed through that new culinary adventure, Susan pondered what had just taken place: *Language? Tongue? Ah-ha! "Lengua" means both.* There are two main words for language, and Mexican Spanish speakers almost always opt for *idioma* over *lengua.* The *señor* had interpreted that she was professing her enchantment with beef tongue *(lengua),* and gallantly gave her the opportunity to sample his own recipe.

I had to take some responsibility for this communication snafu because I had given my students both *idioma* and *lengua* for "language." You can see which one stuck, even though *idioma* is by far the preferred choice in Mexican Spanish. Susan laughed heartily over this misunderstanding—it had resulted in a free taco, after all—and then waded right back into deep and unpredictable linguistic waters, always convinced that everything would turn out just the way it should, and maybe provide entertaining moments en route.

If you are game to sample exotic tacos, some authentic Mexican eateries offer, in addition to *lengua*, *tacos de tripa* (tripe, or the lining of the first of the cow's three stomachs); *tacos de sesos* (beef brains—but why just beef? Are the pigs, sheep, and goats not smart enough?); *tacos de oreja* (pig's ear, with nothing left over for the silk purse); *tacos de rabo* (bull's tail); *taco de cabeza* (roasted meat from the cow's head); and lastly, *tacos de ojo* (eye) and *tacos de mejilla* (beef cheeks)—two specially prized parts of that head. As your mind's eye is already revealing to you, nothing is wasted from ears to tail.

At the mention of words with multiple meanings, *taco* brings to mind only one thing to all of us influenced by Mexico and its cuisine. But remember, there are 21 Spanish-speaking countries in the world, and for Spanish speakers from other parts, *taco* can mean a "plug/wedge/ramrod/blowgun/calendar pad/gulp of wine/confusion/dirty word/obstacle/heel of a shoe/short, stocky person/pool cue." Welcome to the labyrinth of lexicon!

Our English word *tongue* has its roots in old German, Dutch, and Norse. It seems to be a word that English speakers and learners alike do not like to spell, and just might confuse with *tong* and *thong*. This is evidenced by Internet images of bakeries in America with hand-lettered signs instructing customers, "Please use *tongues* to pick up cookies, not your hands," and "Do not touch bread with hands. Please use *tongue*," and even "Please do not touch with hands. Use bread *thongs*. Thank you."

I remember well a potluck with my Spanish-speaking friends in Sacramento in which the main dishes were *lengua* prepared in three very different ways. Zheyla from Ecuador prepared her country's characteristic version of tongue, as well as a second dish of *lengua a la italiana*, stuffed with a mixture of prosciutto, olives, and garlic. Lilia's was the famous Mexican version, baked with onion, garlic, bay, mint, and salt, then chopped and served with corn tortillas, tomatillo salsa, and lots of cilantro and lime. Previous to this culinary triple revelation, I had only sampled the Basque-style pickled tongue during my formative Bakersfield years, and I remained slightly prejudiced in favor of it, though (if the quantity of tongue I consumed that evening is any measure) very appreciative of these new lingual experiences.

What got me thinking about all this *lengua* lore was an ancient legend from the Afro-Cuban spiritual traditions. I used it for years as a reading in Spanish classes because it is a simple but powerful story that relies on the very same play of the dual meaning of *lengua* as "language" and "tongue." To conclude this section, here is the legend in translation as best I remember it:

> Obatalá, the supreme god of all creation, observed that his secretary, Orula, was very creative, imaginative, and unusually wise despite his youth. Obatalá wondered if

he could lighten his own workload and delegate some responsibility onto Orula's shoulders, but knew he had to test the youth's maturity and judgment before giving him such a big job. So Obatalá commanded Orula to prepare him the best meal possible.

Orula, obedient and willing, went immediately to the nearby market and filled his shopping bag with a bull's tongue and all the spices and ingredients he needed for a most worthy dish. When he presented it at Obatalá's table, the supreme leader enjoyed it and his appetite was sated. Licking his fingers, he asked his secretary why he had chosen to prepare *lengua* as the best meal. Orula replied, "It is with the tongue that praises are sung, virtue is exalted, and good works are revealed and emulated, and that *aché,* the mystical energy of the universe, is manifested."

A short while later, Obatalá instructed his secretary to prepare him the worst meal possible. Orula gave no reply but went straight to the market and again filled his shopping bag with a bull's tongue and all the accompaniments. When he served the dish and his master saw the same plate before him, Obatalá said, "How is it that you serve me the same meal as the best as well as the worst of all dishes?" Orula replied, "I told you then that it was the best, and now I tell you it is the worst because with the tongue reputations are destroyed, slander ruins lives, and whole populations are lost. With the tongue, the most vile acts are committed."

Amazed and pleased at the intelligence and wisdom of his secretary, Obatalá gave Orula rule over the world.

And we've been speaking, eating, and wagging tongues ever since.

Pigments of Our Imagination

What's your favorite color? What hues energize you, make you feel tranquil, optimistic, or elegant? Have you ever pored over chips at the local paint store and wondered who dreams up names like Cozy Cover, Copper Beach, Taffy Crunch, or Swiss Coffee—and how much they get paid for doing this? Is there any doubt in your mind that at a traditional wedding, the bride wears white, and you should not show up in black?

What color is your envy as you watch your neighbors leave for a tour of Tuscany, waving *arrivederci* from your ladder while painting the exterior of your house Stonegate Taupe in the August sun? Is there a color for your mood at the end of a week of Maui surf and sunsets as you fly home to face a pile of bills and the morning roll call at the office? Would you wear your green pants and red sweater to a party after the month of December has passed? What color were your "gills" on the fishing boat in the rocky bay? When you realized what the dog did to your fine Italian leather shoes, what color did you "see"?

A single color (pink vs. blue on a baby announcement) or color combo (orange and black in the fall) communicates unmistakable meaning via our culture and conditioning. Color is a form of language. It evokes reaction, creates mood, and expresses experience. This is true all over the world, but what is evoked or expressed by the color yellow to a German might seem as foreign to us Americans as their word for the color itself: *gelb.* While most countries in the West (the United States, Canada, and Western Europe) associate yellow with optimism, warmth, and good cheer (as well as cowardice!), Italians, Germans, and French turn yellow with envy alongside our American green. In Egypt and Burma, yellow is a color of mourning, and for the Cherokee Nation, yellow is a symbol of conflict and strife.

In Western countries, white is the color of purity, peace, safety, and health, and let's not forget that good guys used to wear white 10-gallon hats and ride white horses—"Hi-ho, Silver, away!" (Heroes of the 21st century mostly prefer the power and intimidation of black.) Food is perceived to taste better and be fresher and healthier served on a white plate. The bride's dress and flowers are white, and so is the frosting on the wedding cake. As we go East, though, while white still suggests peace and purity, it begins to speak a very different language of sadness and mourning. In China, Japan, Korea, and other Eastern countries, white is the color of death and funerals. In India, it is traditionally the only color a widow is allowed to wear.

Red is a bold color that can mean excitement, passion, danger, love, anger, and "Stop!" Studies show that sports teams wearing red uniforms have a competitive advantage, and that the color actually makes people stronger during competition. Western countries have red-light districts of prostitution and sex-paraphernalia shops. However, if we "paint the town red," we might wake up hung over but probably just had a night of good, clean fun. In the East, red denotes good fortune, prosperity, and festivity. It's the color worn by brides in China and India, but in South Africa it's the color of mourning. Superstition compels Spanish bullfighters to shun yellow, green, and purple but to wear hot-pink stockings for good luck. As for the matador's red cape—all cattle are colorblind, and the bull will charge at anything that's waved in his face.

America has exported "the blues" worldwide and, while the color can stand for depression and sadness, it also communicates calm, trust, and authority. American financial institutions inspire trust, suggest strength, and promise success with logos of blue. In the West it's a masculine color (and most men's favorite); in China, it's a feminine color. Also on the subject of color and the sexes, although it's almost impossible to imagine anything but pale pink for little girls and powder blue for baby boys, it was just the opposite in Belgium until recent decades.

In many countries, blue is the color for pornography, as in the now-outdated American reference to "blue movies." (In Italy, those racy movies are "red.") Another bygone American expression, "to turn the air blue," meant to swear up a storm. What people used to call "blue jokes" we now just call "off-color" or "dirty." In Spanish, it's the color green that suggests risqué behavior; a "dirty old man" is a *viejo verde.* In Australia, if the couple next door is "having a blue," they're having a fight; and "he made a blue" means he made a mistake.

The bright red of Coca-Cola's signature and Target's bull's-eye suggests excitement, youth, and energy. In America, orange is a cautionary color (think road hazards) as well as one of good cheer, confidence, and approachability (Nickelodeon, Gulf Oil, and Hooters). Orange doesn't give a "hooter" about trying to be subtle or sophisticated. It's the preferred color for fast food joints and discount retailers (McDonald's, Burger King, and Payless Shoes). Just as Mickey D's customizes its menu to offer McLobster rolls in New England, McZpacho chilled tomato soup in Spain, and McKatsu sandwiches in Japan, the mega-retailer also adjusts its website and color strategy for specific areas of its worldwide market. While staying heavy on the red-orange-yellow color scheme, there's a celestial blue background for most of the Middle East (virtue and protection) and a green one for Europe (luck, health, and environmental awareness).

In Holland, orange is the color of the royal family (House of Orange), and whenever the Dutch are vying for the World Cup, the entire country drapes its farmhouses and gabled buildings in bright orange fabric. There will even be an occasional sighting of orange cows. When the big, fluffy marigolds bloom in Mexico, orange speaks of death as people celebrate *el Día de los Muertos* (The Day of the Dead) in early November.

While Americans go green with envy, the French are green with fear. With hair standing on end, an Italian might be blue with fear but green with rage. In U.S. print and publishing, "yellow journalism" alerts us to a publication rife with scandal and exaggeration. In Italian publishing, *un giallo* ("a yellow") is a detective thriller. A "white night" is a sleepless one in French, Italian, Spanish, and other Romance languages.

In my high-school sewing class, Sister Mary Harrold rhapsodized about the existence of 500 different shades of black. We were unimpressed because black, along with white, was the only color she was ever allowed to wear, and we were just kids in uniforms dying to sport *anything* but the requisite forest-green plaid skirts and crisp, white blouses. The possible shades of blue and green might be infinite. Only 50 shades of gray? How unimaginatively dull, in a world full of colors and the foreign languages they speak.

Between the Sword and the Wall

As I started to write about this delightful but vast and slippery subject, I felt rather backed up against a wall with a sword at my throat, wild-eyed yet engaged at the prospect of a challenging duel of words between Spanish and English. Our American expression "between a rock and a hard place" comes close, but doesn't nearly suggest the pounding heart and darting eyes conveyed by the Spanish predicament of being *entre la espada y la pared* ("between the sword and the wall").

Proverbs and popular expressions provide insights into the deep cultural conditioning of attitudes and beliefs, and of course these come and go with changing times. We no longer hear Spaniards describing the order of things as *el hombre en la plaza y la mujer en la casa* ("the man in the plaza and the woman at home"), any more than we hear the phrase "barefoot and pregnant." Thank goodness and amen to that.

The vastness of this topic of proverbs and expressions also stems from the fact that there are 21 Spanish-speaking countries, each with a unique culture and individual linguistic style. You've invited all your international friends to party on your yacht in the Mediterranean for a month. To express our approval and excitement, we say: "Cool!" (Americans), "*¡Chido!*" (Mexicans), "*¡Chévere!*" (Ecuadoreans), "*¡Regio!*" (Argentines), "*¡Guay!*" (Spaniards), "*¡Pura vida!*" (Costa Ricans), "*¡Genial!*" (Peruvians), and "*¡Enpingao!*" (Cubans). With all that spicy variety, a grand time is a guarantee!

You don't have to be bilingual to appreciate the similarities and differences between English sayings and their Spanish counterparts. Some are even exactly alike, though we can't claim that one language poached and translated the expression from the other. We say, "A rolling stone gathers no moss," and Spanish says, *Piedra que rueda no cría moho*; "Better late than never"—*Más vale tarde que nunca;* "Love is blind"—*El amor es ciego.* As tempting as word-for-word translation is, it almost never works. Try commenting to a Spanish-speaker that it's raining *gatos y perros* ("cats and dogs") and they'll think you've got "bats in the belfry" or, as they might put it, *ratones en la azotea*—"rats on the roof."

When the subject of your conversation unexpectedly walks into the room, don't translate "speak of the devil," for it is *el rey de Roma* ("the king of Rome") you were talking about. Forming a direct translation of "wet blanket" won't transmit the image of a party-pooper, even though there *is* "water" mixed with "party" in the parallel term *aguafiestas.* That said, from here on, I will translate the Spanish expressions into English as exactly as possible, even if it comes out a bit awkward, just so you can match up the words in the two languages.

Some sayings carry basically the same elements but include slight differences that might raise our eyebrows. "A bird in the hand is worth two in the bush"—*Pájaro en mano vale cien volando.* ("A bird in the hand is worth 100 flying.") In a rash act, he "jumped out of the frying pan and into the fire," but the Spanish speaker says some variation of *Por huir del fuego, dio en las brasas.* ("Fleeing the fire, he fell into the hot coals.") Another way to say, "To go from bad to worse" is *Salir de* ("to leave") *Guatemala para entrar* ("to enter") *en Guatepeor*—not complimentary to that country, but clever word play, switching out *mala* (bad) for *peor* (worse). In Spanish, you're not "pulling my leg," you're "pulling my hair"—*Me estás tomando el pelo.*

Things really get fun and colorful when the expression

communicates the same basic idea but with totally different imagery. We all know the boring old adage, "Silence is golden," but Spanish instructs that *En boca cerrada no entra mosca.* ("Flies don't enter a closed mouth.") We attempt to brighten a difficult time by saying, "Let's make the best of it" or "Every cloud has a silver lining," but I am far better cheered by the Spanish saying, *Ya que la casa se quema, calentémonos.* ("Since the house is burning down, let's warm ourselves up.") Talk about black(-ened) humor!

One of my mom's favorite retorts to my missteps has always been, "It serves you right!" The *mamá* of another land might say, *Quien con perros se acuesta, con pulgas se levanta.* ("If you lie down with dogs, you get up with fleas.") That certainly offers more color, if not more consolation. Another of mom's favorites in my childhood, "Go fly a kite," is *Vete a freír espárragos.* ("Go fry asparagus.") "To each his own" (with a roll of the eyes) is the beloved Spanish expression *Cada loco con su tema.* ("Every nutcase with his theme.") That reminds me of one of my forever-favorites that hasn't a match in English at all: *De médico, poeta, y loco todos tenemos un poco.* ("Of doctor, poet, and nutcase, we all have a little.") That simple philosophy about the human condition probably holds true for all.

This next one is very Mexican, referencing the famous dish called *mole.* If something is "a dime a dozen," they might say *Es ajonjolí de todos los moles.* ("It's the sesame in every mole.") While we "sweat bullets," someone somewhere farther South will *sudar tinta* ("sweat ink"). We might be left "holding the bag," but pity the unlucky guy who has to *cargar con el muerto* ("carry the cadaver"). What costs me "an arm and a leg," to Lupe, will extract *un ojo de la cara* ("an eye from the face"). Big decision to make, and you need to sleep on it? Time to *consultar con la almohada* ("consult the pillow").

I love the facile rhythm and rhyme of some Spanish sayings. To be "two-faced" is to have *cara de beato y uñas de gato* ("the face of piety and the claws of a cat"). "You snooze, you lose" is *Camarón que se duerme, se lo lleva la corriente.* ("The shrimp that falls asleep gets washed away by the current.") "Look before you leap" is expressed by *Antes que te cases, mira lo que haces.* ("Before you get married, watch what you're doing.") "You can't make a silk purse out of a sow's ear" or "put lipstick on a pig" parallels *Aunque la mona se viste de seda, mona se queda.* ("Even if the monkey dresses in silk, it's still a monkey.")

Two more favorites: "a horse of a different color" is *harina de otro costal* ("flour from a different sack"). "To run off at the mouth" is *hablar hasta por los codos* ("to talk even through your elbows"). I never understood what talking had to do with elbows, but my godson Jaime Rocha informed me that it means talking so much that the words come out of even the least likely place, the elbows!

I've found that the fastest way to extricate myself when I'm "between a rock and a hard place" *(entre la espada y la pared)* is "not to have hairs on my tongue" *(no tener pelos en la lengua),* that is, to speak my mind truthfully. If talking my way out fails, I might have to *echar la capa al toro* ("throw the cape at the bull") in a last-ditch effort to get out of those proverbial *calzas prietas* ("tight britches")—or "hot water," as we know it all too well this side of the Atlantic and the Rio Grande.

Stereotypes in Stereo

I was put to the test many times on my study/travel program to Siena, Italy, but there were joyful experiences that preceded and followed the trying ones. Once installed in our lodgings, my small group and I showed up on Monday morning at the Dante Alighieri Institute to take the placement test and be assigned to our classes. I was put in the advanced class—though convinced I didn't belong there—and the two-week immersion experience began. It was a rough start, because the other 10 students in my class had already been at the institute perfecting their advanced Italian for at least two weeks, and up to three months.

When I took study/travel groups to Oaxaca, Mexico, nearly all the other students at the schools were from the United States. In Siena, I was the only American in my class, immersed in an exciting diversity of worldwide cultures and viewpoints. There was, however, one topic on which they all agreed, and it had to do not with me personally but with Americans in general. We'll get to that shortly, but a bit more background first.

I had become fast friends with Rita from Germany, and the other students in my class included two Frenchmen, a Brazilian girl, two Japanese girls who looked like fashion models, a woman from Switzerland, another from Denmark, a businessman from Canada, a teenager from Mexico, and a foreign ambassador to the Vatican. Our teacher, Alessandra, was the school director—statuesque, fashionable, no-nonsense, and rather fearsome. I could hold my own in conversation, and she was forgiving of my *molti errori* with vocabulary and verb tenses, but when she played a recorded narrative and I hadn't even a clue what it was about, let alone how to answer the content questions, her patience began to wear thin.

In my Spanish classes at Mendocino College, we often explored the topic of stereotypes because it gave rich opportunities for cultural perspectives as well as practice with descriptive adjectives. I was excited when Alessandra announced we were going to work individually to list stereotypes for several nationalities and then compare and discuss our work with the class.

First we explored how such stereotypes originate, and how they might play out in attitudes and actions. Then she presented us with nationalities: *francese* (French), *arabo* (Arabic), *tedesco* (German), *svizzero* (Swiss), *svedese* (Swedish), *cino* (Chinese), *giapponese* (Japanese), *italiano*, and *americano.* This was a big order, and to come up with at least three stereotypical traits for each we combed the memory bank for words and phrases and, when that failed, the dictionary for new vocabulary.

The follow-up conversation was lively, interactive, and punctuated by laughter and surprise, for example, at how different were the stereotypes recorded by the Asian students about Germans compared to those listed by the two Frenchmen. More often than not, the combined class lists included both positive and negative ideas, and general agreement from one student to the next.

Before I tell you how this turned out, I should mention by way of historical context that the United States had just re-elected George W. Bush to the presidency. In his first term, Europeans looked on us with some compassion, especially since Bush had lost the popular vote to Al Gore but had won the electoral vote. When he was elected to a second term, I knew from reading international news and talking with family and friends in Europe and Latin America that most of the Western World had slapped their foreheads, thrown up their hands, and concluded we were next to hopeless. I had been traveling abroad regularly since 1967, and this was the first time I felt goodwill replaced by dismissal at best and animosity at worst.

Back in the classroom with Alessandra and our own mini-United Nations, the other students were now called upon to reveal stereotypes about Americans. (One was exempt from naming stereotypes about one's own nationality except as part of the discussion.) There were at least a dozen different adjectives, and unanimous agreement among my classmates. For a moment, I felt panic and the urge to run from the room while listening to the litany of negative stereotypes coming from all sides. I really had to take hold and remind myself that this was not about (or against) me: *senza gusto* ("bad taste"), *maleducato* ("rude"), *forte a bocca* ("loud-mouthed"), *ignorante*, *disinformato* ("uninformed"), *egotista*, *arrogante*, *dispendioso* ("wasteful"), and *inelegante.* They were apologetic to me for such a harsh barrage, and to lighten up a difficult moment, I made a joke and said it was "inelegant" that hurt the worst.

Apart from any discussion about whether they are true or false, how do we acquire or develop stereotypes? I have the idea (fixed in sand rather than stone) that the Japanese are formal, very proper, esthetic, disciplined, fit, self-modulating, and respectful. However, since I've never been to Japan and I'm not on a first-name basis with a single native Japanese person, what is my evidence for these impressions? I am really thinking hard about this; I am "thinking aloud" as I write. I believe most stereotypes have some basis in reality, and come from films, books, newspaper and magazine articles, histories, photographs, and, to be honest, other people's opinions. All this adds up to cultural conditioning, and our exposure to it is deep, vast, and varied, considering that the many cultures we partake of and contribute to are national, local, familial, and so on.

If I express an opinion that Ecuadoreans are some of the most cheerful, friendly people I've encountered, I am probably contributing to someone's stereotype somewhere. When I tell the story of how some Parisians reacted to my rudimentary, Spanish-accented French, I'd wager I was doing the same. We seem to rely on stereotypes to try to better understand the world—not realizing that, especially in the case of the negative ones, we are reinforcing our separateness, perhaps even asserting our rightness. Isn't it fascinating that we can usually hold a negative opinion of a group of people only until we meet one individual face to face and start exchanging a few words?

On Friday of thc second week at Italian school in Siena, I was saying warm goodbyes to Alessandra and all the students in my class. The two gentlemen from France were effusive with their hugs and good wishes for my future success. In parting, one of them spoke for both, "Finally, we have met an American we like." How was I to respond to that backhanded compliment? I just smiled, accepted one last hug, and walked away knowing that—whether by a millimeter or a mile—the landscape of our cultural stereotypes had experienced a shift.

The Language Police

In a previous title or two, I mentioned the GPTBiA, the Grammar Powers-That-Be in America. Of course, it's all a bit tongue-in-cheek, but I'm half expecting that some wise, all-knowing English professor will descend from the ivory tower of a prestigious university to enlighten me that *of course* there is a language police for English—one single body of sage grammarians and lexical heavyweights to adjudicate the dangling of prepositions and splitting of infinitives, to definitively establish the true meaning of a "bromance," and to determine whether or not "selfie stick" is hyphenated.

But said professor has not materialized, and the only thing my research has definitively established is that no such organization exists for English in either America or the U.K. The question remains: who/what/where is the mysterious power over our language—the one that gave us the green light to tag a preposition onto the end of a sentence after centuries of torturous admonishments to intone, "This is the moment *for which* I have been waiting" and "*With whom* are you going to the prom?"

In the United States, there simply isn't an officially recognized authority invested with decision-making powers over grammar and the lexicon, but is there such a thing anywhere else in the world? Yes. Spain has The Royal Academy of the Spanish Language, which was founded in 1713 and has followed the same motto for over three centuries: "*Limpia, fija, y da esplendor.*" My best loose translation of this charge is: "Keeping it clean, regulating it, and making it shine,"

Today, there are 22 branches of the Real Academia Española

(RAE), each sworn to maintain the legacy and integrity of Spanish: the mother academy in Spain, one for each of the other 20 Spanish-speaking countries of the world, and one for the Spanish spoken by an additional 40 million or so people living in the United States. Of course, there are dialectical differences between the Spanish of Peru and that of Cuba, as well as between the pronunciation and some of the vocabulary of Equatorial Guinea, an officially Spanish-speaking country on the West Coast of Africa, and that of Argentina. Despite regional variations, however, populations of all 21 Spanish-speaking countries plus the United States intercommunicate pretty darn well with only minor glitches.

Glitch sample a): A *guagua* is a toddler in most of South America, but in Cuba and the Canary Islands, the word refers to a bus. This could be quite the deal-breaker in romantic communication for the Cuban suitor boasting to his *novia* (fiancée) about his fleet of a half-dozen *guaguas* if she understands him to be the father of six toddlers.

Glitch sample b): In most countries, the handy verb *coger* means to "catch or grab something": *coger un taxi*; *coger un resfrío* (catch a cold)—but don't utter that verb in Mexico or Argentina, where it's a sexual vulgarity, for you will scandalize your listeners, or at least give them a good laugh after the shock wears off.

This intercommunication in Spanish among 21 countries and the United States is unique and remarkable, especially when we consider that in many countries of the world, linguistic differences are so radical that they prevent communication altogether. In Germany, for instance—a country slightly smaller than the state of Montana but boasting as many as 250 different dialects—folks from one area can't *sprechen* with those from another region reliably at all. China, with an area slightly smaller than that of the

United States, has 297 *living* languages, according to *Ethnologue.* Also, just for the record, India has 122 major languages and 1,599 others.

In the United States, there is regulation of Spanish by the RAE, of Yiddish by the YIVO Institute for Jewish Research, and of Cherokee by the Council of the Cherokee Nation, but neither the U.K. nor the U.S. has any official say in the English that is spoken worldwide. Surprisingly, the only English-speaking country in the world with a language academy is South Africa.

According to Wikipedia's list of language regulators, there are 130 organizations, like the three mentioned in the above paragraph, tasked with exerting control over 110 languages in 187 countries and regions. Do they rule with an iron fist? A jerk of the chain? A wave of the hand? A shrug of the shoulders? I refuse to accept the vast research assignment required to answer those questions unless it comes with a limitless travel budget. At least for now we shall look into some of the recent regulatory activities in Italy, France, and Spain.

The highly respected Dante Alighieri Society, promoter and protector of Italian language and culture, has politely asked Italians to stop using so many English words when a perfectly good Italian one will suffice. However, for the most part, Italians continue to look forward to *il weekend* as a time to relieve *lo stress*—and that's just during their free time! In the workplace, *Anglitaliano* is so frequently used that one might assume no business can be transacted without English words: *Il manager italiano* deals with *il marketing, lo staff, il brand,* and *la competition.* Daily *multitasking è un must!* I have studied at the Dante Alighieri Institute in Siena, Italy, and I deeply admire their mission and dedication, but can they win the battle against ever more English creeping into Italian? È *impossibile!*

The French, rather more determined and heavy-handed than Italians or Americans, have done more than recommend; they have actually outlawed the use of terms like "email" and "hashtag" in official documents, and decreed these must be expressed as *courriel* and *mot-dièse,* respectively. The Académie Française is a powerful council of the French government that rules on all matters linguistic and rails against the sullying of the language with English words. The Académie and the French Ministry of Culture continue to resist the invasion of *le weekend,* "blog," "Twitter/tweet," "e-book," "parking," "chewing gum," and dozens more. The rejection of many terms including "fast food" and "binge-drinking" is every bit as sociocultural as it is linguistic.

In Spain, the RAE has declared war on the gratuitous use of English words in advertising that the purchasing public perceives as sounding more powerful, beautiful, sexy, valuable, affluent, etc. than their native Spanish. The anti-English-in-advertising ad campaign created to appeal to women shows a come-hither beauty with flowing blonde hair moving provocatively as she holds a pink rosebud against her cheek. In the background, a sultry female voice in Spanish promises "new fragrance, new woman," sensually repeating the name of the perfume, "Swine."

In a follow-up commercial, the same model gyrates in slow motion, and the disembodied voice returns with that sexy Spanish whisper, to reveal to audiences, "Swine—the perfume whose name in English tells you that you smell like a pig, but since it was in English, you smelled like Swine, a fragrance of pigs that penetrates your dreams. It sounds very good, but it smells very bad." In the final scene, she's in the arms of Mr. Tall-Dark-Handsome, and they gaze at one another with knitted brows as the realization of their surrounding stink begins to dawn.

A second ad for men is designed to combat the tsunami of

English words in Spanish publicity: After donning a pair of dark glasses called "Sunset Style with Blind Effect," the debonair man in the elegant black suit proceeds to knock over a chess game and crash into a room divider while the suave, male voice purrs in Spanish, "The only glasses that don't allow you to see anything. Dark, like all the words in English, put there just so you can hear them in English. Did you see that clearly, 'great man'? It sounds good, but you can't see a thing!"

The tone of both ads seems almost intentionally hokey, and it may be just that dash of corny over the veneer of elegance and beauty that captures imaginations and creates two viral cult classics. Obviously, the RAE has put not only mouth but a lot of money into these productions. Being somewhat of a linguistic purist myself, I admire the organization's passion and commitment to maintaining the integrity of the language. They might be successful in diminishing the use of English words in Spanish ads (*disappearing* is out of the question), but I won't bet on it. With the world's embrace of English ever broadening, that would be like going to a bullfight in Madrid and betting that the poor *toro* will come out alive.

At the beginning of the 18th century, Jonathan Swift of *Gulliver's Travels* fame proposed the establishment of an academy of the English language in Great Britain because, in his words, "Our Language is extremely imperfect . . . its daily Improvements are by no means in proportion to its daily Corruptions [and] in many Instances it offends against every Part of Grammar." The idea died with the demise of Queen Anne, his most enthusiastic and influential supporter.

In the following century, a bill to establish a national academy of American English was unsuccessfully introduced into the U.S. Congress in 1806. In 1820, the American Academy of Language and Belles Lettres was launched with John Quincy Adams as its president but failed in short order, having received little support from the government or the American people.

It's unlikely we'll see another attempt at the formation of an English language-policing agency anytime soon. I personally believe this is a good thing, because English is a world language, and the fact that it now has more non-native speakers than native ones will make for even greater absorption of outside influences. The American dialect in particular is so embracing of foreign words and welcoming to trendy inventions that it seems destined to continue its wild romp along the linguistic trail, and it surely would not respond well, if at all, to any heavy hand that tried to rein it in.

Rum and Revolution, Part I

March 22, 2015. It was my last day in Cuba, and I was savoring every step of a solo walk around Old Havana when I locked eyes with a skinny, wizened old man savoring a magic moment of his own as he pulled deeply on a fat, six-inch cigar. He regarded me with a twinkling gaze as he blew out the smoke, unhurriedly and obviously delighting in that phase of the breath as well.

"*¿Canadiense?*" When I shook my head and said, "*norteamericana*," he snatched the cigar from his lips, threw his arms skyward, and did a happy dance right there in the street. I couldn't help but do the same! Tourism, especially from Europe and Canada, has been under development as the golden egg of the economy since the collapse of the Soviet Union in 1991. Since direct travel from the U.S. had been severely restricted for decades, Cubans naturally tended to assume we were Canadian, but when they found out we were actually American, they would be invariably welcoming and curious.

The group I was traveling with was organized through the junior college in Santa Rosa, California and sponsored by Global Exchange, an international human-rights organization dedicated to promoting social, economic, and environmental justice worldwide. Our official mission was the study of Cuban nature and culture—quite flexible, but still structured enough to comply with U.S. law. Several people-to-people meetings were scheduled for us that were informative, warmly personal, and mostly satisfying, each in its own way.

I give the trip an A+, not for the comforts, cuisine, or amenities but because of all that I experienced and learned, everything that challenged, delighted, or worried me, and every person that I was privileged to meet along the way. Twenty of us, mostly northern Californians, traveled by tour bus with our dependable driver, Boris, and our superb guide, Tatiana. Their names were a surprise, but she explained that with the profound Russian influence in Cuba prior to 1991, it was trendy to give children Russian names. It's not uncommon to find people of a certain age with names like Vladimir Moreno, Natasha Álvarez, Svetlana Valdez, and so on.

The Revolution is still alive and well in Cuba, though given the shambles of the economy it seems undeniable that the Communist experiment has failed in the most fundamental of ways. On February 23, 2015, a month before we left for Cuba, the Associated Press reported that 150 to 200 dissidents had just been imprisoned there. The timing seemed dreadful, given that in January President Barack Obama had called upon Congress to lift the embargo and travel restrictions. I figured there was a backstory to the arrests, but was unable to dig it up before departing.

Oddly, neither our very knowledgeable guide nor any other Cuban I talked to had heard about the obvious violation of human rights that the worldwide press had reported. The international relations official we met from The Cuban Institute for Friendship Among Peoples (ICAP) knew nothing about it either, but assured us that no one is ever arrested for speaking out against the government, though subversive or criminal acts are punishable by imprisonment. Well aware that a few dozen of the arrested dissidents were women who regularly demonstrated against the government in marches in Havana, I had to wonder about the Revolution's definition of "subversive and criminal acts."

It was already dark when we arrived at the appointed hour in a very small rural town called *Polvo Rojo* ("Red Dust") to attend their monthly assembly of the Committee for the Defense of the

Revolution. I was expecting a political meeting of sorts, perhaps with militant exhortations of the kind Fidel Castro made famous in his hours-long speeches. We learned from Tatiana and our group organizer from Santa Rosa JC, Professor Gino Muzzatti, that every community has such a *comité* that serves as the guardian of the social order at the local level.

One website I consulted claims that these committees are charged by the regime to promote social welfare and report on counterrevolutionary activity—in effect, that they are the "eyes and ears of the Revolution." In this case, and throughout the entire evening, not one revolutionary word was spoken. The whole town had turned out to feast from the enormous and bountiful table of food in the middle of the main road, while salsa music was provided by two boom-box deejays on a nearby front porch. We added our contribution of several bottles of rum, and everyone proceeded to meet and mingle, eat and drink, dance and make memories into the night at this rural Cuban block party.

The teachers at the elementary school where we spent an afternoon told us they had never been visited by an American group before; the kids were seeing their very first Americans. I couldn't help but wonder if they were worried we might be brutes with horns, and surprised that we looked so normal, smiled a lot, and applauded their performance with genuine enthusiasm. One classroom was equipped with 10 computers but only two were still functional, as repairs and replacements were not an option.

The children sang patriotic songs for us, including "Guantanamera" (from the poetry of the Cuban national hero José Martí), and a homage to the national hero Che Guevara. Afterward, they presented us with adorable drawings and heartfelt poems. One little boy, shy and proud, with shining eyes, gave me his masterpiece: a big blue origami bird. It was a sweet and satisfying afternoon, and I will always hold this beautiful experience in my heart.

We passed a slow-motion afternoon in the colonial city of Trinidad, a UNESCO World Heritage Site in central Cuba, its charming cobblestone streets and pastel-colored houses built on the 18th- and 19th-century commerce of sugar and slaves. Then we spent three days in a mountain reserve called Topes de Collante, where we took nature walks (including some deep spelunking), met and talked with locals, bought coffee beans, and of course, like everywhere else we went, got to hear vibrant, zesty salsa music. How could we hear that beat and not *move* to it?

My fellow traveler and good friend Titus had been taking salsa lessons in Santa Rosa, so we had fun dancing together on a few occasions. At our hotel in Topes, the talented Trio Tradicional entertained just a few of us in the lobby, and I grabbed my three minutes of fame and adulation when I got up the nerve to take to the microphone and sing along to the old Cuban standard, *"Quizás, quizás, quizás."*

In Santa Clara, we visited the memorial where the remains of Che Guevara and 29 of his *guerrilleros* were sealed in vaults after being returned from Bolivia where they were killed in 1967 while fomenting armed revolution. The museum was moving and fascinating, filled with photographs of Che and company in the Cuban Revolution against the Batista government in Cuba and during the Bolivia campaign, as well as a display of documents and his personal belongings.

Che remains the most romantic, dashing, and saleable icon of the Revolution. Countless books about him are hawked by vendors on every plaza, and his is the most frequent image on postcards, billboards, and refrigerator magnets. Of course there are huge images of Fidel Castro everywhere too, accompanied by his best-known revolutionary pronouncements. After visiting the Che mausoleum, we met with families at a nearby cooperative farm, who generously laid out a bounty of almost surrealistically huge and colorful fruits and vegetables from their harvest for us to feast on with eyes and palates. As we experienced with everyone else we encountered, they welcomed our presence and encouraged the dialogue.

Many of my friends thought I would see all of Cuba from east to west, but if we had set out to do that in a mere 10 days, we would hardly been able to leave the bus! Cuba is approximately the same length as California, but the fact that it's an island leads people to assume you can drive around it in a day. It is the largest country in the Caribbean, and includes over 4,000 smaller islands and "keys" *(cayos).* During two days at a resort in Cayo Santa Maria in the Atlantic Ocean, we basked on an exquisite beach of fine white sand and crystalline turquoise waters. That made up for the fact that the resort was huge, all-inclusive, and packed with Europeans and Canadians on package holidays. Though it was fun to take in a little glitz, mojito in hand, I was happy to leave that scene and head back to the *real* Cuba for our last three days in Havana.

It's a long bus ride, so here is a lexical note as we bounce down the highway: How did Ernesto Guevara come to be known as "Che"? If you saw the movie *The Motorcycle Diaries* (highly recommended), you'll remember that he was originally from Argentina where *che* is the most frequent word they utter. It's untranslatable, but something like "Hey!/Man!/Wow!/Like..." at the beginning of a sentence to get the listener's attention, and might pop up elsewhere as a filler word ("so... /well... /y'know..."). Hearing him say "che" 100 times a day, how could his non-Argentine pals have called him anything but that?

Now move on to the next page to discover more adventures

in Havana, crumbling architecture, reflections on the economy (a 30-cent taxi ride and a $4,000 lobster dinner), and those fabulous old cars. *Hasta pronto*. . . .

Rum and Revolution, Part II

The streets of Havana, or La Habana ("lah-BAH-nah"), were full of rickety bicycle cabs, the occasional farm animal burdened with produce, and really old cars—a few of them in cherry condition but most wearing every rip, dent, and wrinkle of their 50-plus years. We had to pinch ourselves to remember it was 2015. Marcos, my Cuban friend back home, says that when you look under the hood of one of these pre-Revolution relics, you not only won't see original equipment, but most of what's there won't even be an actual car part!

Before my trip, I bought *A Quick Guide to Cuban Spanish* and even invited Marcos over to practice some slang with me. When I said I didn't anticipate trouble understanding Cuban pronunciation, he just smiled, rolled his eyes, then set me straight. As he had wisely predicted, when people were speaking directly to me, I could understand everything, but to capture even the gist of a conversation between two Cubans—forget it! They break all speed records of speech, and I would have had to commit that entire book of Cuban slang instant-recall memory to even catch their drift.

It's well known that in Cuban Spanish, the *s* isn't pronounced in some positions, especially at the end of words. So while I am still Susanna, Marcos is *Marcoh* when he visits his family and friends. *Los amigos* comes out as *loh amigoh* in Cuba and other parts of the Caribbean. This isn't likely to inhibit understanding, but I had to giggle when the speaker from the Ministry of Science and Environment spoke to us about *pescadores* (fisherman) but, with the first *s* disappeared, it sounded as if she were repeatedly referring to *pecadores* ("sinners"), making for welcome moments of lexical levity in an otherwise dry discourse.

Well-known architect and University of Havana Professor Miguel Coyula was very young when the dictator Fulgencio Batista escaped with his life and a pile of money as Fidel Castro and the revolutionaries took power on January 1, 1959. Under the new Socialist order, renting housing as a business was declared illegal. Everyone was allowed to move into houses and apartments that had been abandoned by Batista supporters fleeing the country, but no one could own an apartment building or charge rent to others. A space that used to house one family was now occupied by several. My understanding is that people paid rent to the government for a period of time, and then were declared the owners of whatever they called "home."

However, in the absence of landlords, no one was responsible for repairs and maintenance. All over Havana we saw crumbling, overcrowded, filthy-looking buildings alongside lovingly tended elegant residences and many buildings of great architectural beauty. The most shocking thing Mr. Coyula told us is that an average of more than three buildings a day collapse in Havana. He didn't address the personal costs in sudden homelessness, to say nothing of injury and death, but one can only imagine!

Despite seediness, power outages, and shortages of things you and I would consider essential, La Habana seduces with vibrant flavors, colors, and rhythms that lead visitors through winding streets and keep them turning yet another corner to discover more. I knew three nights would not be enough to even scratch the surface, yet my experience of the city was memorably satisfying because I got to meet Marcos's cousin Jorge, see Old Havana through his eyes, and view the economy from his perspective.

What is accessible to a tourist and what a Cuban can afford

are so far apart that the mind can hardly compute it. Some actual figures, given in dollar equivalents, will illustrate what I mean. A Cuban professional makes the equivalent of $20 a month (although doctors' salaries were recently doubled to around $40). Under the Castro regime, university education has always been free, and used to be accessible to everyone, but applicants must now pass entrance exams.

Still, the country's 25 universities continue to turn out massive numbers of doctors, lawyers, architects, teachers, and so on. These waves of newly minted professionals face a huge challenge to find jobs in the first place, and then to live on the meager salaries once they do. I spoke with Cubans working in restaurants and hotels, or selling crafts in the plazas, who had given up their professions to work in tourism so they could earn a better living. I'd wager that even a hotel maid can finish out the month with more than $20 in wages and tips combined.

Jorge and I made plans to have dinner in Old Havana at the restaurant where our group had eaten the night before because the food was great, the prices were very reasonable, and it didn't seem touristy. At $12.50, the most expensive item on the menu was the divine trio of lobster, shrimp, and octopus, which I recommended to Jorge. Add to that a glass of wine, a *cafecito,* and a tip, and one diner has just spent a whole month's Cuban salary. Granted, I paid the bill—but can you imagine spending a whole month's income on a single meal? Picture yourself sitting down to a $4,000 seafood trio with a glass of wine and a coffee. Feeling the impact of this economic disparity, you'd probably choke on that lobster.

Unlike a decade or two ago, Cubans can now frequent any restaurant or hotel in their country, but this point is mostly moot because, for someone who is paid in Cuban pesos, such places might as well be on another planet. The next night, fellow traveler

Titus and I walked for hours with Jorge along the sea wall, the legendary Malecón, Havana's favorite 'round-the-clock hangout. At midnight, we unanimously opted to hail a taxi to take us back to our hotel and then take Jorge on to his suburb.

It didn't even occur to Titus and me that there was an alternative to the tourist taxis we'd already taken around town, so we started waving our arms at the passing traffic. Jorge stopped us, adamant that it was unthinkable to pay the exorbitant $7 fare. We walked four blocks inland to a busy corner where loaded taxis—very beat-up vintage cars from the 40s and 50s—were whizzing in both directions. One stopped to let out three of its five passengers, and we hopped in the back seat. It cost 10 Cuban pesos per person (about 30 cents) to go anywhere in the city. That was dirt cheap for us Americans, but still an extravagance for a Cuban making a maximum of $20 a month.

Toward the beginning of the trip, we arrived at a rural hotel, only to be unexpectedly switched to inferior lodging with torn curtains and crumbling cinder blocks—"basic" at best. In our first two hotels, I could only get vaguely lukewarm water in the shower. Vegetables served in restaurants were almost always overcooked, and often canned. In moments of disappointment or frustration, as well as celebration, our ebullient group organizer, Professor Gino Muzzatti, prescribed doses of "vitamin R"—Cuban rum, preferably Havana Club, aged 7–15 years.

Our Cuban guide for Global Exchange, the delightful Tatiana with the unforgettable smile, taught us the principle of TIC: "This is Cuba (and that's just the way it is)." She said Cubans have a way of laughing and making jokes about reversals, shortages, and loss, not out of optimism but as a survival mechanism. They live with such daily hardship over aspects and objects of life that we in the United States take so completely for granted that cheer and a chuckle in the moment may be the only cushion between them and despair. That discussion put torn curtains and soggy vegetables into perspective.

Many Cubans I spoke with were excited and optimistic about a future without the embargo and travel restrictions against Americans, and they hoped to better their economic lot as a result. Some were proactively converting a part of their residence into a bed-and-breakfast, or planning other ways to profit from the promise of increased American tourism. Everyone was waiting for the influx of products from essential medicines to luxury electronics but, truthfully, it may be a very long wait. Legislation still holds the U.S. trade embargo in place and, even given the green light, that could take years to untangle. Congress must vote to lift the embargo, and the Republican Party remains strongly anti-Castro. Those are the facts, but optimism for "normalization" is fading.

Fidel Castro died on November 25, 2016 at age 90, and with his brother Raúl as president (2008-2018), the Revolution lived on, though with mostly welcome if tentative liberal advances for the Cuban people. It seems a profound irony that, in the very same month as the death of Fidel—the firebrand of revolutionary and anti-American ideals for almost half a century—Donald Trump was elected U.S. president and immediately began closing the doors to the normalization of Cuban-American relations that had been initiated by Barack Obama and Raúl Castro.

At the time of this writing (early 2018), the future of those relations are uncertain. With the administration of Donald Trump, all bets are off, and it appears that the thaw of a developing détente may again freeze into acrimonious relations and even harsher restrictions on travel and trade.

CHAPTER FIVE

The Wonders of the Bilingual Brain

Riding the Silver Tsunami

Baby Boomers, grab your surfboards! We'll see what being bilingual can do for aging brains, and find out some good news about regenerating neurons, self-repairing dendrites, and 100 ways to protect against Alzheimer's.

The Best Brain Elixir

What are London cab drivers and some Swedish military recruits doing to grow bigger brains? Do infants remember sounds they heard in the womb? Why do some children show accelerated development of problem-solving skills, reasoning, focus, and memory?

The Blooming Brain

The benefits of bilingualism accrue throughout life, and it's never too late to start learning a foreign language. Of course, considering that a baby at birth can distinguish all 800 sounds of the world's 6,500 languages, the earlier the better!

The Tongue May Falter, But the Brain Purrs

You studied a foreign language in high school and now you're sure you've "forgotten everything." Is that really possible? Learn the secret to where it is and how you can get it back. Plus, uncover the four big myths about learning a foreign language—herein revealed and debunked!

The Job-Seeker's Competitive Edge

What is the single most overlooked job skill, overlooked and underrated by the applicant but avidly sought by the employer? Here's how to capitalize on it and earn up to 20% more over the course of your working life.

Riding the Silver Tsunami

I will not be coy with you, dear reader. This is about Alzheimer's disease, and although there is very good news herein, some of what your eyes will take in will not be pretty—fascinating, yes, but not pretty. The lack of photos and pie charts on these pages is a plus because it frees you to use your imagination, and that in itself is an excellent anti-Alzheimer's exercise.

For starters, picture the holes in a chunk of Swiss cheese. A slice of Alzheimer's brain actually does look like a piece of Swiss cheese, with gaps in the tissue caused by—in highly simplified language that this author can understand—abnormal deposits of neural "gunk" that prevent neurons from transmitting and receiving messages, and eventually trigger an autoimmune attack on the brain itself. Assailed by inflammation, neurons die. Holes form, the brain shrinks, and the outward manifestations of the disease increasingly express as horrible symptoms: inability to remember, think clearly, compute, recognize loved ones, manage emotions, and live independently. This degenerative pattern becomes all too familiar as we and our friends care for aging loved ones.

We're still on this page together, so let's take an early reward in the form of some good news. The lifelong prognosis for humans, though it still ends in death, is not nearly as bad as most of us grew up thinking it was. Until very recently, science firmly held that brain cells cannot regenerate. Remember the sinking feeling that came with that so-called knowledge? What researchers have now discovered is that new neurons are continually being added to the cerebral cortex, the brain center responsible for learning and higher decision-making.

What a welcome revelation! The brain actually can grow new cells and repair itself, and there really is hope for future effective treatment of brain disorders and injuries. For now, though, while a good orthopedic surgeon and about three dollars' worth of titanium can get you a new knee or replace a hip, a partial- or full-brain transplant is not an option, and we are best served to dedicate ourselves to coddling—not curdling—the one we've got.

Engage your long-term memory once again, and recall your high-school or college biology class in which you learned that the average adult brain is home to some 100 billion neurons. Some of you might also remember making a mental review of the presumed fact that each shot of alcohol kills about a million brain cells, and then doing the math at the end of a particularly wild weekend.

Here's more good news: In 1993, scientists making cell counts of alcoholic vs. nonalcoholic brains came to the conclusion that this idea of alcohol-induced cell death just isn't so. Yes, a large amount of alcohol does impair the brain, but not by killing cells. Rather, it damages the dendrites—those branched extensions at the ends of the cells—thus inhibiting neurons' ability to communicate with each other, and causing loss of coordination, garbled speech, scrambled thoughts and, possibly, Alzheimer's and other forms of dementia. Even though dendrites can self-repair, it's still not advisable to pour a martini, light up a smoke, and camp on the couch, confident that genius scientists and profit-motivated drug companies will soon produce the magic pill or potion to disappear the plaque that causes the Swiss-cheese effect.

Before we get to the best news of all, let's investigate the numbers because all of us—whether we're the surfers on the so-called "silver tsunami" of aging Baby Boomers, or buff young bystanders on the beach—will see our lives affected in some way by Alzheimer's. Many of the 76 million Boomers (defined as babies born post-WWII between 1945 and 1964) have already celebrated year 65, the age after which most cases of the disease begin to manifest. The Alzheimer's Foundation reports that one in nine people (11%) aged 65 and older has Alzheimer's disease. Today's count of nearly 5.5 million sufferers could explode to 14 million by 2050, when the number of senior citizens will have doubled in the United States. Imagine the traumatic impact that will have on families, nursing homes, and the Medicare budget.

How can we turn the tide? Neuron by neuron, one brain at a time. A friend recently recommended a book entitled *100 Simple Things You Can Do to Prevent Alzheimer's*, by Jean Carper. Her search for simple but scientifically backed ways to accomplish what the title says was motivated by the discovery that she is among the 25% of Americans who carry the ApoE4 gene, which makes them more susceptible to Alzheimer's. Realizing that this means vulnerable but not condemned, she applied herself to devising a game plan and probably created a billion or so new neurons in the process. Here are titles of some of her 100 very readable, two-page chapters:

"Be a Busy Body"
"Say Yes to Coffee"
"Grow a Bigger Brain"
"Eat a Low-Glycemic Diet"
"Learn to Love Language"

Given as I am to loving language and promoting bilingualism, I am drawn to this last topic because of how the manipulation of words and language enhances the brain, and strengthens the structures and processes that will keep it firing fresh and fast for the rest of your life. Carper exhorts, "Read widely and write extensively to express your thoughts," and states, "Handling more than one language constantly exercises and strengthens the brain."

Every list of anti-Alzheimer's strategies gives a high rank to learning another language, and if you've ever tackled one, you have firsthand experience as to why this is so. You can almost feel those neurons pushing out their little dendrite branches as your brain, forced to reject its easy path to the English word "neighbor," darts down endless corridors and turns away from numerous fruitless dead-ends in the mind-maze before it finally produces—Eureka!—the Spanish equivalent, *vecino.* It's a beautiful, wondrous process, but it can also be a highly frustrating one if you are that struggling foreign-language learner.

The case for learning a foreign language is compelling. Scientists using MRI technology examined the brains of people who were studying foreign languages and those of others who were studying non-language subjects with equal dedication. Scans showed increased brain size in certain areas (the posterior hippocampus and cerebral cortex) among the language students, but not in the brains of the control group. Studies have established that speakers of more than one language score higher on academic tests in both math and reading, and they are able to better tune into their surroundings and focus on important facts. Do you have to speak your second language fluently to reap the brain benefits? My decades of experience teaching foreign language to English-speaking adults tell me your cerebral cylinders fire even more enthusiastically if you find yourself struggling.

Since I dedicate my professional life to helping people become bilingual, I'd like to return to the subject of frustration, which we touched on briefly in the previous paragraph. For the vast majority of us, frustration is simply an unavoidable, permanent feature of speaking a language that we weren't born into. Yes, I am saying that frustration will *always* be a part of your bilingual experience, in varying degrees of intensity. Once accepted, that's actually great news, because now you know to embrace it, dance with it, live and breathe it—do anything except fight it. Remember, too, as we've already seen, that dealing with unfamiliar challenges is all part of the brain's healthy and regenerative impetus toward new neural production.

If you are already bilingual, I encourage you to become even more so by honing your reading and writing skills. If you dream of speaking a second language, you've put it off long enough in the hopes of finding the elusive "right time." Just start now, already! The brain loves big challenges, fruitful frustrations, and bold new beginnings.

The Best Brain Elixir

Did someone say "brain elixir"? Let's make it something we can drink, especially if it tastes like a piña colada—or eat, preferably with the flavor and texture of fine, dark chocolate. Lacking that, at least give it to us in pill form; after all, this is 21st-century America, and we expect things to be fast, effortless, and effective.

What? There's no such pill? Okay, then, how about a surgical procedure? You know—risk-free, quick recovery, and lift this saggy jowl while you're at it.

Actually, there are many substances we can drink, eat, and pop that might benefit the brain. Ginseng is tops among several herbs that are said to improve memory and mental performance. *Gingko biloba* is another, known as a memory booster, and widely used in Europe to treat dementia. The list of "brain foods" tacked to your refrigerator door probably includes blueberries, wild salmon, avocados, nuts and seeds, leafy greens, whole grains, and yes, dark chocolate. (Finally, a guilt-free obsession!)

It is suggested that coffee and tea not only improve mood but also enhance memory and general cognitive function as well. There are claims for wheatgrass versus brain fog, and pomegranate juice versus forgetfulness. Of course, exercise is one of the most effective, cheapest, and most accessible ways to maintain brain health into old age. Studies show that people who walk just five miles a week increase their brain volume and show less development of Alzheimer's and other forms of dementia. Along with that green light for dark chocolate, here's a welcome piece of news for aging knees: some studies indicate that brisk walking is preferable to heavy aerobic exercise.

The subject of growing a bigger brain captured my attention when I read a BBC report about a scientific study of the brain size of London cab drivers. Interns undergo three to four years of intensive training, then take a test to determine the accuracy of their mental map of the city's 25,000 streets and thousands of landmarks, and their ability to quickly calculate routes and avoid jams. Only about half of them pass to become taxi drivers in one of the world's busiest cities and craziest street grids. In each of the individuals in the study, MRI imaging showed that a specific part of the brain, the posterior hippocampus, had grown remarkably and continued to develop as the cab driver spent hours each day behind the wheel mentally mapping the quickest route between two points.

Another recent landmark study in Sweden used recruits in the Swedish Armed Forces Interpreter Academy who were tested before and after a three-month period of intensive foreign-language study. Compared to the control group, the language students showed growth in the hippocampus as well as in three areas of the cerebral cortex. Since the hippocampus is responsible for learning new material and for spatial navigation, and the cerebral cortex is related to language learning, the findings in both studies seem logical in retrospect. What is truly stunning is the realization that the brain actually behaves like a muscle, increasing in size and strength with mental exercise.

Let's focus closer on foreign-language learning and bilingualism, and go deeper and further into the past. In fact, let's go all the way back before birth, into the womb. In years past, science assumed that a baby is born as a *tabula rasa,* a "clean slate" that can be imprinted and begin to learn only *after* birth. More recent studies overwhelmingly demonstrate that, at least during the last three months of pregnancy, unborn babies are tasting, smelling, and feeling their way around. (The amniotic fluid babies float in actually enhances their sense of smell.) Perhaps they are even seeing changes in light, and for certain they are hearing, remembering, and responding to sounds, especially those of Mom's voice vibrating into her body from her vocal cords, as well as passing from the outside air through her abdomen into the womb.

Testing of newborns' brainwaves showed that they recognized an invented word, *tatata*, which had been recorded and played to them thousands of times during the last trimester of pregnancy. An early study showed that the theme song of Mom's favorite soap opera could be imprinted on her newborn's brain. Moms-to-be started putting headphones on their bumps to play Mozart, Berlitz language courses, and recordings of *The Great Books*—but the medical field believes this amplification is too much noise, and could actually cause unhealthy overstimulation of the fetus's developing organs.

There is no longer any doubt that language is imprinted on the fetal brain, and landmark studies counting the frequency and speed of sucks on a pacifier connected to a recording show that babies, even on their first day of life outside the womb, can distinguish between Mom's voice and an unfamiliar female voice. Amazingly, and within minutes, they adapt their sucking patterns to connect with the sound of their own mother's voices. Pacifier experiments also suggest newborns can distinguish between native and foreign languages. In another study, Swedish babies sucked harder on pacifiers to hear more of the unfamiliar American speech sounds, and American babies did the same to hear more new sounds in Swedish. I've yet to find a study where the fetus was exposed to the two native languages of a fully bilingual mother but—you can already guess—I would be betting on newborn recognition of *both*.

Now, let's say at least one of the parents is bilingual, and the newborn infant, far too young to utter a word, is sponging up the sounds of two languages because Grandma has come to live in America and there's regular Skyping with relatives in the old country. Researchers say that just growing up in a multi-language home can produce enhancements of memory, problem-solving, reasoning, creativity, interpersonal relationships, communication and, of course, language development. If all that comes from just passive exposure, imagine what happens to brain development when the child starts *speaking* a second language! Then there is a whole category of neurological-based skills, known as "executive functioning," which is now being studied in infants and found by researchers to accelerate in development as well. These include: impulse and emotional control, flexible thinking, working memory, planning and prioritizing, and task initiation and organization. If the bilingualism is maintained and developed, neurological benefits continue to manifest throughout life.

Being bilingual is no guarantee of higher intelligence, let alone happiness or success, but it can undeniably offer the proverbial leg up in life from babyhood onward. We've looked at some of the benefits that have been observed and measured during infancy and childhood. Now we'll take a speed-ride through the next phase of life.

The Blooming Brain

Thanks for joining me as we hover in space, far above Earth. We look down on our planet from a great distance, and listen in with very powerful audio equipment to 7.4 billion people speaking some 6,500 different languages. Our computer deciphers them into individual sounds, and we discover that there are around 800 unique "phonemes," or distinct units of spoken sounds, that produce all the languages of the world, with each language composed of about 40 of these.

In a compelling study by research scientist Naja Fernan Ramírez, a research scientist at the University of Washington, we learn that babies at birth can distinguish all 800 of these sounds. That seems impressive, but it is simply essential since every baby must be capable of learning whichever of the 6,500 languages it is born into. If this malleability persisted through life, we would all be able to learn any language quickly and produce it with a perfect accent. Alas, it is not so!

Have you ever struggled to produce the Spanish *j* sound from the back of your throat, or the French *r* with just the right balance of palate and uvula? Have you ever noticed how much trouble some English learners have with the "th" of "this" and "that"? My Dutch father *(vader)* mastered perfect English grammar, but said "dis" and "dat" throughout his entire English-speaking life. The click is one of the most common consonants in many Southern African languages. If you've ever heard it in speech, you know it's not a sound the English-speaking mouth can easily reproduce.

By the time infants are 12 months old, they have become specialized in the sounds of the language spoken around them, and they are well on their way to losing the potential to distinguish the other 760 or so. Predictably, babies in bilingual households can process the phonemes of two languages, but what about exposure in the form of recordings? It seems logical that hearing the sounds of other languages in any form at a young age would afford at least some linguistic advantages. There is no hard science here, but I can share some personal experience of this.

Not only did Dad and Grandma *spreken* Dutch throughout my childhood, but the family's favorite (and only) Christmas album featured traditional songs in several different languages that we played endlessly from Thanksgiving through New Year's. My Italian mother recalled a few sentimental Neapolitan folk songs from her childhood, and she sang them to us when Grandma wasn't around. Between church, school, and choir, there was a soundtrack of ecclesiastical Latin running in the background for the first 15 years of my life (until Catholic Mass was said in English).

I didn't pick up Dutch, despite all my visits to the aunties in The Netherlands, but Romance languages do come easily to me and, in the case of French and Portuguese, disappear pretty quickly too for lack of practice. When I was in Tanzania, it was great fun to learn bits of Swahili. My adorable exchange student from Denmark, Ida, commented that my mimic of a long, gnarly Danish word was the best she'd ever heard from an American mouth. I attribute that to my Dutch *vader* and *grootmoeder,* my Italian mamma, the Catholic liturgy in Latin, and of course, Mrs. Domínguez, my high-school Spanish teacher.

Undeniably, growing up in that petri dish of language sounds has given me some advantage, but even so—and in the same category as my longing to be able to dance, ski, type, and play the harp—I deeply wish I'd started a second language in my very early years. As we have already seen, ample research reveals the marvelous benefits of bilingualism for the brain—improved communication and interpersonal skills, creativity, focus, higher reasoning, and memory.

All the revelatory research on what's called "the bilingual advantage" raises a big question: In the United States, why does foreign-language training usually not begin until the teen years, if even then? A depressing note: a large majority of states do not require any foreign language in high school at all, and the Modern Language Association (MLA) reports a 6.7% drop in foreign-language enrollment since 2009. That's bad news in the long-term economic and political pictures, but it can mean good positioning for the students who *do* gain a degree of fluency and for bilingual-born children who keep up their speaking skills and also learn to read and write well in both languages.

Second-language ability may not be a sizeable advantage in college admission, but if the student has tutored or used the language in some capacity to help others, it *will* give them a boost. The benefits of being bilingual in the job market are undeniable. What many applicants don't realize is that second-language ability is what employers in both the public and private sectors are screaming for. Federal agencies especially need speakers fluent in Eastern and African languages, but even local and state governments and private businesses still can't find enough qualified Spanish-speaking staff.

Here is some practical advice for high-school and college students: Pour on the coals in your foreign-language classes as if your professional life depends on it. It's not easy to become bilingual, but even starting in high school, as I did, isn't too late. Find opportunities outside of class to practice speaking in "real life," and sign up for a total-immersion program, preferably in another country. Expensive? Not necessarily. Scary? You bet! But only until you actually dig in and begin. That's when the second language starts to come alive, and you'll have a life-changing experience—and fun in the process.

I'll never forget how terrified I was to move in with a family of total strangers in Guadalajara for a two-week immersion program after four years of high-school Spanish. I couldn't understand a thing they said until finally I heard "tacos" and "tamales" and realized the *señora* was asking me which I preferred for my first meal in her home.

I was perfectly happy with either, and that's what I thought I'd told her, but her quick step backward and the rather shocked expression on her face told me it hadn't gone well. It took a while to unravel my mistake, and lunch was further delayed while she taught me what I should have said instead of, "I don't give a hoot."* It surely wasn't my only embarrassing moment, but I survived and even thrived outside the comfort zone of the classroom. Those two challenging weeks improved my speaking ability by at least 100%, and gave me my first deeply satisfying feeling of, "Wow—I can't believe I did that!"

---

* I said, *"No me importa"* ("I don't care"), which comes across like "I don't give a d***"—when I meant to say something more gracious, like *"Me da igual"* ("It's the same to me") or *"Me gustan los dos"* ("I like both").

The Tongue May Stumble, but the Brain Purrs

The most common claim I heard from students showing up on the first day of class was, "I took Spanish in high school, but now I've forgotten everything." A former student remarked to me that he wanted to get back into Spanish, but that all he had gained those several years back was now "all gone."

In fact, a lot of it is still there, in something akin to suspended animation—just not on the tip of your tongue anymore due to lack of recent exercise. Class starts, and you pour some magic elixir, in the form of simple exposure to the language, on the stuck hinges and—lo and behold!—the door swings open, though creaky at first. Words and phrases in that "forgotten" foreign language start springing back to life into your memory and onto your tongue. This happens almost comically sometimes, when a student who took, say, French in high school believes she has forgotten everything, decides to take up Spanish a few years later in college, and is shocked that for the first few weeks every time she intends to say *sí* it comes out *oui,* and every morning starts off with *"Bon jo*—oops, I mean *buenos días."*

Is it really true that one can learn language at any age? So often, I hear something like, "Oh, I'm too old for that. My memory just isn't what it used to be." We all wish we'd started in early childhood, but there are also advantages for adults: we can apply preexisting knowledge to any new subject, can choose from and combine a variety of learning methods, and have access to travel and other ways to apply and practice skills. Adult language students are also highly likely to be able to read and write what they learn to say with a minimum of additional effort compared to children.

In addition, much research suggests that the "failing" memory needs, and responds to, stimulation like language learning to remain sharp and focused. Scientists are seeing anatomical changes in even the brains of the elderly who make an effort to exercise the body and the brain. Important research has been carried out on adults with Alzheimer's, and it indicates that being bilingual appears to be a powerful buffer against the disease and can even delay its onset by four years or more, as well as slow the progress of some forms of dementia if already manifesting. This claim has intriguing potential and, since it has been challenged by subsequent studies, the research dollars will flow in; doubtlessly, this will be studied and tested further in the coming years. Wherever the proof ultimately lies, I'd wager there's great truth in that canned message I recently saw taped to a friend's wall: "You don't stop learning because you get old; you get old because you stop learning."

Years ago, I coined a saying inspired by the number of times I was asked a question I could not answer: "How long will it take me to become fluent?" My adage, *"No hay destino, sólo camino"*—"There is no destination, only the road"—is the best answer I know. There's no arrival point, because it's always an ongoing process.

Every one of us is already fully multilingual, with at least 100 words from several foreign languages—words that we have heard and repeated so many times that they have become fully ours. They materialize from mental concept straight to tongue, without the intermediate stage of translation. This feat is called "thinking in a foreign language"—and we do it all the time. In English, in addition to *tacos, tamales, salsa,* and *enchiladas,* witness *sushi, hari-kari, à la mode, baguette, cappuccino, biscotti, arrivederci, wiener schnitzel*, and *gesundheit*. In effect, when we say these words, we are thinking in a foreign language—and that's fluency, my friend!

Mastery of a language is the repeated act of becoming fluent with more and more words, expressions, phrases, and language patterns. Sure, it can feel difficult, frustrating, and slow going, if that's what we focus on; but why suffer and rush if the process itself can be fun, enlivening, and delicious? Why not savor becoming bilingual throughout life?

Once and for all, let's debunk the four big myths about learning a foreign language that have just been begging to be blown out of the water:

1. "It costs too much." Debunk: Yes, private tutors and Rosetta Stone programs can be pricey, but there are good language programs available free online, such as Duolingo. Community-college classes are still a bargain, and language-immersion courses in other countries can be quite affordable, to say nothing of fun and deeply rewarding.
2. "I just don't have enough time." Debunk: Even five minutes a day of doing anything in the target language will keep it alive and accessible, and keep you progressing. It's the daily consistency that makes a dream come true. (See "The Secret to Everything" in Chapter 7.) For example, one Duolingo lesson takes only about 10 minutes, but be sure to practice everything out loud, because that triples the value of your lesson time. The more active your activity, the better. A three-minute conversation in fractured French, with hands flailing to make up for your lack of words, can boost your skills better than an hour of staring at pages of grammar explanations. Sing along in Italian with Andrea Bocelli, make your ATM transaction in Spanish, order

your meal in your new language, and chat up the German lady around the corner. Mix it up! Do something fun, and venture out of your comfort zone every day.

3. "I'm too old; my memory isn't what it used to be." Debunk: Enough said about this; but if you've forgotten, just backtrack a few paragraphs.
4. "I don't have a flair for languages." Debunk: There is no hit of linguistic angel dust visited upon others but not upon you. There is no foreign-language gene. Some people do better in math, while others gravitate more toward language. The real deciding factor in who becomes functionally bilingual and who does not is this: the bilingual person sticks with it, and the other person doesn't. No judgment is intended there, but what come into play are factors like motivation, need, perseverance, and personal circumstance. The hard truth is that many people give up because they grow impatient with the process and gradual results, expecting some magical osmosis to occur without nearly enough exposure to and repetition of the language on their part.

There is great excitement over studies demonstrating that *plasticity,* the brain's ability to change throughout life, is available, yes, throughout life. It is enhanced by good nutrition, adequate sleep, regular exercise, and the amazing elixir of creative, communicative brain-feeding activities like playing a musical instrument, speaking foreign language, and even learning to swing-dance. This has tremendous implications for children throughout their developmental years, for adults as parents and professionals, and for seniors who want to remain vibrant and productive for *all* their years.

It's best to start your foreign-language learning as early as you can. That would be right now—at any age. Yes, it will be challenging, but be prepared to have some fun! Successful bilinguals don't wait until they're "good enough" at it to use their language in the world. As Ralph Waldo Emerson exhorted, "Do the thing and you shall have the power."

The Job-Seeker's Competitive Edge

Let's say you're a recent graduate, or you've just been laid off from a job, or have simply decided to look for a better one. In other words, you're in the job market, and need to maximize every advantage possible: any and all volunteer work and community activity, organizational experience you gained while planning the family reunion, or training skills you developed with the new family dog. I'm almost kidding about that last one, but don't overlook a thing, especially if you're young with a slim résumé.

Oftentimes, after gaining intermediate language abilities, students of mine leave this question blank on their application: "What other languages do you speak? read? write?" Why don't they give an answer? Because they are afraid of overstating their skills, and shy about possibly over-representing themselves since they aren't fully bilingual. I say it's best to always toot your horn, while remaining truthful. You may not be "fluent," but you can be "functionally bilingual," meaning you are able to use a second language effectively in life's ordinary situations, albeit with errors.

On a trip to the local emergency room with a sprained ankle, I sat first in the waiting room and then in the treatment area. I was in great pain but immense joy as I listened to three of my former students who worked there, effectively handling the needs of Spanish-speaking patients. Regardless of whether or not they could navigate a cocktail party in their second language, they were functionally bilingual on the job. Was their ability attributable to my Spanish classes? Only in small part, for their skill and confidence came from seeing a need, being willing to step in, and then, as in most jobs, repeating the same words and phrases time and time again.

In a past life, I interviewed many applicants for jobs in food service, and was always on the lookout for bilingual hires. I often think how powerful it would be for an interviewee in any field to say to the manager, "I took X foreign language in school. I'm not fluent yet, but I speak, read, and write it enough to get my point across, *and* I'm on a daily study and practice program to continue to develop my abilities. I'm committed to being bilingual, and I know I can be an asset to this company with my advancing language skills and my understanding of another culture."

Had someone given me that answer, I would have responded, "*¡Bravísimo!* You're hired and, furthermore, within six months, I'm going to start you on an advancement program to get you that 20% additional pay that you, as a bilingual person, have the potential to earn over the course of your working life."

If you are one of the lucky people with the immense advantage of being born into bilingualism with a foreign language spoken at home, capitalize on that gift by developing your reading and writing skills to match your fluent speaking skills. If you do, your dream job will soon be calling your name, and that additional 20% of earnings will be in your bank account.

No matter your age, if you've taken even one class in foreign language, amazing changes have occurred in your brain, so don't stop now! Your gray matter is becoming denser for better muscle control, sensory perceptions, memory, emotions, speech, decision-making, and self-control. Your white matter, which connects the gray matter areas and carries nerve impulses between neurons, is being strengthened.

You see? It just keeps getting better—but you have to keep it up. It can feel slow and bumpy, but a foreign-language learning curve should be a nice, steady forward trajectory that moves gradually upward. Unfortunately, most trajectories look more like a roller-coaster ride of fits and starts and stops as the language center of the brain lights up (new class! online program! travel!) and shuts down (end of class, forgot about program for two weeks, no money to travel . . . *oh, what's the use?*).

There's a simple trick to even out this craziness, to keep that learning curve on a steady rise, and to ensure a snappily firing brain, to say nothing of moving us in the direction of our goal. My goal is to be ever more fluent in Italian, so I spend a few minutes a day using the free online language program called Duolingo. I receive a daily e-mail reminder, and earn rewards by staying on a learning streak of one lesson every 24 hours. It takes five to 10 minutes to do that.

I triple the value of my short sessions by repeating everything I hear, and reading everything I see *ad alta voce* ("out loud"). Of course, more is always better, but make no mistake—that five minutes a day is more valuable to my brain and tongue than 35 minutes every Saturday afternoon. The language-learning center in my brain—the one with "Italian" on the door—always stays open with the lights on. That's the physiological advantage of the daily-practice rule. There's also the added psychological benefit that, as long as I keep it up, I never feel I've taken a linguistic backslide and lost ground through inactivity.

High-school and college graduations happen every spring, and I wonder where all the students who've taken one to four foreign language classes will be in five years. I am passionate about making language learning a lifelong practice, just like physical fitness, eating a healthy diet, or getting enough sleep. Notice I chose three things that are highly desirable for a vibrant life but also challenging to maintain in our busy world. Let's compare daily language practice to putting a few dollars into a savings account every month:

1. It's not easy to start the discipline and remain consistent with it.
2. Sometimes you might fall off the wagon and succumb to the temptation to cash out all your savings or drop out of your daily language routine. (I have firsthand experience at both!)
3. If you do tumble off the wagon, you can always begin again. The difference in our analogy here is that you'll have to restart with a zero balance in your savings account, while your bilingual brain bank has stored much of the learning and can't wait to dust it off when you begin again.
4. If you follow through with your savings plan, at the end of a year, a decade, or a half-century, you'll have a significant amount of money in the bank. A few minutes a day of foreign language compounds into bilingual abilities that are personally and professionally enhancing.

With a clear commitment and consistent deposits to your savings account or your bilingual bank (better yet, both!), you'll have very concrete results to show, and much to be proud of. The only ingredients to add to the mix are a dash of acceptance for wherever you are in the process, and lots of encouraging self-pats on the back.

CHAPTER SIX

A Life in Words

Make Love, Not War

A bittersweet flashback to the 50s, 60s and 70s: the Cold War, the Iron Curtain, backyard bomb shelters, the Cuban Missile Crisis, Women's Lib, Kennedy's Camelot, Vietnam, and more.

Don the Noose for Biscuits

If you can relate to being a kid learning to sing the traditional hymn "Gladly the Cross I'd Bear" and feeling somehow cheered there's a church song about *Gladdy the cross-eyed bear;* or singing along with the Beatles to "Lucy in the Sky with Diamonds," but always baffled at the part about *the girl with colitis goes by* ("the girl with kaleidoscope eyes"), then this one's for you.

All About Me: The Sequel

This is the story of how I left my freeway-flyer life of multiple part-time jobs in Sacramento for a small city in northern California, where the dearth of malls and restaurants didn't bother me—but I found some street signs, place names, and roadside images truly worrisome.

All About Me: Prequel I

Perhaps my linguistic trajectory through life was launched in my childhood, but we begin this prequel before I was even a twinkle in my parents' eyes.

All About Me: Prequel II

Eight years of foreign language studies, a BA in Spanish and suddenly I'm in a graduate program with native speakers from all over the Spanish-speaking world, and I can't carry on a simple conversation. I could have quit. It could have killed me. But since neither happened, I became bilingual.

Ez Dakite Euskaraz Hitz Egiten Duzu?

No, I don't speak a word of Basque, but I feel as close to this culture as to the Italian and Dutch of my own heritage. Beautiful people, fascinating history, delicious cuisine (though I'll pass on the pigs' feet), and a language that remains one of the great linguistic mysteries of the world.

The Cure by Feeding of Earworms

They worm their way into your skull without reason, but often with rhyme and a catchy tune. Then the same few bars keep playing in your head for hours, perhaps days—or, as some sufferers report, for years. Is there a brain wash to eradicate the earworm?

In Megahurtz, but Knotfurlong

Does thinking of half a large intestine as one semicolon make you groan or grin? It wasn't writer's block but a fractured wrist that derailed me from my writing track. So, I got creative—with other people's material.

A Girl (Not) Named Sue

Can you imagine a 21st-century baby named Ethel or Gertrude, Gaylord or Ambrose? A first name can be inspired by genealogy, religion, tradition, trend, or simply choice. Mine seems to be still a work in progress.

Behind Closed Classroom Doors, Part I

Spanish classes without food? Unthinkable! Then again, maybe we took it too far with inky squid, flying eggs, and possibly poisonous mushrooms.

Behind Closed Classroom Doors, Part II

Cigarettes, alcohol, a near brawl, and thousands of counterfeit bills changing hands—was this a college Spanish class or a den of iniquity?

Behind Closed Classroom Doors, Part III

Simulating imprisonment and torture and contemplating disaster on a massive scale are weighty matters. There's nothing like some explosive pyrotechnics to lighten things up!

Make Love, Not War

Looking back at my childhood in America of the 1950s and 1960s, specific words come to mind reigniting the emotions and confusions they evoked then, along with the impact of history they evoke now: “Sputnik/Cold War/atomic bomb/Iron Curtain/USSR/Communism/space race/JFK/Bay of Pigs/Cuban Missile Crisis/hippies/Vietnam.” Each term is loaded with metaphoric meaning for an era, a way of life, and for how we’ve grown up to be who we are today.

I will add to this list the term “sonic boom,” even though most folks weren’t nearly blown off their feet in their own backyards twice a day unless they lived near an air force base. It’s been decades since I’ve heard a sonic boom, but living in Bakersfield, just 83 miles from Edwards Air Force Base, we got used to the frequent air-shattering “BOOOM!” as merely part of the landscape—or, more precisely, the skyscape. Visitors to the area were often paralyzed with shock, running for cover, screaming hysterically, or engaging all three reactions at the same time.

I was a happy kid in a great home in a friendly town. I believed in Santa Claus and the Easter Bunny, and knew my guardian angel was watching over me and that my parents would always protect me. But two inescapable fears weighed heavily on my scrawny shoulders: the fear of eternal damnation in Hell, and the fear of nuclear annihilation. By early Saturday afternoons, I was already nervous about the weekly trip to church at 5:00 p.m. to confess my sins and pray for my penance—my only protection against an eternity spent burning in Hell, other than the impossible option of ceasing to sin altogether.

As an aspiring saint I had tried that route, but quickly gave up on perfect angelic behavior as an unrealistic option. There were just too many opportunities to be "unkind to my brother and sisters" and "disobedient to my parents." For that reason, Saturday afternoons in the confessional were dreaded but essential purges in an effort to hold on to at least a reasonable shot at gaining a place in Heaven.

On those Saturday afternoons before my weekly confession of "Bless me, Father, for I have sinned . . ." the neighborhood gang gathered in our front yard to play a new game we had invented called *Sputnik.* The Soviets had launched the first satellite of that name on October 4, 1957, and by the time my sister Margie turned six, less than two weeks later, it was a household word even to us kids. The game simply consisted of all of us in a circle taking turns to see who could throw the basketball the straightest and highest, while the rest of us yelled at the top of our lungs, "Sputniiik!" We'd inducted the term into our lexicon of play, and into our mental bank of fears that dangerous things from the skies could actually destroy us. We were just regular kids playing games, going to school, riding bikes, and blasting up and down cracked sidewalks on metal skates without a care in the world—except for the threat of nuclear war.

Meanwhile, Dad spent *his* Saturday afternoons sandbagging the basement of the house on V Street, and then stocking it with nonperishables in the event we'd have to take subterranean shelter from bombs falling nearby or, more likely, their fallout from afar. I stood in the doorway of that basement one sunny afternoon when I was not much taller than the doorknob, and asked my father—just to make sure—"Will Spotty get to come too?" When he said that we couldn't bring the family dog into the bomb shelter, I was overcome with anticipated loss and feelings of dread. A few months later, after a happy family camping vacation in Yosemite, I was in the back of the station wagon watching the park recede from view, feeling a hopeless conviction that nuclear bombs would destroy everything, and I'd never see Yosemite again.

At school, we had regular bomb drills. When the alarm bell sounded in a certain pattern, we knew to slide off our little benches and crouch on the floor under our desks with our arms over our heads (as if!). My friend Susan remembers doing the same drill at her grade school in San Francisco, always worrying desperately how she would get home to her mother when the attack came—*when,* not *if.* I know it sounds contradictory, but we were happy-go-lucky children living with a sense of impending doom. I was too young during the Cuban Missile Crisis to understand the circumstances and the potential consequences, but I clearly remember the look on Dad's face that told me this was *dire.*

When I was in high school, the side yard of our big corner lot was excavated, and a 16-foot, cylindrical metal tank with air filters and a spiral stairway was buried alongside the house. We were the first family in America to have that model of bomb shelter because my father had designed and built it at the steel company he worked for. The local TV news team showed up to photograph the event and interview my Dad. By then, the Cold War was such a given in the fabric of life that I was more worried about the appearance of my flip hairdo on camera than in the threat of nuclear annihilation.

When President Kennedy was shot on November 22, 1963, the nuns led us in prayer for his recovery. I grew up watching TV hospital dramas like *Doctor Kildare* and *Ben Casey, MD,* so I was naïvely sure he would be saved. Besides, JFK was Catholic, and I still believed God favored us as the true chosen ones. The announcement of his death came to us from our teachers in the early afternoon, and we were stunned. I watched the reactions of some of the upper-class students, and felt my own confusion and wordless anguish. Helplessness. All I remember after that is being at home in the late afternoon; Mom cooked dinner while Dad locked himself in the hall bathroom because he couldn't stop crying. Maybe we didn't *really* believe in Camelot, but on that day another part of our optimism and innocence was irrevocably blown away.

* * *

The Vietnam War came with a whole new vocabulary list: "Vietcong/Da Nang/Ho Chi Minh/Gulf of Tonkin/hawks and doves/My Lai Massacre/napalm/Agent Orange," and more. Words foreign, macabre, and menacing. If these terms still evoke horror in me, I can imagine what they must create in the minds of those who actually served there. As I went away to college at UC Davis, my parents threatened to cut off my funds if I participated in antiwar demonstrations. At first, I complied with the letter of that law, but at the end of my first year away, even that became impossible.

On April 30, 1970, President Nixon announced the need for 150,000 more troops to expand the war and invade Cambodia, and protests broke out on campuses nationwide. Four days later, on May 4, 1970, National Guardsmen fired into a peaceful antiwar demonstration at Kent State University in Ohio, killing four students and wounding nine. Outrage was the emotion, and protest was the call to action. Universities shut down for several days, and many professors and most students devoted ourselves full time to marches in Sacramento and antiwar rallies on campus.

I remember feeling deep anger and frustration as well as an awakening awareness of how easy it could be to resort to violence.

But we didn't choose that route. Instead, my friends and I joined an antiwar information group; we educated ourselves, and then went into the residential streets of nearby towns to knock on doors, hear others' views, and speak ours, which were wholeheartedly against the war.

The year 1970 was an amazing one, full of triumph and tragedy, with the Women's Lib movement roaring like an avalanche in the background of it all. On April 17, the Apollo 13 crew landed safely in the South Pacific after its aborted mission to the moon. A week before President Nixon's announcement to escalate the war in Vietnam, the very first Earth Day was held on April 22, and 20 million Americans of all walks and persuasions celebrated and rallied for a clean, sustainable environment. The Beatles had already announced their breakup, and their last album, *Let It Be,* was officially released on May 8, four days after the Kent State massacre. Jimi Hendrix died of an overdose on September 18, right before I went back to college for my senior year.

The 50s and 60s were over, although the Cold War would last through the next two decades. Clearly, 1970 was a watershed year of endings and new beginnings. It sounds trite to say the world would never be the same again, but it also rings true: it wouldn't, and it wasn't, and it never will be. Even so, for those of us who came of age in that era (and aren't we all always "coming of age"?) the words and images live on in deep visceral memory, and that world within us remains forever vividly alive.

Don the Noose for Biscuits

Every childhood is replete with legions of misunderstood words, invented meanings, and big questions in little minds trying to discover, "Just what are those tall people trying to say?" Anytime an adult speaks, there's a high probability that children, always negotiating with what little they know of the world and its words, will fill in mental blanks with creative meaning-making. Adults take a lot for granted, having long forgotten how many dots must be connected for a single concept or act to be understood.

My mother was working on a project in the garden of our house on V Street in Bakersfield (I perceived it as a mansion on an expansive estate; I was only five), and she told me to run and get "a couple" of empty coffee cans. Anxious to be useful, I raced across the yard, through the house, out to the garage and to the shelf where—*Oops!*—I realized I was missing an important piece of understanding. I retraced my steps back to the garden at twice the speed and, gulping air, asked, "Mommy, how many is 'a couple'?" Even today, I can still hear the impatient disbelief in the tone of her reply, and the sense of wonder in my brain that there was another word for "two."

We went to Catholic Mass every Sunday, and it ultimately got to where I could practically speak Latin. At that tender age, I didn't recognize it as a different language. My brain tried mightily and constantly to figure out its meaning by mentally searching out the closest word in the limited lexicon that I *did* know. I just assumed the priest was pronouncing English badly, and so it was up to me to compensate my way to some level of comprehension.

Over and over in the Mass, he would say, *"Dominus vobiscum,"* to which the congregation responded, *"Et cum spiritu tuo."*

I hadn't yet learned that these phrases meant, respectively, "The Lord be with you," and "And with your spirit," so my brain went to work on them: *"Dah-mu-nuus"—hmmm . . . something about "dominoes"?* I knew that was unlikely, as I hadn't seen my favorite game played in church yet. *Maybe something about a "noose"? Then that "vobiscum" part could be about "biscuits." Is that what people get on their tongue when they take Communion?*

Unanswered questions loomed with the first phrase, but less so with the second. The meaning of *"Et cum spiritu tuo"* was obvious to me, hearing it just as the priest said it: "Eh, come, Spirit 2-2-0." It seemed neither magical nor wondrous but entirely practical that the Holy Spirit had a contact number. I assumed my parents phoned him a lot, and I hoped they were telling him mostly good things about me.*

My grandmother emigrated from WWII-ravaged Holland and came to live with us when I was a toddler. She and my dad conversed in Dutch, and my Italian mom learned to catch the gist of these unfamiliar utterances so she could follow what her hyper-critical mother-in-law was saying about her. My little sister Margie and I didn't understand anything of those chats between mother and son, so we made up nonsense sounds and insisted to Grandma that we, too could speak her language: "*Ownsee kownsee blamla floop*." She was neither impressed nor amused.

At the age of six, I started the first of 12 years of Catholic school at St. Francis Elementary, and the rain of unfamiliar words

---

* My poet friend Dan Barth reports that, as a child, he was pretty sure that *Et cum spiritu tuo* had something to do with Tootsie Rolls. After he learned to sing "Silent Night, holy night, all is calm, all is bright 'round yon virgin mother and child . . ." he drew a picture of Jesus's babyhood friend, Round John Virgin.

turned into a deluge. We learned more prayers in addition to the ones we already knew for reciting the Rosary. The nuns taught us the Act of Contrition, to express penitence for our numerous and oft-repeated sins. It begins, "Oh, my God, I am heartily sorry for having offended Thee," and with true repentance and abiding fear of eternity in Hell, I prayed it at least twice a day, especially after tripping Margie or telling Karen she was a meanie: "Oh, my God, I am *hardly* sorry . . ." I was vaguely aware of the discrepancy between that mistaken adverb and my sincere intent, and I briefly wondered if God or the nuns had made a mistake. We just didn't question that sort of thing, though, for fear of having yet another sin to do penance for.

In the second grade, we learned about a place called Limbo, where the souls of innocent babies who died before they could be baptized were warehoused for all eternity. They were not tortured, like the sinful ones damned to burn in Hell, but they were forever denied the sight of God for lack of a sprinkle of water and the requisite incantations. This affected me deeply, and I badgered parents, relatives, neighbors, and even strangers on adjoining city blocks for donations to the St. Francis collection for pagan babies, so that the innocents in Africa could be baptized and thus saved from the fate of being trapped in Limbo for all time. I recently asked a devout Catholic, "Whatever happened to Limbo?" and she replied with firmness and finality, precluding further query, "They *closed* it."

In the third grade, my teacher announced that we were going to learn *homonyms.* I was in orbit with joy, because I thought we were going to practice the "harmonies" that Mom had taught us kids to do, fantasizing that we would become the next Lennon Sisters on the Lawrence Welk show. (We never missed a Saturday night!) My sibs and I had been singing "You Are My Sunshine" in harmony for as long as we could remember. Back in the classroom, the announcement about *homonyms* was a moment of intense excitement, followed by deep disappointment—though I admit to getting pretty interested in "two/too," "mail/male," "pail/pale," and so (/sew) on.

Kids are literal-minded little meaning-makers. One boy, when asked if he knew the name of Mother Mary's husband, replied with confidence, "He's called 'The Verge.'" The *Verge??* "Yeah, you know, 'The Verge 'n' Mary.'" Another child applied her best artistic skill to depicting Pontius Pilate coming in for a landing outside the palace where he was to condemn Jesus to death by crucifixion. It took the teacher a minute of head-scratching to make the connection. When Bob was a fifth-grader, he took a teacher's note home to his parents that read, "Bobby has outstanding work in art." He remembers thinking, *Wow! How did that happen? I never even turned anything in.*

This next anecdote isn't about a misunderstanding of meaning, but perhaps just of misplaced context. When my baby sister Liz was four or five years old, she would race past the bedrooms (I was a teenager trying to ignore her), repeating under her breath all the lines she was about to deliver to Mom when she reached the kitchen. She did this regularly with speed, intensity, and accuracy. Although it just seemed like an annoying part of the homescape at the time, I'm now impressed with her language practice that was training her for articulate verbal delivery.

One day, after too many exposures to Betty Crocker biscuit-mix commercials on TV, she completed her rehearsal while racing through the hallway and the living room and arrived in the kitchen to announce with enthusiastic affection, "Mommy, you're so moist, so light, so flakey!" In adulthood, Liz is articulate and exceptionally clear on what she means to say. For my part, perhaps

I should have spent more childhood time rehearsing lines in the hallway and less time writing in my diary.

About to graduate from the eighth grade at St. Francis and move on to Garces Memorial High School, we had become cocky and were prone to making silly jokes about 1) *Ejaculations,* 2) the *Diet of Worms,* 3) *Papal Bulls,* and 4) the seventh planet from the sun.† At Garces, my vocabulary grew and became more accurate; I memorized soliloquies from Shakespeare, wrote reports on everything, and joined the Speech and Debate Club. Better late than never, I started learning my first foreign language in Mrs. Domínguez's Spanish 1 class, and stuck it out through Spanish 4, partly because that was the only class at the high school that was co-ed—although, in the year I took it, we were 25 girls plus Vincent.

I wasn't obsessed about Limbo and pagan babies anymore, and most of my extracurricular attention was focused on boys. To my knowledge, the Pope hadn't yet closed Hell or Purgatory,‡ and I was given to guilt and worry over where *my* eternity might be spent—useless concerns, really, but definitely formative as a rite of passage into the adulthood of erroneous beliefs that one must be very careful and/or very good, and the misguided conviction that life is *serious* business.

---

† 1) Short prayers repeated throughout the day; 2) the assembly (diet) of the Holy Roman Empire to which Martin Luther was summoned to Worms, Germany in 1521 to renounce his heretical teachings; 3) official letters issued by the Pope; and 4) Uranus.

‡ A place of suffering where souls go to atone for their sins before being allowed entrance to Heaven.

All About Me, the Sequel

There was a lot of linguistic history in my life prior to 1988, but I feel compelled to set the stage starting with that landmark year, and reveal the rest in the prequels. That was the year I left the third-floor Victorian apartment in midtown Sacramento, assorted part-time teaching assignments, and the moonlighting job that had enabled me to weather the financial ups and downs, even if it was a profession some considered inappropriate for a college teacher. (Hmmm, a prequel, yes...) It was the year I moved to Mendocino County for a full-time teaching position in Spanish at the community college. But I am already ahead of my story, because first I had to venture into uncharted, northern territory for my interview.

I'd heard of Ukiah, and even had a friend in Sacramento who grew up there, but I hadn't a clue about its location. To a majority of Californians, the cities named Ukiah, Eureka, Yreka, Yucaipa, and sometimes Yuba City thrown in as well, form a mystery map of vague, interchangeable, geographic generalities. When I told friends from Sacramento down to Southern California that I'd moved to Ukiah, the conversation usually proceeded in one of these five directions:

1. "Wow! You're all the way up there on the Oregon border?" (Yreka: 285 miles north)
2. "Are you going to teach part-time at Humboldt State, too?" (Eureka: 160 miles north)
3. "Can you walk to the beach from your house?" (Mendocino, the town: 63 miles west)

4. "Isn't that close to Chico?" (Yuba City: 120 miles east)
5. "So you've become a desert rat?" (Yucaipa: 560 miles south)

I'd say, "No, Ukiah is on Highway 101, about two hours north of San Francisco," only to be met with glazed eyes as friends visualized a complete topographical blank. I'd add, " It's up in the wine country," to which they knowingly nodded: "Oh! You mean Napa Valley" (100 miles southeast). Oh, well, I didn't want houseguests anyway.

I could hardly blame them because that was me, too, before the spring of 1988 when my dear friend Liz G., who was my colleague and mentor at Sacramento City College, encouraged me to apply for a teaching position at Mendocino College. First, I had to find Ukiah on a map, then contend with the fact that there is no simple and obvious way to get there from Sacramento. I ended up choosing the most traffic-laden route (Highway 80 West, then through the wine country and up the 101—don't do it! Go north on Highway 5 and then west on 20). Well, to make a long story short, I made it to the interview with little time to spare, and had to rush back to Sacramento afterward for moonlighting in aforementioned questionable profession.

Lucky me! I got the job. My brother offered to accompany me on a road trip to Ukiah to go apartment-hunting, and he chose an only slightly better highway route. Once we were within the city limits, the fun really began. We wanted to get off the freeway and into downtown Ukiah, so I voted to take Perkins Street. We passed up the Gobbi Street off-ramp in part because we couldn't settle a debate as to the pronunciation of "Gobbi." He thought it should be a long "o" as in "oh," and I disagreed, with a lengthy argument about how that would be the same pronunciation as the Gobi Desert, and "Gobbi" with the double "b" surely rhymes with "knobby"—like "globby" without the "l." That seemed phonetically logical to me even though the idea of a major street pronounced either way was vaguely disconcerting.

We let it go to deal with later, because soon enough we were at the stoplight of Perkins and State Streets. I looked at the store windows across the intersection and over at my brother, then said in amazement, "This must be a really progressive place. Just look at that—they have a Frederick's of Hollywood on the main street of downtown!" I wish I'd snapped a photo, but in my mind's eye I still see a sensuous display of mannequins clad in flimsy red lingerie, seducing passersby from the picture windows of what I later learned was the Palace Dress Shop.

No, it wasn't Frederick's of Hollywood on State and Perkins, but Ukiah continued to reveal surprises, and I have never forgotten my first impressions—those moments of elation and despair—as I tried to relate to my new home. The search for an apartment that was both desirable and available turned up zilch, and I ended up renting one burg north, in Redwood Valley. But driving around town was entertaining and even had its linguistically exciting moments. After seeing the name "Yokayo" pop up several times, I theorized that it had to be a corruption of the Native American word *ukiah*. It wasn't long before I learned I had it backward: "Ukiah" is actually a corruption of the Pomo word *yokayo,* meaning "deep valley."

By day's end, we'd seen many of the neighborhoods in Ukiah and, despite my high degree of directional challenge, I was starting to get the lay of the land. My mind excitedly raced ahead to the start of the school year in September, just as my brother made a left turn off Talmage Road onto South State Street, and the big, gaudy sign for the Ron-Day-Voo diner and cocktail lounge (now the site of Jalos Mexican restaurant) came into view in garish hues of red and blue neon. It first struck me as entertaining, but then sunk me into deep doubt about the linguistic ambiance in the town where I would henceforth teach foreign language.

Well, to make the long story of my career at the college short, that doubt was unfounded, and I enjoyed 25 years of teaching thousands of enthusiastic and delightful language learners, many of whom I count as friends today. When I started my job in the fall of 1988, my first students taught me that the pronunciation of the name of a nearby town is "CO-ve-lo," and not "Co-VE-lo," and that the Mendocino College athletic teams were not named after those big black birds with the red wattles circling overhead. In fact, those were turkey vultures, not the eagles I was rhapsodizing about.

It was easy to leave behind multiple part-time teaching jobs and freeway flying between Sacramento and Davis and move to the land of simpler life and fewer choices. For the first time ever, I had only one job—full-time with a monthly salary—no overtime pay, but with benefits. Although there was no more need to moonlight in that questionable profession, I admit that it was the one thing I missed.

All About Me, Prequel I

The sequel began as I left Sacramento to take a teaching position at Mendocino College in 1988, but my life in words started long before, perhaps even in the womb, because English was not the native language of either of my parents. Caterina Gambardella Crai, my Italian mother, was born in the Bronx to immigrant parents from Naples and Calabria. She started learning English in grade school, via the unenlightened but very effective "sink or swim" method of bilingual education.

Friedjof Johannes Christie Janssen, my father, came from the Netherlands with the Dutch Merchant Marines during WWII. Since he was tall, blond, and handsome, and loved dating tall, blonde American girls when his ship was docked in U.S. ports, he was highly motivated to learn the English language and adopt American ways. He wasn't prejudiced against darker-hued women, but he was understandably attracted to and exclusively dated the ones who resembled the Dutch girls he grew up with and regretfully left behind at age 17.

So how did this tall, blond, handsome Dutchman cross paths with a short, dark, beautiful Italian *signorina?* Where else but in front of the church? His best friend and shipmate, Dirk, was getting married to her best girlfriend, Elsie. Caterina was running late for rehearsal—literally running across the street to St. Raymond's in the Bronx at a fast trot. Friedjof's eyes went dreamy and his stomach flipped as he said to Dirk with the certainty that only lovers at first sight can know, "Dat is du voman I am goving to marry." And so it was to be. They were engaged in two weeks, and exchanged vows within two months, despite the dire warning from Caterina's Italian cousins of the dangers of marrying a foreigner, and from Friedjof's Dutch shipmates about what happens to petite Italian girls after a giving birth to a couple of babies. Neither prediction came true, in the short or the long run.

They headed west to California, still a relatively sparsely populated land of cheap real estate and golden opportunity in 1946, where an elderly Dutch couple in Artesia, just outside of Los Angeles, had agreed to sponsor Fred for citizenship. Yes, Friedjof became Fred, and Caterina became Kay, and they embarked wholeheartedly on postwar American life, leaving the ways of the old countries behind and contributing regularly to the Baby Boom.

When Dad's mother immigrated in 1952, she was allowed to take only a small amount of cash, around $400, out of war-ravaged Holland. She had her household treasures packed and shipped in a 5' x 4' x 8' wooden crate. (Later, Dad added windows, door, and roof and—voilà—the ideal playhouse!) It arrived months later to U.S. shores: grandfather clock, china cabinet, throne-like chairs, assorted copper coal buckets and candle holders, an ancient spinning wheel, and a late 1800s vintage church pew.

What little English Grandma knew when she arrived improved only slightly during the decades of her life in the United States. Given to telling inflated stories of her circumstances and social position in Holland, she was haughty and of the opinion that the Netherlands sat at the top of the European hierarchy, and Italy at the bottom. That should give you an idea of how she regarded my mother who, hungry for family roots and traditions, never failed to include Grandma in Sunday dinners, summer vacations, and every single religious or secular event my Catholic family ever thought to celebrate.

Dad and Grandma often spoke Dutch, so I grew up hearing a foreign language but rarely captured a word of it. My sister and

I used to mimic the phrases in babbly-baby blah-blah. Grandma was deeply insulted when she heard us carrying on in our invented lowlands lingo, not appreciating that we were only trying to sound like her. It seems ironic that I was exposed to so much Dutch in childhood, but no Italian, because Mom had no family to talk to in the West. Yet it was Romance languages that have been absorbed into my brain like water on parched earth. It's also worth noting that I gave up my early attempts to learn Dutch because, even though I traveled to Holland often, all the relatives and friends there spoke English comfortably, and enthusiastically preferred speaking it with me over their native language.

At Garces High School in Bakersfield, foreign language was a requirement, and the options were French, German, Latin, and Spanish. It's hard to believe, but in the mid-1960s Californians still didn't think of Spanish as a very useful second language, let alone a necessary one. The César Chávez farm workers' movement in nearby Delano was soon to explode, and would focus the nation's attention on the plight of exploited Mexican laborers. In 1964, however, French would have been my path, except for one crucial factor: Mom's dear friend Mrs. Domínguez from Puerto Rico was the high-school Spanish teacher. I started on my second-language path through no clear selection on my part, but rather because of maternal insistence.

We lived on a street called Loma Linda (Spanish for "Pretty Hill"), and nearby lanes were named Pasatiempo ("Pastime"), Alta Vista ("High View"), and La Colina ("The Hill"). We already knew lots of Spanish words—*enchilada, burrito, fiesta, siesta, tortilla*—so how hard could this be? Well, to tell the truth, I barely survived the first few weeks of Mrs. D's class and, given the option, I would have quit altogether and taken anything other than Spanish—anything! She was using a new methodology in which students heard and repeated but never actually saw words written in the language. We were mired in frustration, parroting phrases day in and out (*"Escuche y repita"* said the disembodied voice through my headphones in the language lab: "Listen and repeat"), trying to decipher their meaning, and wondering all the while where one word ended and the next one began.

Our ability for second-language acquisition changes dramatically around the time of puberty, and I was already past the stage of carefree, unquestioning absorption, assimilation, and regurgitation of foreign sounds, as were the rest of the adolescent students in my freshman Spanish class. I remember it as something of a mass revolt that ultimately motivated Mrs. D to produce handouts with written words, leading to "ah-ha!" moments as we connected the letters to the sounds, and then to the meaning. (As a teacher myself, I now appreciate the value of her all-audio method as an approximation to how a child learns its first language.) My first foray into foreign language suddenly took a turn for the better, and I sailed through four years with Mrs. D, earning straight A's but, in the predictable high-school process and outcome of that era, I never had any actual conversations in Spanish, and I graduated without even enough linguistic finesse to comfortably respond to the prompt, *"Hola. ¿Cómo estás?"*

After that, it was two years of community college and more Spanish. It just seemed like the thing to do, since I'd already invested four years in it. I also took all the general education requirements; I loved biology and botany but really struggled through math (a pattern well established in high school) and chemistry. By the time I transferred to the University of California at Davis, it was evident that I could not cut it as a science major no matter how deftly I could pith and dissect a frog. I declared Spanish as my major, completed all the upper-division requirements in my junior and senior years, and hadn't a clue what would come next. Maybe a K–12 teaching credential? The feminist movement had begun, but I could not think beyond traditional careers.

As I was applying for the fifth-year credential program, a totally unexpected event occurred—one that that sealed my future as a college Spanish teacher. I had continued to earn good grades in my classes. Never mind that I still couldn't actually carry on a conversation in Spanish, because a perfect grade-point average spoke louder than even rudimentary fluency in the foreign language. Along with my bachelor's degree, I was given the Academic Excellence award by the Spanish Department, accompanied by an invitation to the graduate program to work toward a master's degree in Spanish literature while teaching one class per quarter. How convenient, since I was now to be severed from the parental financial feedbag and had no plan as to how I would manage.

As it turned out, on just a teaching assistant's salary, I could get by very nicely. As crazy as it sounds in this era of hugely inflated college costs and student loans soaring into the tens of thousands, from 1971 to 1973, I earned something around $365.00 a month as a teaching assistant at the University of California, but still managed to pay my tuition and room and board, with a little left over for macramé supplies and a bottle of cheap Spañada wine for the Friday afternoon apartment house party.

Winning the award was the easy part. The reality I was about to face in graduate school would prove to be the hardest test of all.

All About Me, Prequel II

As I was saying in "Prequel I," getting into graduate school was the easy part; the day-to-day reality of it was devastatingly difficult. I was one of only two non-native speakers of Spanish in the MA/PhD program at UC Davis. *Gringa Número Dos,* Susan W., had just returned from a year in Spain and spoke beautiful, lispy, peninsular Spanish as if she'd been born there. The other students in our graduate program were from Chile, Argentina, Bolivia, Mexico, España, Perú, and Uruguay, striving in their native language toward postgraduate degrees in Spanish and Latin American literature.

The fist of fate had plucked me from the top of the undergraduate ladder and flung me to the bottom of the graduate-school barrel. Eight years into my second-language study, I still could not comfortably carry on a conversation. This was so painful that I intentionally ascended and descended nine stories of stairs in Sproul Hall three to five times a day to avoid being stuck with professors in the elevator. All it took was their amiable invitation to small talk—*"Hola. ¿Cómo está usted?"*—and my throat would close up, and I'd feel like I was going to pass out.

As painful and shaming as my experience felt, there was surely similar suffering going on at higher levels in this ivory tower of academia, and that too had to do with the fact that the conversational approach in foreign language teaching still had not become the favored methodology. It seems almost impossible to conceive of this now, but in those days languages were taught mostly to be read and written rather than spoken and heard.

When I peeked out from the bottom of the barrel, I noticed

that two of my grad-school professors were perhaps suffering similarly. One was a well-regarded authority on the 16th-century Spanish novelist Miguel de Cervantes and his masterpiece *Don Quijote.* The other was equally established in the arcane field of the 19th-century South American essay. They could produce flowing Spanish prose in the articles they wrote for publication, but were not at ease during casual conversation—something I realized when I met them on the stairs to the ninth floor. Their academic training had never prepared them for something quite so mundane as chat-in-the-elevator Spanish. What a fate to be erudite but not comfortably conversant in a second language! I am forever thankful that fate was not to be mine.

That first year felt like it would be the death of me, but I hung on for dear life because I didn't have a Plan B. First of all, no "assisting" was involved in being a teaching assistant. I was actually tasked with solo-teaching an undergraduate class, effective immediately. I remember walking into the classroom on the first day of the fall quarter of my first year of grad school to teach my first Spanish 1 class. It consisted of a dozen or so freshman girls, one older female student, and half the college football team. The "How-to-Teach-Spanish" graduate seminar hadn't yet begun—but never mind the fine points of methodology; the larger problem was my shaky grasp of the basic grammar and vocabulary I was to teach.

What I lacked in ability I made up for in sweat, many candles burnt out at both ends and, eventually, true enthusiasm. During that first year, for my Monday-through-Friday one hour a day in front of the class, I prepped for at least three hours daily. I didn't know the answers to most of my students' "How do you say . . . ?" and "What's the difference between . . . ?" questions, but I always came back informed the next day. It would be understandable if you are shocked to learn that someone as incompetent as I was teaching a university class. I too was in disbelief, but after a few weeks I felt more relaxed and started to truly enjoy the classroom experience.

My graduate literature classes were an even stiffer challenge. Since I couldn't competently speak the language, I sat in the back of the classroom taking reams of notes, afraid of being called on or being engaged in a chat with the professor before or after class. But we were a small group of graduate students (around a dozen), all sharing the same large office, and there was no way to protect my torched ego or hide my sorry plight. The thing that terrified me the most—having to speak Spanish with all those native-speaker professors and students—turned out to be the very thing that nudged me toward fluency. Between teaching one class a day plus prepping and grading homework, taking several graduate seminars, studying, and writing papers, I was hearing, speaking, reading, and writing Spanish for 10 hours a day.

My *compañeros* were patient with my inadequacy, and generous with their help; I was taken under a lot of wings, especially that first year. My new Chilean friend Santiago sat with me for hours at a time correcting my writing before I submitted my papers. There were frequent group-study sessions, constant conversations, and regular social mixers that often included the professors. It was like living in total immersion in a Spanish-speaking country, and I came to feel moments of linguistic buoyancy. Gradually, there was less flailing to keep from drowning, and more time treading water (though still quite furiously), to stay afloat—and finally, I was starting to swim.

I learned more Spanish in that first year of grad school than I did in eight years of high-school and college classes combined. I developed the knack of seldom making the same mistake twice, especially if motivated by embarrassment—like the time at a party at the department chairman's house when I walked around the roomful of professors and grad students with a plateful of homemade goodies, offering them *gallinas.* Finally, someone quietly but pointedly thanked me for the *galletas,* and it was all I could do not to drop the plate and slap my forehead when I realized I had been offering not "cookies" but "barnyard chickens."

Despite linguistic missteps and mishaps, after two of the hardest years of my life I received my master's degree, moved from Davis to Sacramento and launched into my new career as . . . a waitress! Well, what's a girl to do? I had to make a living, after all. At least I chose a Mexican restaurant, one of those upscale El Torito-type places. We had to wear short skirts with off-the-shoulder peasant blouses, and greet each table in Spanish. I'll never forget the time I approached a table at lunch with my usual cheery "¡Buenas tardes!" The girl's head shot up from her menu in shocked recognition of my voice. She was a former student of mine from UC Davis, and she had heard me say those same words as I walked into the classroom every day for 10 weeks.

Within a few months, I was hired to teach part-time at Sacramento City College, and had also been retained by UC Davis for similar assignments. Those two jobs, plus waitressing shifts and, later, a five-year stint managing a health-food restaurant, carried me from 1973 to 1988. It was a period of dearth in full-time teaching positions in the California community college system, given that many of the schools were fairly new and their faculty still young. I clung to my restaurant jobs as a way to support my teaching habit, and I actually loved the fact that the physical work balanced out the more cerebral life of academia. Though my family and colleagues thought it questionable that I taught college by day and waited tables on nights and weekends, I managed to support myself, and Sacramento was a big enough city that it allowed me to keep my two professions mostly separate.

In the spring of 1988, Mendocino College advertised for its first full-time Spanish teacher—the only such opening in the California community college system that year. Good fortune shone upon me; not every underemployed Spanish teacher was willing to move to a small city in rural Northern California. I was hired in the spring, and launched into the next 25 years of my career that September. It was a fantastic opportunity in a town I soon came to call my own, with people I easily came to know and love. Ukiah was a world away from Davis and Sacramento, but as I made friends among my new colleagues, students, and neighbors, I settled in with the warm feeling that we were all, in essence, speaking the same language.

Ez Dakite Euskaraz Hitz Egiten Duzu?

No, I don't either—speak Basque, that is—not a single word. I can't even pronounce that title! It seems a shame, since I grew up in Bakersfield, surrounded by Basque people, Basque food, and Basque sheep ranches. The big immigration from far northwestern Spain and far southwestern France had begun with the American Gold Rush in the mid 1800s, but most Basques didn't feel suited to mining so they turned to what they knew best—ranching sheep—thus ensuring waves of immigrants well into the 20th century. As a result, I had classmates at the Catholic school named Ansolabehere, Echeverry, Echinique, Etchechury, Eyherabide, Bidart, and Anchordoquy.

After our move from a tiny cottage in a Los Angeles suburb to what my kindergartener eyes deemed a mansion in Bakersfield, my parents became fast friends with the Anchordoquys, who lived at the other end of V Street. I and my siblings—only two of them at the time—joined in playing with Tommy, Arnie, and Vivi every day at their house or ours: bikes, ball, Monopoly, Pick-up Stix, and diving into piles of leaves that my dad raked up from the huge sycamore trees in front of our house. I remember gazing in spellbound horror at an enormous jar in the Anchordoquy's garage, full of small animal legs suspended in murky liquid, hooves and all. Having an Italian mom had exposed me to a few unusual things on the fork, such as raw clams on the half-shell and the stomach lining of a cow (in a rolling boil, it looked to me like a ruffled bathing cap), but I still could not fathom the culinary allure of pickled pigs' feet.

Our moms took turns driving us to St. Francis Elementary

School every day. I loved riding in Rose's car because it was a big, brand-new, red sedan with shiny upholstery and long, exotic finlike things that jutted out the back. Besides her car, I loved everything about her. She was pretty and stylish, gave only the gentlest of scoldings (at least to the neighbor kids), and spoke accented English with a sweet lilt from the French side of the Pyrenees.

Tom was a sheep rancher outside of Bakersfield, a dark, stocky, barrel-chested man—the exact opposite kind of handsome as my father. Their shared experience of being immigrants from European countries must have forged their friendship. Not the types to bond over Friday-night poker or Sunday beer and TV football, they were the kind of friends who simply and enduringly admired and respected each other and would always lend a hand when needed. I remember Tom as a man of kindness and few words. There was always a twinkle in his eye—one that was inherited by his son Arnold. He was the epitome of what my dad admired in the Basque as "the gentlest people in the world."

Although it's distant and blurred, my earliest memory of life in Bakersfield is of a visit to the sheep ranch, with Rose behind the wheel and all us kids tumbled all over the Naugahyde, before the legislated advent of seatbelts. The excitement had been building for days, because it was to be an adventure into the unknown, and also because my parents would not be there to supervise. We arrived to flat, dry, ranch land with hot dust hanging in the air and clinging to our sweat, and thousands of "bahhhhhs" in all directions. It was shearing day, and Rose joined the women leaning over big pots on open fires while we kids took off on an adventure that I can still replay with all five senses, even through the long lens of time.

My older sister and I tagged after Tommy and Arnie, who were headed for the pen where tightly packed sheep waited their turn to be relieved of their wool. The boys climbed up the fence, and Karen and I clambered to follow their lead. At the top of the barrier, they slid down to land their feet firmly on the backs of sheep, docile now with nowhere to bolt in the tight herd. We followed, found our footing, and flitted behind them over the thick wooly backs, to the bleating of the animals and the shouts of the herders. I felt no fear, only the rush of excitement in one of those high-adrenaline, is-this-really-happening? moments.

Why is this ovine experience so unforgettable? Well, for one thing, I had a deep and abiding crush on both boys and, beyond that confessional detail, this was way more exciting than growing the award-winning giant radish in kindergarten or jump-skating the cracks on V-street sidewalks. After our walkways of animals found their turn under the shears, I saw nicks on their back and bellies releasing trickles of blood, and I remember feeling sorry for the sheep, now shorn of their protective coats.

That was my most dramatic memory, but the Basque way of life permeated my childhood in permanent, memorable ways. After the church ceremonies of first communions and confirmations, the celebrating families repaired to Noriega's on the other side of town, one of several family-style Basque eateries clustered around the old railroad station of East Bakersfield. My dad thought nothing of propping us little kids on stools at the bar while we waited to go in for dinner. I loved sipping my Shirley Temple, but insisted that what I really fancied was Picon Punch; the name sounded enchanting, and it was what all the Basque people at the bar were drinking. I didn't realize it was a cocktail and had nothing to do with nuts or punch.

Noriega's was our hands-down favorite restaurant because the grown-ups would excuse us from the table to romp around the three-walled ball court attached to the building. The Basque game it was built for is called *pelota,* which is similar to handball. The commercialized version of it, *jai alai* (billed as "the fastest sport in the world" because of ball speeds approaching 200 mph), used to be a popular gaming attraction in Las Vegas, and still is in Florida.

All of my family's big events were and still are celebrated at the Wool Growers or Noriega's, both legendary family-style Basque establishments whose renown has grown from local to national. The first course is minestrone soup with brown beans, served with spicy red salsa on the side, a simple green salad dressed with oil and vinegar, and a tomato salad. It's very tempting to devour multiple helpings from the big communal bowls, accompanied by fresh, crusty bread and satisfying red table wine from an unlabeled bottle, and just call that dinner; but no one in my family would dream of passing up what follows: thinly sliced, pickled beef tongue, so popular and addictive that refills at the Wool Grower's are no longer free.[§]

Served with the tongue are a vegetable plate, spaghetti, and french fries, and *all* of these plates are just the starters. I remember taking some friends to a Basque restaurant in San Francisco, and being so enthralled with the taste of home that I neglected to tell them to save room for the main course: your choice of pork chops, roast lamb, steaks, veal, chicken, halibut, scampi, or oxtail stew.

Francisco Franco, the dictator who iron-fisted Spain for 40 years after the Spanish Civil War (1936–1939), tried mightily to obliterate Spain's secondary languages and regional customs. This suppression was particularly brutal against Catalonia (capital: Barcelona) and the Basque region, banning the languages and imprisoning anyone caught speaking them in public. Spain's return

---

§ My brother Fred sweet-talks the waitress into an extra plate or two because he has "come all the way from Seattle" just to indulge his passion for their pickled tongue. He's been known to buy a pound or so of the delicacy from Luigi's deli and tuck it—very well sealed—into his suitcase when returning to Seattle from trips to Bakersfield.

to democracy in 1975 after Franco's death fueled a resurgence of interest in diversity and the preservation of ancient customs and linguistic variations from the dominant tongue.

Before that, the Basque language, officially named Euskara, was one of many that was feared to become extinct in our lifetime. Will it survive? As a world language, Basque is one of a kind, not related to any of the Indo-European branches from which many (with exceptions such as Basque, Korean, Ainu, Sumerian, and Burushaski) of the world's languages evolved. It is believed to have its roots much earlier, in Stone-Age Europe, but there appears to be no link between Basque and any other known language, current or extinct.

This is a linguistic phenomenon of mind-bending magnitude, leading to many theories of its origin, some remotely plausible and others downright fantastical, like the Lost Continent of Atlantis. The Basque people are proud, strong, individualistic, independent, and committed to preserving their history and heritage. Their language, no longer considered endangered, is on the "vulnerable" list, and may, we hope, be headed back toward vibrant health through literacy and fluency among younger generations.

* * *

My sisters, our mother, and I had a long-overdue reunion in the garden of Rose's care home with our old playmates Arnold and Vivian when their matriarch was in her early nineties. I last saw her shortly after she celebrated her 94th birthday, and she even regaled me with a few phrases in her native Basque. Rose passed away in December of 2015 at age 96, after having enjoyed visits from one or more of her kids and grandkids every single day while she resided in assisted living.

Even though it evolved into an important part of my vicarious linguistic and cultural identity, the Basque culture didn't mean much to my young mind way back then on V Street in Bakersfield. It was simply woven into the tapestry of my childhood, and the Janssens loved the Anchordoquys to pieces, as dear friends and close kin. Still do, always will.

The Cure by Feeding of Earworms

I've had an annoying earworm in my head for over a week, and I am hoping that writing about it will at least begin the exorcism process. First, though, I have to wonder if you know what an earworm is, because I didn't until recently, when I came across a mention of it in something I was reading online. Eureka! This is a word we have needed for a long time to describe the universal phenomenon of our least-favorite line in a song we really don't like, perhaps even espousing a sentiment we don't agree with, playing over and over in our heads like a broken record.

As I was packing up the house to prepare for my big move away from the "undesirable" West Side of Ukiah to the "desirable" West Side, the Beatles kept my spirits high, my feet hopping, and my lips syncing while I loaded my life of accumulations into U-Haul boxes. Now I can't get Paul McCartney to stop singing in my ear, though in the listening, I was transported to a time when I would have invited him to do just about anything in my ear. Over and over again, I mentally hear the same line from the song, "You're Looking Through Me" (from *Rubber Soul):* "Love has a nasty habit of disappearing overnight."

It is said that what we resist persists, and that may be a clue to the creation and persistence of earworms. Love is supposed to last forever, and I resist the possibility but have had the experience—as we all have—of love "disappearing overnight." As the word suggests, the earworm burrows in through the ear, and I theorize that it goes deeper into the brain each time we hear our own mental replay—and wish we hadn't; wish we could make it go away; or wish it were a perfect world in which love does last forever and always, and doesn't just disappear overnight.

Meaning, however, is not requisite to an earworm invasion. Manfred Mann sang, "There she was, just a-walking down the street, singing '*Do wah diddy diddy dum diddy do*,'" and while I know I'm dating myself, I admit that nonsense still rattles around in my brain. My contemporaries may also remember with fond bewilderment, "*Papa-oom-mow-mow*" (from the Rivingtons, sometime in the past century) and, also from ancient history, "*Supercalifragilisticexpialidocious*"—even though the sound of it really *is* something quite atrocious.

Here's what I learned while opening the proverbial can of earworms that I thought worth sharing with readers, because the phenomenon is such a universal annoyance. Borrowed and literally translated from the German term *ohrwurm* (pronounced "oar-vorm"), it's now an American colloquialism, according to the *Oxford English Dictionary*. Anticipating your next question—yes, you *can* use it in Scrabble play!

There has been scientific study and copious writing about pieces of music looping endlessly through the brains of all but 2% of us. Some researchers offer remedies that include: brain work with Sudoku or crosswords, reading novels, listening to a different "cure" song (great—now I've got the "Karma Chameleon" ditty stuck in my head), taking OCD medication, or—the two universal cures for whatever ails—chewing gum and meditating (though not simultaneously).

I searched further for real people's experience with strategies on how to kill the pesky earworm. Melanie of Vancouver, Canada reports: "The cure we have tried—and this is dangerous, so we only use it when desperate—is to start singing 'New York, New York.' That usually clears out the stuck song—but occasionally takes over like a dictator after a revolution." To follow up with another great metaphor, Anthony of Birmingham in England likens his years-long earworm (the theme from *The Addams Family*) to a screen-saver in the brain because it pops in when his mind is blank. Other reader recommendations include doing long division in one's head to mentally "take the needle off the vinyl." The problem with this last strategy is that an increasing number of younger folks have never actually seen a record player, let alone placed a large vinyl disk on a turntable and then a needle on top of it.

According to a short story titled "The Imp of the Perverse," penned by Edgar Allen Poe about earworms, "It is quite a common thing to be thus annoyed with the ringing in our ears, or rather in our memories, of the burthen of some ordinary song, or some unimpressive snatches from an opera. Nor will we be the less tormented if the song in itself be good, or the opera air meritorious." Earworms have burrowed their way into the plots of books, films, sitcoms (notably, a *Seinfeld* episode called "The Jacket"), and legions of science-fiction stories because of the viral nature of the worm and the possibilities for crazy-making and mind-control.

Long ago and far away, I learned that to make something unwanted disappear, the trick is to consciously create what is happening unconsciously. I have the habit of flexing the very powerful muscles between my eyebrows—commonly known as frowning—sometimes causing people to think I am worried, upset, or mad at them. Of course there's always Botox, but a noninvasive and totally cost-free procedure is to knit the brows purposely and repeatedly, perhaps even while looking in the mirror. Over time, the habit can be broken.

After I saw the movie *Jaws,* I experienced visceral terror every time I stuck even a toe into a body of water larger than a bathtub.

A wise friend counseled that I should watch the horrific flick over and over again, explaining that this was like pressing the shock button so many times that it would finally lose its impact. I couldn't bear to actually do so, but I did see the logic behind his advice—simply a call to exercise the opposite of resistance.

If you're a chronic nail-biter, perhaps you stress over it, searching for a way to break the habit once and for all. At one time, a straitjacket might have been attempted as a cure, but with the influence of Eastern wisdom, we are learning to surrender and embrace what is instead of fighting against it. I'm just theorizing here, but it seems very likely that you could affect a major shift in that nail-biting by standing in front of the mirror every day to knowingly, purposefully, and even creatively chew your fingernails to the nubs, until you don't anymore.

So my strategy for excising this Beatles earworm from my brain is simple enough: I will consciously, and at the top of my lungs, sing that particular line to extinction. I may be free of the earworm, but the couple next door to my uptown house may think their new neighbor has a screw loose, or is having a nervous breakdown over love's "nasty habit of disappearing overnight." If that doesn't work, I'll try alternating song-and-dance rounds of the "Hokey-Pokey" and the "Locomotion," with chants of "*bibbidi-bobbidi-boo.*" If my persistent earworm isn't vaporized by that interference, at least I'll have developed a more interesting looping repertoire. I'll let you know how it goes. In the meantime, here's wishing you a "*Zip-A-Dee-Doo-Dah*" day!

In Megahurtz, but Knotfurlong

For a very long time, I have been toying with the idea of getting a Dragon—no, not the fire-breathing kind, but the computer-dictation variety, so that everything from emails to grocery lists to whole book chapters could roll melodically off the tip of my tongue to magically appear on the screen before me.

The concept of computer-dictation software is already obsolete, at least according to Mac users who have had this function built into their computers for years. Having failed to find the Mac as very intuitive as everyone rhapsodizes that it is, I cut my losses, sold the beast, and returned to the world of PC with a sigh of relief. Well, I'm just not very tech-savvy, OK?

In the best of circumstances, I type with four fingers, never taking my eyes off the keys, three typing classes between the ages of 14 and 44 notwithstanding. (Is "typing" still an extant word?) A colleague at Mendocino College tried her best with me in my third attempt at learning to type, and I passed her class by the skin of my fingertips at a whopping 34 words a minute (including *a, of, the, or, but,* and *oops!)*—with accuracy at some percentage pretty close to the number I just mentioned. Keyboarding is something I just couldn't master, and this challenge badgers me daily, from two-word email responses, in which I commonly have a 100% error rate as in *Thakn yoou,* to this book you now tenderly hold in your hands.

Grandma despaired when she gave me piano lessons for 10 years, holding out hope that I would miraculously exhibit a burst of talent somewhere along the way, but insisting that I look at the music book and not at my hands on the keys. I could not do it. I could not both look straight ahead and know where my fingers were down below, even in the simplest of compositions. I could not make that brain-hand connection. The resulting cacophony finally became too much, and Grandma finally had to resign herself to the fact that I didn't possess musical talent, but what I *do* possess is some kind of a spatial-learning impairment. To this day, when I watch someone type or play piano without looking at the keys, I am awestruck, overcome with wonderment and confusion at how it is possible that so many are doing what for me seems impossible.

Keyboarding is not the only type of boarding at which I have failed. I've also flopped (literally, onto concrete and into ice banks) at skateboarding and snowboarding. Most recently, I proved my ineptness with fast-moving flat, slick surfaces by way of a running plant of my left foot on a 10" x 14" piece of hard royal-blue plastic located—right where I had carelessly flung it—on the stone step of my house. I took that tumble while zippily carrying in items from the U-Haul boxes in the garage.

In retrospective analysis, as the unintended sled took off, my left foot left the ground, and my body went airborne, heading east-southeast. I picture myself suspended horizontally in mid-air for one *bananosecond* before plummeting to stone in the following order of impact: heel of left hand, outer bone of left hip, and inner right ankle. Despite the *megahurtz,* I only suffered a compression fracture to my left wrist, and luckily I'm right handed. For a time, though, with my left arm out of action, I was challenged by everyday maintenance acts like washing my face (forget flossing!), opening a can of cat food, pulling my yoga pants all the way up to my waist, and other less mentionable acts.

Now, about that limited-fingered typing: Since three of the four "boarding" fingers belong to my left hand, try to picture what I did for weeks with the middle finger of my right hand. Yes, typing with a single finger was slow going, and I was feeling a bit beat up on the outside; but in my heart I had to shout my thanks to the heavens.

Though I am no longer a churchgoer, I have a long ecclesiastical memory (as you might recall from the piece "Don the Noose for Biscuits"), and now I cannot help but recall the consoling promise, in the words of Psalm 91:12, that "(angels) will bear you up lest you dash your foot against a stone." Well, those angels still get top billing in my life because, while I did dash my wrist (and bumped bum and ankle) against that stone, they saved my head and let me off with merely a non-separated radial fracture, and nary a word of reproach for my careless fling of the plastic lid in the first place, along with a self-promise to retrieve it "before someone gets hurt." I hereby renew their contract through 2050.

That's it for one-fingered typing today. Harking back to the piece entitled "The 'U.S. and Them' View of the World" in which I explored America's way of making measurements and recording things, I want to share with you these wonderfully funny and delightfully clever definitions, sent by a friend who makes it his business to keep me well supplied with laughs and lexical fodder. Not only do these draw smiles (and a few groans), but they also illustrate how very versatile, unpredictable, flexible, and risible our language can be when it falls into the "wrong" hands that chop it up and reassemble the pieces for our willing ears and eyes.

Useful Conversion Units

- Ratio of an igloo's circumference to its diameter = Eskimo pi
- Ratio of a jack-o'-lantern's circumference to its diameter = pumpkin pi

- 2,000 pounds of Chinese soup = won ton
- Statute miles of intravenous tubing at Yale University Hospital = one IV League
- Weight an evangelist carries with God = 1 billigram
- Time it takes to sail 220 yards at 1 nautical mile per hour = knotfurlong
- 365.25 days of drinking low-calorie beer = 1 lite year
- Half a large intestine = 1 semicolon
- 1,000,000 aches = 1 megahurtz
- 1 basic unit of laryngitis = 1 hoarsepower
- 2,000 mockingbirds = 2 kilomockingbirds
- 1 kilogram of falling figs = 1 Fig Newton
- 1,000 cc's of wet socks = 1 literhosen
- 8 nickels = 2 paradigms
- 2 wharves = 1 paradox¶

Surely this has multiple authors, and I admire them all for their imaginative twists. Can you hear the sound of one hand clapping? I'm still undecided about whether to get that word-breathing Dragon or to just keep doing keyboard aerobics with the middle finger of my right hand.

¶ Bonus originals: by me—Male instinct to periodically hole up in man cave = mens' troll cycle; and by my lexi-fodder friend—Two crows hanging out with a raven = an attempted murder.

A Girl (Not) Named Sue

Yes, it's true: I made a unilateral decision (i.e., did not consult my parents) to change my name from Susan to Susanna, for reasons I believe to be more defensible than reprehensible.

The name on my birth certificate is Susan Janssen. That's it, no frills. Just one first name, and one last name. Mostly, that has simplified my life, except that people often think there must be a middle name lurking in the shadows, maybe one that I'm embarrassed to disclose. My father had two middle names, so he had to write four names on official documents. As for my mother—well, those Italian names have enough syllables to fill several bowls of alphabet soup. After naming their firstborn "Karen Mary," they quit the middle-names business, nevermore to revisit the subject with their four more additions to the family.

I used to be kind of jealous of my older sister Karen for getting something that I didn't. First it was the middle name; then it was braces in high school. Heaven knows I didn't want to go around looking like a horse with all that metal gear in my mouth and the strap around the back of my neck, but in retrospect it would've been a worthwhile investment of my suffering and my parents' money for the long-term esthetics of my teeth. Now that I've got that off my chest and out of my mind, we can get back to the issue of names.

It used to be that many Catholic parents baptized their child with a saint's name. This was a custom that began in medieval France and Germany and was widely accepted and followed, though never a part of the Church's official Canon Law. My parents were strict Catholics, and I theorize that my older sister got the middle name of Mary (after the Holy Mother) because they needed to compensate for the fact that there is no saint named Karen, even though it's a name derived from Catherine. Ah, but there is a Saint Susan—Santa Susanna, actually—the third-century virgin martyr whose story I won't even mention because it reads like a tabloid and may even be spectacularly fictional.

When my little sister was born two years later, Mom and Dad concluded that Marjorie was sufficiently close to (Saint) Margaret that the middle name could again be dispensed with. With the subsequent offspring, Frederick and Elizabeth, there was no doubt that their names came directly from the official roster of saints. When I made my confirmation, the saint's name chosen by half the little girls in my sixth-grade class and me was Therese ("The Little Flower") of Lisieux. A confirmation name is a devotional name, not a legal name, nor is it ever actually used. That said, for years my mother addressed letters to me as Susan T. Janssen, perhaps regretting that no middle name had been bestowed at birth.

Nobody ever called me Susan until I was in college, with the possible exception of the parish priest when he visited our second-grade classroom to quiz us on the Catechism before we made our first communion. I was Susie to everybody, and that was fine with me. My mother personalized a popular song from her era for Karen, Margie, and me. Mine was, "If you knew Susie (. . . like I know Susie, oh, oh, oh, what a girl!)." It was cutesy and catchy, and always put me in a happy mood. It wasn't until I was in high school that I became restless with my moniker and felt compelled to at least give it a bit of an edge, so I modernized the spelling to Suzi. My friends caught on fast. The family was a harder sell. Mom still begins her letters to me, "Dear Susie . . ."

To everyone in the family, and most of my friends from Bakersfield, Davis, and Sacramento, I am Suzi (Aunt Suzi to a dozen or so of them), and I can't imagine it any other way. However, in and after graduate school, it just seemed natural to transition to the more mature and professional Susan. By then, I was living a lot of my life in Spanish, and in that language, people usually called me Susana or Susanita.

I liked my given name, Susan Janssen, but found two faults with it. First, I never cared much for the monotonous quality of the repetitive schwa—you know, that *uh* sound that any one of the vowels can make. As illustrated in "The Law of Schwa," whether we spell my name Susan, Susen, Susin, Suson, or Susun, it will be pronounced the same. There is a second schwa at the end of my last name, so altogether it comes out "Su-suhn Jans-suhn," with a dull, rhyming quality to it. I know it sounds silly to make a big deal over this, but I always longed for a three-syllable name—Samantha, Alexa, or perhaps Juliana, after a queen of Holland.

The second fault is both fun and fraught. In the 1950s, "Susan" was the fourth-most popular girl's name, after Mary, Linda, and Patricia, and close to a half million of us bear it. The fun part is that when I first moved to Mendocino County, there was a Susan Club as well as a Susan Marching Band. The downside is that everywhere I go there are legions of us. As an occasional visitor to the Mendocino coastal tango community, I am Rita because there are already four other long-term dancers in the group named—you guessed it. As I prepared to go with friends to Tanzania a few years ago, there was another woman in our group named Susan, so I researched Swahili names and chose to be called Jamila for the duration of our safari. I very much enjoyed those three syllables and the *JJ* alliteration.

A few years ago, I started traveling to Italy to connect with my mother's language and heritage. I now teach basic Italian, and have become comfortable with being called Susanna. This, by the way, sounds notably different from the Spanish *Su-SA-na* because, in Italian, there is a "z" sound that Spanish lacks, and also because whenever there is a double consonant in Italian, the voice must rest there for an extra fraction of a second—a significant amount of time in the pronunciation of a word—to pronounce Susanna as *Su-ZA-nnna.*

In a single moment of early April 2016, I was suddenly galvanized to alter my appellation. Just a few days before leaving for New York to attend Steve Harrison's National Publicity Summit. I received an email that this was the last day to submit or change personal information for nametags, directory, etc. In a sudden bolt of clarity, I pictured 100 nametags arranged on the welcome table, and the name Susan jumping out from at least a half dozen of them. I emailed the organizers to change mine and became the only Susanna in a group of attendees that included, yes, a half-dozen Susans.

Since then, it's worked out just fine, except for the time or two when someone called out "Susanna!" and I didn't respond, or else I looked behind me to see who they were calling to. Except for some friends who now don't know what to call me. And except for TWK, a fellow newspaper columnist, asking me in the middle of our respective morning walks, "So what's the deal with Susan here and Susanna there?"

The simple answer is that you can call me anything, as long as you don't call me Sue!

Behind Closed Classroom Doors, Part I

Over a Japanese lunch with Joanne and Esther, two dear friends who also happen to be former students, we laughed at a memory they brought up of me telling a story in Spanish class involving a perfectly ordinary word, *bicho.* In standard Spanish, it simply means "bug," but *bichos* are something quite out of that ordinary meaning in some Latin American slang lexicons.

A pest-extermination company, hoping to increase its business in heavily Cuban-American Miami, translated into Spanish the slogan that promised to "kill those *bichos* for good!" The reaction of the population was somewhere between horror and hilarity as the collective mind flashed first to the colloquial meaning of *bichos* as male genitalia, long before it registered the standard dictionary definition of the word.

Joanne, Esther, and I then joked about what would be revealed if I did a survey asking, "What do you remember best from señora Janssen's Spanish class?" With a mixture of fear and delight, I suspect it might be one of these incidents in the following pages. Along with the language acquisition that occurred in my college classrooms over the years, what follows are some entertaining moments I'll never forget, that perhaps some of my students haven't either.

It isn't surprising how many memorable experiences involved food. We did a lot of eating in Spanish classes: salsa competitions, holiday burrito buffets, flan, Spanish tortilla-making demonstrations, and end-of-semester potlucks. Of course, Dove dark chocolate was always passed around on Mondays, before tests, and whenever else the energy level needed a lift.

* * *

I never actually cleaned a squid in class, but I have a great how-to diagram. Sometimes I passed it out while describing the famous dish *calamares en su tinta* (squid in its own ink). Wednesday's class ended with a particularly enthusiastic response of mostly, "Ew, gross!" On Monday at eight a.m., I walked in to greet the same group of students, and my *"Buenos días, clase!"* caught in my throat when I saw a plastic baggie on my desk containing something dark and squishy. Not accustomed to pranks in college classrooms, I tried to remain calm and cheerful as I gently poked the watery black blob. A closer examination revealed white, fleshy things floating in it. *"¿Qué es esto?"* I asked.

The whole class was in on the answer to "What is this?" and the perpetrator, a star athlete with a strong academic record, came forward and proudly announced he had found a recipe for the squid in ink that we were talking about last Wednesday. He had bought the ingredients, cleaned the squid, carefully emptied the ink sacs to make the black sauce, cooked it all up and served the dish to his friends, thoughtfully setting aside a portion for *la profesora.* That night, I prepared white rice, heated up the contents of the plastic baggie, and had an unforgettably authentic Spanish supper of *calamares en su tinta.* In the following class, I gave the dish a glowing review, and to the baseball player-cum-chef, a big dollop of extra credit.

* * *

Half of the final exam in conversation classes consisted of an oral report that students gave as a presentation on a subject of their choosing, trying to stick to known vocabulary and structures as much as possible. For the beginning classes, the time limit was one to three minutes; for the intermediates, it was three to five minutes. Most moaned at the anticipated impossibility of speaking Spanish for even 60 seconds straight in front of an audience, but then they usually went on for 10 minutes or more when their turn came.

Food was often involved, particularly in levels I and II: *cómo preparar guacamole, mi abuela's* recipe for salsa, the world's best flan, etc. As a side note, my forever-favorite flan recipe that I have been preparing for over 30 years came from Crystal's final exam presentation at Sacramento City College.

In one memorable presentation, Sheryl used full-color illustrations to explain wild-mushroom hunting. Of course, the audience of students wanted to know how to tell the difference among the edible ones, the ones that make you violently ill, and the ones so lethal that you would drop dead in the forest. Sheryl pointed out differences in the photographs but, to many who were uninitiated in the art of foraging for fungi, this teacher included, the toxic and the table-worthy were indistinguishable.

At the conclusion of her talk, Sheryl presented me with a plastic bag full of wild mushrooms, large and small, smooth and swarthy, and with names I no longer recall. The other students had a field day: "You're not going to eat those, are you? I wouldn't, if I were you. If you're not here for the written final on Tuesday, we'll know what happened. It could be a plot to make sure you don't come back!" Sheryl and I had already become fast friends, and I knew her experience of the natural world was informed and profound. That night at home, I sliced, sautéed, and savored that whole fungal assortment—an experience my taste buds have never forgotten.

* * *

Reaching back to the ancient history of my Sacramento City College days, I recall an oral final exam involving food that had a not-so-happy—but unintentionally funny—ending. A young man's presentation was about how to prepare the Spanish omelet called *tortilla.* In addition to the perfectly browned and set version he'd made at home, he brought fresh ingredients and arranged them on the table as he described the process: *huevos* ("eggs"), *cebolla* ("onion"), *papas* ("potatoes"), *y aceite de olivo* ("and olive oil"). Everything went just fine until, at the very end, he picked up the three eggs and theatrically announced his intent: *hacer malabares* ("to juggle"). I was being laissez-faire in the back of the room when, sure enough, a second later three eggs flew into the air and splattered onto the classroom carpet. We cleaned up the mess as best we could, but for the rest of my years at Sac City, I pretended to know nothing about the mysterious omelet-sized stain on the floor in front of my desk.

* * *

Students often went all-out with their presentations, and took to heart my encouragement to use props and engage audience participation. My colleague Skip had everyone up on their feet practicing tennis serves. A lovely lady fashioned a time capsule out of cardboard and presented the what and why of an assortment of 20th-century items to be shot into outer space. A lawyer instructed the class with a how-to of constructing a basic last will and testament. A grape-grower demonstrated the art of pruning vines. One very large dog was smuggled through the side door of MacMillan Hall, delighting everyone as he obeyed his owner's commands in Spanish to sit, roll over, and shake hands.

* * *

I recently ran into Yvonne at the local bookstore, and we again shared a laugh over how, in my first-semester class, she shot down my romantic naiveté about the big black birds circling overhead. I remember her telling me in my first class at Mendocino College: "Those aren't eagles, they're turkey vultures!" From the same class, I fondly recall sweet Marge in the front row wearing adorable little ladybug earrings, and Cheryl announcing $99.00 fares to Mexico via Alaska Air, which resulted in the first of my 20 trips to Oaxaca and a study/travel program for the college.

I should have taken better notes in my classes, as I'm sure many incidents have slipped my mind. But my memory is still darned good, and I haven't yet told all. In fact, you've only heard the third of it. Move to the next page for part II and tales of an end-of-semester toast that turned unexpectedly alcoholic, a near fist-fight, and a whole lot of smoking going on.

Behind Closed Classroom Doors, Part II

While we were students at UC Davis, in addition to working hard for our graduate degrees, participating in antiwar activities, and enjoying great camaraderie among professors and students, we smoked in the classrooms. I know this is unthinkable now, just as it's unimaginable that there were ashtrays in clothing-store fitting rooms, and lots of clothes that went on the sale rack with cigarette burns in the fabric.

It was the 70s, and you could light up anywhere. Professor Rogers walked into classes with a mug of coffee in one hand and a cigarette in the other. Professor Scari was an Argentine romantic whose good looks were distracting enough, but what really caused us not to remember anything he lectured about was his habit of drawing a cigarette from the pack and then spending the next 15 minutes lighting match after wasted match that burned down while he talked, gesticulating with the unlit cigarette, and flinging spent matches from his singed fingertips.

Unlike the dressing rooms at Macy's and JC Penney, our classrooms did not have ashtrays. Professors and students lit up, flicked ashes on the floor, then stamped out the butts and left them for janitors to sweep up at night. I never taught my classes with a cigarette in hand, but I do recall lighting up when my students were taking tests. I cringe even as I write this because I think of how awful that smelly environment must have been for nonsmokers, and how unimaginable this must seem to anyone who didn't live through that era, and even those of us (now, I hope, ex-smokers) who did.

* * *

On dozens of occasions, I dragged the two-burner stovetop from my office into the classroom to heat the tortillas for our burrito buffet, or to whip up Mexican hot chocolate. On the study/travel trips that I led to Oaxaca, Mexico, I discovered the best brand of chocolate for making the drink, and would return every summer with at least 10 pounds of Mayordomo in my suitcase for the next school year. Once or twice I made a Spanish *tortilla* (an egg, potato, and onion omelet eaten as an appetizer or a light supper), but I never attempted a *paella* because the timing and number of ingredients in this spectacular Spanish rice dish—sausage, chicken, seafood, and vegetables—are too daunting for in-class preparation.

* * *

Before finals week, my students and I always wrapped up the semester with a party that included food and beverages. At the end of a particular Sacramento City College class, everyone had chosen a potluck item to bring, and one woman had volunteered to bring drinks for the group. On the evening of the on-campus party, she arrived with six chilled bottles of what she thought was sparkling apple cider, so proud to have chosen the perfect beverage for the Spanish class party because it was *from Spain.* Yes, it certainly was!—hard cider from Asturias, in northern Spain. "Hmm . . . what a dilemma—either an alcoholic beverage, or the drinking fountain. Since I'm more pragmatist than purist, and the students were all over 21, I swore them to secrecy and invited the beverage hostess to pour her cider enthusiastically, but not liberally, into the plastic cups, and we shared a toast:

"*¡Salud, amor, dinero, y tiempo para disfrutarlos, amigos!*" ("Health, love, money, and time to enjoy them, friends!")

* * *

At Mendocino College, I remember a particularly lively Spanish II class that, within the first month of the semester, had developed into a wonderful multi-aged community of highly communicative people. As was my pattern, every class started with a stand-up exchange of students circulating around the room asking each other a specific question. I don't recall what the question was on that particular day, but my memory is crystal-clear about the fact that, while the students were moving about on foot, our college president was seated as an observer in the back of the room.

Suddenly, in the middle of the activity, some sort of altercation broke out, and I heard one young woman yell, "It was *you*!" Then she hauled off and hit the guy standing in front of her. She whacked him pretty hard in the shoulder, and continued to berate him while he shrank back, wearing a half-guilty, half-amused, sheepish expression on his face.

We didn't have to pull them apart, but it did take some unraveling to get to the story. They had been happy classmates for the first several weeks when suddenly a chance exchange in their second language clued her that he was the knave who, at the stop sign exiting from the campus onto State Street, had braked, accelerated, then braked again, resulting in her rear-ending his car and having to pay for the damages. I thought I had chosen the perfect class to showcase for the president, but instead he witnessed a near-brawl.

* * *

Nearly every semester, we held an auction day in my classes—*una subasta.* The evening before the big day, I assembled stacks of paper money that my student assistant had photocopied and cut for me, before that employment category became extinct in the succession of budget cuts during the 90s. There were color-coded denominations of $500, $100, and $50 bills, bearing grainy images of Antonio Banderas, Pablo Picasso, and Penelope Cruz. These were *dólares* and not *pesos* because, ironically, Americans find the names of both our country *(Los Estados Unidos)* and our currency *(el dólar)* to be among the most challenging words in Spanish to pronounce. *Dólares* usually came out sounding like the name "Dolores" as well as *dolores,* the Spanish word for aches and pains.

Students received their stacks of bills and immediately counted their money to make sure they had the full $30,755 and not *un dólar* less. They had been instructed to bring a belonging they were willing to part with—something that others might want. Those who had forgotten to bring something beat a path to the vending machine for Snickers, Skittles, or M&Ms—popular auction items that incited serious bidding wars into the thousands. Of course, the whole point was to practice saying larger numbers in Spanish, and the student auctioning an item had to repeat the number each time a bid was shouted out.

When the bidding slowed, they said, "$1,565 *una vez . . . dos veces . . . tres veces. . . .* ¡Se vende!" ("$1565 once . . . twice . . . three times. . . . Sold!"). The money changed hands, as did the book, vase, mug, baseball cap, candy bar, colored-pencil set, or mini stapler. One student auctioned off an intact wasp nest, minus insects, that the purchaser intended to display as a work of art in his office.

A real estate agent had the winning bid for a transparent green-plastic watch, which he then wore daily for years. I was afraid I'd have to stop my winemaker student from auctioning off the bottle in his hand, but it turned out to be a gift for the teacher, and was accepted graciously.

It all sounds so clean, neat, and perfectly orderly in the telling, doesn't it? Maybe it started out that way, but about halfway through any given auction, when a few students had a towering stack of bills and most had too few to buy anything more, things inevitably began to deteriorate. With the wink of an eye and the nod of a head, wads of money were passed across the classroom, and purchasing cartels spontaneously formed to acquire the coveted bag of M&Ms (which could be shared) or the baseball cap (which couldn't), more for the sake of sport and strategy than actual attainment. Those were delightful days when I just sat in the back row, coaching them on their use of higher numbers, and laughing as one by one they took to the front of the room to extol the virtue and value of a used shopping bag, a Beanie Baby, or a Disney-character Christmas ornament.

The *subastas* sure didn't teach anything about the value of money, but numbers came alive and, after all that practice, they could begin to imagine themselves in an open-air market somewhere in Mexico, holding their own with the vendor as they negotiated the price of a wool poncho and a pair of huarache sandals. Mission accomplished.

Behind Closed Classroom Doors, Part III

The fourth-semester Spanish class at Mendocino College wasn't a literature class *per se,* but I'd long since given up on following textbook dictates, and had instead designed conversation-based learning activities that included culture and literature, and *didn't* involve buying a $130 textbook. These classes were unique and delightfully unpredictable because students at that level were capable of so much linguistic creativity.

In a turn-of-the-century spring class, we had read several pieces of prose and poetry by Latin American writers who lived under repressive regimes. Students learned about *los desaparecidos* ("the disappeared ones") of Chile and Argentina in the 70s. They watched a film about the mothers who marched every Thursday from 1977 through 2006 in the Plaza de Mayo of Buenos Aires, demanding that the military dictatorship of Rafael Videla reveal what it had done with the thousands of sons and daughters who were summarily detained between 1976 and 1983, never to be seen again. We absorbed heart-rending first-person accounts of those who had survived imprisonment and torture by the regimes, and read poetry by dissidents against the Cuban Revolution, imprisoned for years or for life—unfortunate souls with no legal recourse.

I had never intended to present an extended course on such an emotionally wrenching subject, but once we started pulling the thread of the so-called "Dirty War" in Chile, one thing kept leading to another. Given all that weighty material, even past-subjunctive verb conjugations became a jovial topic. In truth, we were all deeply moved by the experience and, when it came to the final assignment, they were inspired. Each took the viewpoint of one imprisoned by a dictatorship for their beliefs, then poured their thoughts and experiences into a poem in Spanish. I was awed, humbled, and deeply moved. I still am, after all these years.

* * *

In mid-December of 1999, we were reviewing before finals when there was a sudden campus-wide blackout. Our classroom had one south-facing window that didn't provide enough light to see either the textbooks or the board. I was going to cancel the class and let them join the streams of students already heading for the parking lot, but the electrical failure spawned a spontaneous conversation about Y2K (the possible technological disasters anticipated at the turn of the year 2000)—and in their foreign language at that! Soon we were creating a list of the items that everyone thought should go into a survival kit in case the world-wide computer systems that enable most aspects of our lives crashed at 12:01 a.m. on January 1, 2000, since it was suspected and feared that they weren't programmed to recognize "00" as the next sequence after "99." In the daily business of prepping lessons and correcting homework and compositions, I hadn't given this possibility a lot of my attention. However, many of my students had, and this sparked a provocative conversation in Spanish during which I wrote in huge letters on the board the items they recommended for our hypothetical survival box.

Though the Y2K angel of doom has long since passed over us, I still keep a student-inspired box of emergency supplies, *en caso de que* ("just in case"): *botellas de agua* ("bottles of water"), *comida enlatada* ("canned food"), *un abrelatas* ("a can opener"), *cobijas* ("blankets"), *una almohada* ("a pillow"), *curitas* ("Band-Aids"), *velas y cerillos* ("candles and matches"), etcétera. ¡Ah! y *una botella de cognac* (for medicinal purposes only, of course).

* * *

Colleagues often signed up for my evening Spanish conversation classes, and in one particular semester I had the chemistry professor as my student. He was the last in the line-up to take the stage for his final presentation, and what came next was explosive, unprecedented, and probably illegal—and had consequences. Forgive my memory lapse on the technical details, but I do recall that he faced his audience with a rolled-up newspaper in one hand and a glass bottle in the other. He lit the end of the newspaper wad, talking in Spanish all the while about the exchange of gases, combustion, and who-knows-what-else (for I was far too busy watching the torch burn down towards his hand as he waved it around to make his points). I had no idea how this was going to turn out, but it had to end soon, because his mini-inferno was moving quickly, and that torch was over 50% ash and cinders.

Then he drew our attention to the glass bottle, and put the flame to whatever was inside it. A sudden second later, there was a loud, sharp "BANG!" that lifted us two inches off our chairs. I wondered, *Should I stop this now or let him go on?* He was, after all, a professor of chemistry, and had a decade and a half more tenure than I. Surely he knew what he was doing with gases, fire, and whatever else he had up his sleeve. As it turned out, he did, and two seconds before the torch flame reached his hand, he doused it in a bucket of water hidden beneath the desk. Once the grand finale was over, we could all breathe again. With relief and admiration, we broke into applause, and the evening of presentations ended with calls of "¡Chido*!*" ("Cool!") and claps on the back. After rounds of "¡Felicidades!" ("Congratulations!") and *abrazos* ("hugs"), we called that semester class a wrap, and exited for the parking lot.

End of story? Ohh, no—at least not for the teacher, who found out through college email first thing the next morning that the maintenance and security personnel had searched all of MacMillan Hall the previous evening after several staff reported smelling smoke in the offices and classrooms. They found nothing to account for the worrisome odor, but the Fire Department was called in to search the building again, just to be on the safe side. It was determined that smoke had circulated through the ventilation system of the building, but the source could not be identified. This occasioned much shrugging of shoulders and scratching of heads, but luckily no investigation into the shenanigans (in the service of learning foreign language) behind the closed doors of Room 1260.

CHAPTER SEVEN

Marking Moments in the Year

Have a *Feliz Navidad* and a "Diglot" New Year!

Perhaps like me, you resonate with that Spanish phrase in the title more readily than the English word "diglot." Following a brief discussion of diglotism, you will be treated to a bilingual poem (complete with glossary) that's meant for December but might even provide cheer in August.

May Your Days Be Merry and Bright

Whether you're reading in December or May, this section will put you in high spirits, especially if accompanied by a slice of (last year's?) fruitcake and a favorite libation. As for the reindeer—no matter the month of the year but, especially in spring, they would want you to know the truth.

High Notes on Highway 99

Christmas always finds me driving south to visit family, and by New Year's Day I'm plying the same highway back north to redwoods and wine country. Here I share with you some memorable slices of the central California valley culture as expressed through its billboards, road signs, place names, and rural geography. Hold on for a fast, fun ride!

And the Word of the Year Is . . .

Lexophiles wait breathlessly for the annual announcement of the Words of the Year by various dictionary companies and academic societies. Enjoy a little background and history of the American Dialectical Society's selections since 1990.

"Reach Out and Open Your Kimono": A Lexical Review

There is yet more to be said about those Words of the Year. I am interested not only in how far you "open your kimono" but also in knowing whether the kinds of news items about words and language that I gravitate to are the same ones that grab a share of your attention.

The Secret to Everything, Part I

It's the key to realizing your dream of you-name-it, and it will come as no great surprise. Then why is it that that over 95% of us don't do it?

The Secret to Everything, Part II

Four sub-secrets and an inspirational true story will help us ride out the rough times and finish with the elite few who *do* make their dreams come true.

Around the World in Cupid's Quiver

Honey, *Babe*, and *Boo* might seem a bit bland when compared to foreign terms of endearment that translate *My Heartbeat*, *Little Treasure*, and *Gold Nugget.* To some lovers, there's even romantic sentiment in *Breadcrumb*, *Microbe*, and *Meatball.*

Mary and the Merry Month of May

We count on spring to bring flowers and rebirth—but what about snake-parades and cheese-racing? We'll take a whirlwind tour of some unusual seasonal rites from around the world, then look more deeply into the Christian celebrations of Mother Mary in the month of May.

The Yodeling Dutchman: a Father's Day Tribute

This is a story of my father, with my mother in a supporting role, though in reality it was a pretty equal partnership in parenting, education, and discipline. Since this book is dedicated to them both, it seems a most fitting section with which to conclude.

Have a *Feliz Navidad* and a "Diglot" New Year!

That's a new word I learned the other day: "diglot." In the absence of context, when I first spotted it in a book title, I thought it had something to do with a "dig" and a "lot." I was completely off the mark. We are perhaps more familiar with the word "polyglot," referring to one who speaks, reads, and writes several languages. Besides English, I can converse well in Spanish and passably in Italian, but I am flummoxed to read about someone who is fluent in those two languages as well as English, German, Arabic, and Farsi. *Mon Dieu!*

In the United States, we're usually quite impressed by people who are bilingual, or *diglot*, because most Americans aren't, although a great number have had enough experience in a second-language high-school class to appreciate the challenges of acquiring *lingua* #2, let alone #3. My aunties in the Netherlands were fluent in German and English on top of their native Dutch and, dedicated travelers that they were, they devoted themselves to learning Spanish, French, Italian, and a smattering of the local language in whatever country of the world they visited on holiday.

In over a dozen trips to Holland, I never picked up any Dutch because most Netherlanders speak, read, write, and watch TV in English. I consider my Italian friend who lives in Barcelona a true polyglot. Ludovica has mastered English, Spanish, French, and Catalan, the language of Catalonia (of which Barcelona is the capital). On the job, she translates in all five languages. I am ever in awe of her mastery and fluency, but as an American I feel fortunate to have at least more than one language on the tip of my tongue. My linguistic bent is towards Romance languages, and I will always prefer the mellifluous flow of the Latin-origin word *bilingual* over the Germanic guttural thud of *diglot.*

* * *

To celebrate the season as well as our second-commonest language in America, I would like to share with you my personal version of an anonymous diglot poem that never ceases to delight (see glossary that follows, if clarification is needed):

’Twas the night before Christmas
and all through the *casa*
not a creature was stirring . . . *¡Caramba! ¿Qué pasa?*
The stockings were hung by the chimney *con cuidado*
in hopes that Ol’ Santa would feel *obligado*
to leave a few *cosas aquí y allí*
for *toda la familia,* but especially *para mí.*
While *mamá* worked late in her big *oficina,*
papá was shopping at the corner *cantina,*
buying milk and Doritos and a can of *cerveza*
for Santa to find on the dining-room *mesa.*
Now the *niños* are snuggled all safe in their *camas,*
some in their *’chones,* and some in *pijama.*
Those little *cabezas* are filled with sweet dreams—
they’re all *esperando lo que* Santa will bring.
Then out in the yard, there arose such a *grito*
that I jumped to my feet like a frightened *gatito.*
I ran to the window and looked *para afuera,*
and who in the world do you think *¿quién era?*

St. Nick in a sleigh and a big red *sombrero*
came dashing along like a crazy *bombero.*
And pulling his sleigh, instead of *venados,*
were eight little burros approaching *volados.*
And holding the reins was a quaint little *hombre,*
shouting and whistling, calling them by *nombre:*
¡Panchita y Pepe! ¡Nacho, Lupita!
¡Ey, Beto y Chata! ¡Nieto y Flaquita!
¡Adelante! ¡Arriba! ¡Abajo! ¡Y vamos!
We'll park it right here on the lawn *donde estamos.*"
Then standing up straight with his hands on his *pecho,*
he flew to the top of our very own *techo.*
With his big round *panza* like a bowl of *jalea,*
he struggled to squeeze down our small *chimenea.*
Then, huffing and puffing at last in our *sala,*
with soot smeared all over his red suit *de gala,*
he filled all the stockings with lovely *regalos,*
for none of the *niños* had been *muy malos.*
He nibbled *galletas,* took a sniff of *cerveza,*
and cleaned his round *lentes* with the cloth on the *mesa.*
Then, chuckling aloud, and feeling *contento,*
he turned like a flash and was gone *como el viento.*
And I heard him exclaim—and this is *verdad*—
"Merry Christmas to all! ¡*Y Feliz Navidad!*"

Whether you're reading this in July or December, may all our days be merry and bright, may we support the local economy with all our might, may all our credit card bills be light, and may we all sleep tight tonight!

Glossary of Spanish Words

abajo	down
adelante	forward
afuera	outside
aquí y allí	here and there
arriba	up
bombero	fireman
cabezas	heads
'chones	undies
como el viento	like the wind
con cuidado	with care
cosas	things
donde estamos	where we are
esperando	waiting
gala	festive
galletas	cookies
gatito	kitten
grito	shout
jalea	jelly
lentes	eyeglasses
mesa	table
muy malos	very bad
niños	children
nombre	name
panza	belly
pecho	chest
¿quién era?	who was it?
regalos	gifts
sala	living room

techo	roof
toda	all
venados	deer
verdad	true
volados	flying

May Your Days Be Merry and Bright

If it's February or August, best save this read for December when you can imagine that Bing Crosby is again and forever dreaming of a "White Christmas," Paul McCartney is "Simply Having a Wonderful Christmas Time," and Andy Williams keeps reminding us that "It's the most wonderful time of the year." Despite that popular carol, at the moment, I'm only convinced that it's the most expensive, stressful, and high-maintenance time of the year. As the "shoppers rush home with their treasures," they're already imagining what the credit-card company will bring in January.

I can't be the only one who just occasionally gets ever so slightly crabby as the shopping days before Christmas dwindle, the pressure mounts, and I face the fact that my annual resolution to simplify has again met with failure. If you ever experience a moment like that, I recommend building a snowman and engaging him in a game of catch with a fruitcake, singing carols to the neighbors, then lobbing what's left of said fruitcake over the backyard fence, or roasting some chestnuts on an open fire, then throwing in last year's fruitcake for a spectacular burn.

Speaking of an open fire: Christmas was a much simpler affair when my father was a boy in Holland. He and his siblings put out their little wooden shoes, and in the morning they were ecstatic to find that *Sinterklaas* had left each one an orange. Infantile ecstasy over a piece of fruit is hard to imagine for those who never lived in a cold, rainy, flooded country in the early 20th century, ate boiled potatoes and cabbage every day, and regarded an orange as more precious than a Fabergé egg.

Dad told us stories from his early childhood, like the time he was chased around the yard by a giant rooster and fell into the family cesspool. I don't think that had anything to do with Christmas, but it always comes to mind during Yuletide, along with the story about how his wonder got the best of him one late-December evening, circa 1925. His hair caught fire when he leaned in too close to the tree, which was illuminated by real, lighted candles tied to the branches of a real, live tree. It makes one wonder how folks survived the olden days, but I'm sure the number of house fires and hair fires accelerated the invention of electrical-light strings, and boosted product liability as a prime new area of specialization for lawyers.

My Italian mamma, along with being a pro at Scrabble, is a legendary cook, and produces loaves of old-fashioned fruitcake every year, the rich, moist kind that many people actually eat and enjoy. Last year, I got one for Christmas, another for the Fourth of July, and a third for my birthday in November because she always makes extras and stores them in the freezer. She knows I'm going to tell her the same joke every Christmas Eve when I land on her back porch, road-weary but holly-jolly after seven to eight hours en route from Ukiah to Bakersfield. Somehow, her curiosity always kicks in before her memory of last year's telling does:

Suzi: Mom, did you know that a newly discovered Dead Sea scroll has revealed the existence of a fourth Wise Man?

Mom: Really? Why didn't we hear about that in church?

Suzi: Because he was turned away for bringing a fruitcake.

Mom rolls her eyes and laughs as she hands me my first slice.

Before I share this recipe with you, let me be very clear: It's not Mom's. She hasn't yet given me hers, but promises not to take it to the grave. This one is courtesy of the Internet, something I found while trolling around for "the best fruitcake ever." You never know what you'll get with Internet recipes, but this one intrigued me and I thought it worth sharing with you for the holidays:

The Best Fruitcake Ever

Ingredients: 1 cup butter; 1 cup sugar; 4 large eggs; 1 cup assorted dried fruit; 1 tsp. baking powder;* 1 tsp. baking soda; 2 cups flour; 1 tbsp. lemon juice; 1 cup brown sugar; 1 cup nuts; 1–2 quarts aged whiskey.

Preparation Time: between 20 and 120 minutes (plus the next day for recovery).

- Measure 1 level cup of the whiskey into a clear glass to check for color. It should be light to medium golden-brown. Taste a bit to test its quality. Drink the rest of the glass to ensure it possesses the depth and character worthy of The Best Fruitcake Ever. Repeat this step if you are not 100% convinced.
- Now, with an eclectic mixer, beat one cup of butter in a large, fluffy bowl.
- Add 1 teaspoon of sugar, and beat the dickens out of it again. Meanwhile, at this parshticular point in time, make sure that the whixey hasn't oxshitized since offening the bottle. Open second quart if nestessary.
- Add two large leggs, 2 cups of fruit, and beat till high. If the fruit gets shtuck in the peaters, just pry the clods loosh with a drewscriver.

---

* Beware of abbreviations! My little brother, Freddie, was helping in the kitchen, and when Mom's pancake recipe called for 2 tsp. of "bp," he sprinkled two generous teaspoons of black pepper into the batter and fired up the griddle for the family's Sunday breakfast.

- "Example" the whikstey again, shecking confistancy, then shift two cups of floor or Cashcade or whatever—like anyones give a woot. Chample the whitchey shum mor.
- Splurt in some lemming zhoosh. Foold in chopped splutter and strained nuts.
- Add in 100 babblespoons of brown booger and shumma dat shoda and mix well.
- Greash ubben and turn the cakey pan to 350 degrees.
- Now pour the whole blarn mesh into the dwyer and shpin on pertinent presh til dinnerstime.
- Sheck dat whixney wunsh more and pash ou.

* * *

Continuing in a more scientific but no less festive vein, we shall now explore the gender distribution of Santa's reindeer, always depicted guiding the sleigh in sleek, graceful precision with their perfectly symmetrical racks of antlers. A popular urban legend of the past decade enlightens us with information attributed to the Alaska Department of Fish and Game:

> While both males and females of the species grow antlers in the summer each year, male reindeer drop their antlers at the beginning of winter, usually late November to mid-December. Female reindeer, however, retain their antlers until after they give birth in the spring. Therefore, according to every historical rendition depicting Santa's reindeer, every single one of them, from Rudolph to Blitzen, had to be a female.

Every year, Alaska F&G receives more inquiries than Santa gets letters about the sex of Dasher, Dancer, Prancer, Vixen, Comet,

Cupid, Donner, and Blitzen—arguably unisex names for animals, but then there's Rudolph of the foggy nights. The Alaska F&G informs us that, yes, the majority of male reindeer do shed their antlers before December 24, while females don't shed theirs until they calve in the spring. Therefore, it is highly probable that most, if not all, of Santa's reindeer were, are, and always will be female. The urban legend messenger says, in conclusion: "We should have known! Only women would be able to drag a fat man in a red velvet suit all around the world in one night without getting lost." To that I say, you go, girls!

Finally, here are a few words of advice for the holiday season: Don't stick your head in the Christmas tree, even if the lights are electrical; don't accept a gift from the fourth Wise Man unless you fancy fossilized fruitcake,† keep Grandma out of the path of Dasher and Vixen; and keep the cap tightly screwed down on her "whishkey" bottle. Drink smart, and buy local!

---

† In August of 2017, National Geographic reported that a 107-year-old piece of fruitcake was found in an abandoned building in Antarctica, and is believed to have been brought there by the British explorer Robert Scott in 1920. The team who discovered this culinary relic reported that it "looked and smelled almost edible." Keep this in mind when you assemble your emergency survival kit.

High Notes on Highway 99

I love road trips—no talk-radio, no iPod tunes, and no audiobooks, just the thoughts in my head and the scenery before my eyes. It's a long drive from Northern California to Bakersfield in the Central Valley to visit Mom for Christmas, and I usually break it up by stopping in Sacramento to see friends from the old days. After merriment and gift exchanges, I leave the capital city with three hours down and four and a half to go.

Some folks claim that taking Highway 5 instead of 99 will shave off a few minutes. That may be true, but the 5 has way too many big trucks, and offers far too little entertainment for this connoisseur of California roadways. Sure, Highway 99 presents the inevitable proliferation of chain retail, with its towering signage for endless iterations of Bed Bath & Beyond, TJ Maxx, Michael's, and Ross Dress for Less, making every city look alike when viewed from the freeway. But focusing beyond the big corporate, cookie-cutter clutter, things started to get more interesting.

Past the slick urbanity of Sacramento, coming up on Merced, I almost choked on my Triple Threat Power Bar at the sight of Lou Rodman's Barstools and Dining billboard, inviting me to, "Come in and check out our stool samples." A neighboring billboard read, "We want your junk!" and yet another proclaimed, "We buy ugly houses."

On the food scene—though it was hard to consider so soon after Lou Rodman's dubiously beckoning words—IHOP has made a big comeback with pancakes in the heartland, and Black Bear Diners are leaving a big footprint. Jack-in-the-Box kept coming on to me with "MMMM-eaty!" but I stayed with my carrots and apple slices. On down the road, I was as charmed as ever by signs for cafes named Apple Annie's and Blueberry Hill. (I could just hear Fats Domino finding his "thrill"!) I was tempted by a juicy plate soaring in a billboard sky for Salazar's Grill 'n' Bar, but figured there was no telling what they'd serve up at Joe Bob's Barn' Grill. (Was that just an error in spacing?)

It was Christmas Eve, finally raining heavily after four years of drought, and the FedEx trucks were out in full force to land those packages on their designated porches. The Walmart fleet was racing from store to store to fulfill their promise to America: "Save money. Live better." Jewelers had amped up their ad campaigns for the holidays—what better time to shower that special one with diamonds? The Rogers Jewelers billboard sparkled and purred, "Stoke the fires," and a local purveyor promised that with the gift of a glittery rock there would be "A great day for her, a better night for you." Another billboard of bling opted for a fear-and-jealousy pitch: "Your girlfriend wants me. Bad." That one still disturbs me. Also unsettling were the numerous signs by 1-855-FOR-TRUTH (by GospelBillboards.org): "If you die tonight? Heaven or Hell." Soon enough, I found welcome distraction and immeasurable cheer in a long lineup of bare-chested Chippendales inviting me to experience "Fifty Shades of Men." Suddenly, the Valley didn't seem so sleepy anymore.

The Central Valley is still California's premier food-producing region, with 230 different crops including tomatoes, almonds, grapes, cotton, apricots, and asparagus, and providing 8% of the total value of U.S. agricultural output. South of Fresno, livestock operations and huge dairy farms are frequent sights. The perfectly flat land extends eastward toward the Sierra Nevada mountains, which, thanks to valley smog, often can't be seen too clearly.

Billboards abound selling tractors, harvesters, and pesticides: "Stop this bug from killing California citrus!"

Back in 2005, forests of billboards up and down the entire valley promised everyone an easy mortgage with "no down payment!" for homes under $150,000. Those are all gone now, except for one brave and perhaps exaggerated claim in Kingsburg, just north of Fresno: "If you can dream it, we can finance it." All the rest noiselessly disappeared in the disastrous real estate market implosion of foreclosures on the American Dream.

The ubiquitous theme these days is water, and the signs of stress and divisive interests caused by the drought are everywhere: "Irrigation matters!" and "Is growing food wasting water?" After four years of drastically low rain and snowfall, the UC Davis Center for Watershed Sciences reports that the drought cost California $1.84 billion and 10,100 jobs in 2015. With El Niño dangling its promise of winter rains, new billboards exhort, "Build water storage now!"

Farmers may be struggling, but personal injury/defense lawyers seem to be on a roll. With every trip, I see an increase in the number of outraged but confidence-inspiring male faces promising that they can and will fight the system, and win: "Been fired or harassed? Fight back!"; "Fix that ticket!"; "DUI? Crash? injury? We are here for you."

Meanwhile, the economy beer and wine industry entices with billboards every mile or two: "Raid the state of celebration!" (Budweiser); "Go long. Finish light." (Coors); "Stella Rosa: your favorite tailgate wine" and "California loves to Stellabrate" (under $10 a bottle; heavy on the pinks and peaches). A plumbing company promises, "We fix any leak," accompanied by a photo of a toddler with his diaper sagging to the floor, followed by, "Well, almost any." With Coors, Bud, Stella, the plumber, and of course,

Rodman's stool samples, Central California looks like one big party with a couple of trips to the bathroom.

Years ago, on the drive south, Susan, my passenger from San Francisco, commented on the cutesy names of towns and roads in the Central Valley. I was so used to growing up near Buttonwillow, Terra Bella, and Pumpkin Center that I was embarrassed to say I'd never even noticed. Plus, I felt like a hick around my big-city friend from "The City." Now, I revel in the folksy charm of towns named Gustine, Snelling, and Chowchilla. I nod at the faded sign that still heralds Selma as the "Raisin Capital of the World," and drive on past off-ramps for Dinuba, Goshen, Tipton, Pixley, Conejo ("rabbit," in Spanish), Earlimart, and Alpaugh.

The Elmo Highway to McFarland is a sign that Bakersfield is near. The Lerdo Highway to Shafter means I'm getting warmer. Then there's Kimberlina Road, and finally the sign that tells me I have arrived—at least to the northernmost end of greater Bakersfield: Oildale. There's still Merle Haggard Drive and Buck Owens Boulevard to navigate before I reach Mom's place.

Fast-forward five days: Santa and his little burros have come and gone, the prime rib was roasted and consumed, the gifts have been torn from their wrappings, and the fourth Wise Man has been turned away for bringing a fruitcake. I've picked as many grapefruit from the family tree as will fit in the car, and I'm heading back north on Highway 99, immensely grateful for the intermittent 70-mph speed limit that lets me fly.

On the first fast stretch toward Fresno, I strain my eyes to the east for Madame Sophia, in her fourth or so decade of reading palms in a rundown little house alongside the highway. I still think I might stop to meet her someday. A little farther north, around Modesto, I see she has competition: "Hermana Milagrosa" (Miraculous Sister) is obviously in the business of palm-reading as well, with a two-story sign along the 99 beside an equally dumpy little house topped by a huge hand sporting a long and promising lifeline.

Approaching Sacramento, and just about the time I think the roadside entertainment has played out, a billboard for Planet Fitness in Stockton renews my faith in the power of remodeling a hackneyed term to provocative effect. The gym promises that if you sign up for a new membership in January, you'll "Pay diddly for your squat."

Comparing the North Valley to the South, the fields are greener, the sky is bluer, and K–12 recesses aren't cancelled due to intense smog. I can often see the mountains on both sides of the freeway. I admire those views, but miss the entertainment and already anticipate a future foray through California's heartland, a place where I can feel the pulse of the great state and sample what they're serving up on Highway 99.

And the Word of the Year Is . . .

Every year's events, trends, scandals, and tech advances are fertile ground for a new word or phrase to be born, capture our imagination, bounce from our brain to our tongue, and go verbally viral into the vibrant and volatile realm of words and the images they conjure up.

In many cases, an original term must be coined to allow us to refer to the new thing, and generally the new invention will be just a word or two rather than a half-dozen or more. "To smoke an electronic cigarette, inhaling nicotine through a vaporized solution" mercifully simplifies these days to "vape." There is no need to suffer the lengthy awkwardness of writing on your Christmas wish list, "I want one of those collapsible monopods to attach to my camera or cell phone for better selfies," when you can just say, "Dear Santa, please bring me a selfie stick!"

The Word of the Year (WotY) isn't just one contest but several, with widely recognized players including the Oxford Dictionaries, Merriam-Webster, and Global Language Monitor presenting their selections. However, the most prestigious choice of a year's winning word is that of the American Dialect Society (ADS), thus distinguished because it is the oldest such contest, and its WotY is determined by a vote of linguistic experts independent of commercial interests. The yearly selection made by these linguists is also unique and eagerly awaited because it is the last one announced, in January, after all the delights and disasters of the year have been consigned to history.

Perusing this list, we see many terms that are old news at best, and head-scratchers or completely forgotten at worst. But we must remember that the Word of the Year is chosen not because it should stand the test of time, but because it is perceived to best reflect the mood and preoccupations of the preceding 12 months. Mass agreement is, of course, impossible, but now you can exercise your memory of these past years and judge for yourself.

Below are the ADS Word of the Year picks since the tradition began in January 1991.

- 1990: **"bushlips"**—similar to "bullshit," stemming from President George H.W. Bush's infamous broken promise in 1988: "Read my lips: no new taxes."
- 1991: **"mother of all"**— as in Saddam Hussein's threatened "mother of all battles."
- 1992: **"not!"**—meaning "just kidding."
- 1993: **"information superhighway"**
- 1994: 1. **"cyber"**; 2. **"morph"**—to change form.
- 1995: **"newt"**—to act aggressively as a newcomer, like House Speaker Newt Gingrich with the "Contract with America."
- 1996: **"soccer mom"**
- 1997: **"millennium bug"**—the feared computer inability to distinguish 1900 from 2000, expected to create international havoc.
- 1998: the prefix **"e-"** as in "email" or "e-commerce."
- 1999: **"Y2K"**—simply meaning "the year 2000" but resonating with all of its accompanying "millennium-bug" fear and dread.
- 2000: **"chad"**—a bit of paper punched out, for example, in a ballot card, brought to national attention by the 2000 presidential-election controversy in Florida.
- 2001: **"9-11"**—the attack on New York's World Trade Center towers on September 11, 2001.

- 2002: **"weapons of mass destruction (WMD)"**
- 2003: **"metrosexual"**—heterosexual male who likes beauty treatments and fashionable clothes.
- 2004: **"red state/blue state/purple state"**—states identified by Republican, Democratic, or mixed voter majority, from the 2004 U.S. presidential election.
- 2005: **"truthiness"**—quality of an alleged truth that a person claims to know intuitively because it just feels right, without regard to evidence, logic, or facts (popularized on The Colbert Report).
- 2006: **"plutoed"**—demoted or devalued, as happened to the once and perhaps future planet Pluto.
- 2007: **"subprime"**—describes a risky or less-than-ideal loan, mortgage, or investment.
- 2008: **"bailout"**—in the specific sense of the rescue by the government of companies on the brink of failure, including large players in the banking industry.
- 2009: **"tweet"**—short message sent via Twitter.com; the act of sending such a message.
- 2010: **"app"**—abbreviated form of "application," or software program for a computer or phone-operating system.
- 2011: **"occupy"**—verb or noun, inspired from the Occupy Movement of 2011.
- 2012: **"hashtag"**—a word or phrase preceded by an octothorpe (pound sign or hash symbol: #), used on Twitter to mark a topic or make a commentary.
- 2013: **"because . . ."**—abbreviated phrase introducing a noun, adjective, or other part of speech (e.g., "because reasons," "because awesome").
- 2014: **"#blacklivesmatter"**—hashtag used as a protest over blacks killed at the hands of police, triggered

specifically by the deaths of Michael Brown in Ferguson, Missouri and Eric Garner in Staten Island.

- 2015: the singular **"they/their"**—a gender-neutral pronoun to avoid the use of "he/she." Example: Each student has to provide their own email address (more on this in the next section).
- 2016: **"dumpster fire"**—a situation that is chaotic, disastrous, out-of-control—a total mess, in other words. (Needless to say, many a WotY is born from observation of the political landscape.)
- 2017: **"fake news"**—disinformation or falsehoods presented as real news.

In addition to the Word of the Year, the ADS also selects words in other categories that can vary from year to year. I have taken massive editing liberties to present to you those I thought most useful, creative, fun, or outrageous.

Most Creative

- 2008: **"recombobulation area"**—named after an area at General Mitchell International Airport in Milwaukee where passengers who have passed through security screening can get their clothes and belongings back in order.
- 2009: **"Dracula sneeze"**—covering one's mouth with the crook of one's elbow when sneezing (similar to popular portrayals of the vampire Dracula in which he hides the lower half of his face with a cape draped over his arm).

Most Unnecessary

- 2010: **"refudiate"**—blend of "refute" and "repudiate" as used by Sarah Palin on Twitter.

Most Outrageous

- 2012: **"legitimate rape"**—type of rape that Missouri senate candidate Todd Akin claimed rarely results in pregnancy.

Most Euphemistic

- 2010: **"kinetic event"**—Pentagon term for violent attacks on troops in Afghanistan.
- 2013: **"least untruthful"**—involving the smallest necessary lie, used by U.S. Director of National Intelligence James Clapper.

Most Likely to Succeed

- 2014: **"salty"** —exceptionally bitter, angry, or upset.
- 2017: "**newsjacking**"—co-opting *current events or news stories to promote or advertise one's product or brand.*

Least Likely to Succeed

- 2012: **"phablet"**—midsized electronic device, between a smartphone and a tablet in size.
- 2017: **"milkshake duck"**—a person or character on social media that appears to be endearing at first, but is found to have an unappealing backstory.

Of these winners and runners-up, how many survivors are there?

In the next section, we will open wide the kimono to reveal the naked truth about some exciting and controversial years in lexical history.

"Reach Out and Open Your Kimono": A Lexical Review

Sometime prior to 2015, a corporate talking head or two must have decided it was crass to "contact." The taboo spread like wordfire, and now professionals everywhere are, all touchy-feely-like, "reaching out" to colleagues, clients, students, and associates. Many find this usage weird, yet the verb "to contact," which was controversial in the early 60s, is gathering dust in professional-speak circular files everywhere.

Sample memo: "Bob, it's time we reach out to the managers at Acme Excavations and Cronuts, Inc. to see if they're amenable to opening their kimono."

The phrase "open kimono" appears to have first surfaced in the 80s with international business dealings between the West and Japan. To be "open-kimono" or "to open the kimono" means to reveal plans and share information freely; to be transparent. The term is laughable and "kind of creepy," in the words of Bruce Barry, a professor at Vanderbilt University's Owen School of Business, but it was a top contender for Australia's word of the year in the *Macquarie Dictionary* for 2015, occasioning chuckles over visualizations of kimonos in the Outback.

In the end, "open kimono" was edged out by "captain's call," a cricket term that has invaded the world of business and politics to refer to a decision made without consulting one's colleagues. Not very sporting, eh, mate? It's interesting that the two terms represent opposite tactics in the business world: "We hoped he would open his kimono, but he made a captain's call instead."

* * *

Here is the rundown of the Words of the Year (WotY) for 2015, revealed in January of 2016: Oxford Dictionaries WotY is not even a word but an emoji—a smiley face with a big fat tear dripping from each eye. One might be moved to ask how this symbol best encompasses the ethos and preoccupations of 2015, and might then conclude that English speakers are doing less actual verbalizing and more pointing and clicking. Why articulate the emotion we are feeling when we can just find something suitable on the emoji menu?

It's easy to relate to laughing and crying at the same time, and it was a reaction often elicited during the presidential debates of that year, but this particular emoji is called "joy." What went on in 2015 that caused Oxford to assume we were mass-emoting tears of joy? And on that note, I wonder whether that verb "emote" still exists, or if it has joined "contact" in the lexical dustbin, to be replaced by "emojiate," after the model of "conversate," which some people are willing to bet money is in the dictionary.

Merriam-Webster's selection for 2015 isn't a word either; it's merely the suffix "-ism." It was chosen because there are 2,733 English words ending in "–ism" in the *Merriam-Webster Unabridged Dictionary,* and seven of these were among their site's most popular searches during the year: socialism, capitalism, racism, communism, sexism, terrorism, and fascism. Important topics for our time? Of course, but "–ism" as the WotY is lacking in, shall we say, "slexical" appeal.

Global Language Monitor's WotY was "microaggression," defined as "everyday verbal, nonverbal, and environmental slights, snubs, or insults, whether intentional or unintentional, which communicate hostile, derogatory, or negative messages to target persons based solely upon their marginalized group membership."

This is certainly recognizable as a relevant societal preoccupation, especially in the context of worldwide refugee crises and racial prejudice, as well as bullying in the schools, and the move toward extreme political correctness on college campuses.

The American Dialect Society choice is last though anything but least, because in addition to carrying the highest prestige, it resolves a long-standing grammatical problem in the English language. It is *(drumroll . . .)* the singular "they/their"—and I say, "Yay!" Specifically, this is the personal "they/their," used as a gender-neutral *singular* pronoun. This is no grand preoccupation like terrorism or fascism—but before you roll your eyes or throw up your hands, consider this: Do you ever wonder if you must go through the rigmarole of writing, "The applicant should be told how much he/she will have to pay for his/her loan"?

Wouldn't it simplify things to write, "The applicant should be told how much *they* will have to pay for *their* loan"—which is how you would verbalize it anyway? So it's not a moral dilemma or a defining ethos, but this bold move by the ADS, with precedents in Chaucer, Shakespeare, and Jane Austen, is a logical step toward resolving a linguistic gap in our language. In 2015, "*they/their*" used as singular was blessed by the *Washington Post* style guide, and *WP* copy editor Bill Walsh called it "the only sensible solution to English's lack of a gender-neutral, third-person-singular personal pronoun." (Non-sensible solutions have included "s/he" and "'e.")

* * *

According to Oxford Dictionaries, 2016 was the year of the "post-truth," suggesting that emotion and personal beliefs are more influential in shaping public opinion than are objective facts. In counterpoint, The Global Language Monitor's top word was "truth," perhaps because it is becoming an increasingly rare value and commodity in these times. The American Dialect Society presented its selection: "dumpster fire," meaning a disastrous and chaotic mess. The Macquarie Dictionary jumped in with the term that was on everyone's mind and lips: "fake news"; and Merriam Webster aptly summed up the preoccupation and ethos of these times in one choice adjective: "surreal."

* * *

Maybe I'm just looking for a reason to feel optimistic, but I find the 2017 picks more provocative and slightly more upbeat than last year's. Oxford chose "youthquake," a significant cultural, political, or social change arising from the actions or influence of young people. That lands well on a hopeful ear, even though the Washington Post and some other media sources didn't react positively to a word they had never heard used.

The same could probably be said for most of Oxford's other contenders—among them "milkshake duck," "white fragility," "kompromat," "broflake," and "gorpcore." Merriam-Webster's 2017 selection was "feminism," as online searches of the word spiked with the January Women's March on Washington, DC, and affiliated marches internationally; the searches escalated with Kellyanne Conway's statement in an interview that she didn't consider herself a feminist, and skyrocketed with the avalanche of sexual assault and harassment charges against powerful men (many of them no longer) in high places.

The word "complicit" was chosen by Dictionary.com as its Word of the Year after online searches soared with each news story about possible collusion with Russia by Trump and his team before, during, and after the 2016 election; in March, after a *Saturday Night*

Live satire featured Ivanka Trump, played by Scarlett Johansson, unveiling a perfume called "Complicit—the fragrance for the woman who could stop all this, but won't"; and in April, when the real Ivanka, in an interview with Gayle King, said, "If being complicit is wanting to be a force for good and to make a positive impact, then I'm complicit. . . . I don't know what it means to be complicit."

If Ivanka were among the hordes who had looked up the word, she would have found that it means "choosing to be involved in an illegal or questionable act, especially with others; having partnership or involvement in wrongdoing." In October, at least one layer of collusion was lifted when Senator Jeff Flake declared in his retirement statement, "I will not be complicit."

Collins Dictionary announced "fake news" as its pick—nothing novel there, and a reiteration of Macquarie's selection in 2016. Nonetheless, it seems fitting because the expression has taken a more sinister turn as President Trump dismisses unfavorable or threatening information by tweeting or declaring, "Fake news!" All the more reason to hone our critical thinking skills and commit to truth over "false, often sensational information, disseminated under the guise of news."

By the time the last calendar page is torn off, new Words of the Year will have been debated, selected, and presented to the world. What will they reflect about our societal and political preoccupations, and what will they suggest about our future course?

In conclusion, here is my latest set of New Year's resolutions: in the professional arena, more contacting, but no reaching out; on the personal front, choosing to express true emotions over emojicons; in entertainment, playing Sudoku using only Roman numerals; and in life in general, *not* throwing fuel on a dumpster fire, refusing to ingest fake news, and never going about with my kimono flapping in the breeze.

The Secret to Everything, Part I

These next two sections might be an inspiring read around January 1, though it seems that New Year's resolutions have become unfashionable of late. Lest you think my title hyperbolic, I offer the caveat that the secret I am about to reveal will not breathe life into the garage door that suddenly and completely shut down yesterday afternoon. It will not magically disappear the dings in the car door, banish gray hair, or materialize gold coins in pockets or purses. However, it can provide the ticket to a flat belly, make you a great swing dancer, unlock the mysteries of becoming bilingual, and maybe even allow you to read your cat's mind.

It really is the secret to learning *anything* and, even more importantly, to not losing the mastery you gain. It is so simple—even obvious—and not at all mysterious, though definitely elusive. Although I discovered this secret for myself through life experience, it is a fundamental principle of how things work, and has been around for all time. It will not come as a surprise to you.

Did you ever take music lessons as a kid? If your answer is "yes," do you still play that saxophone, guitar, or violin? I took 10 years of piano lessons from my Dutch grandmother, who was a very strict teacher of classical music only, permitting no movie tunes and certainly no improvisation. I practiced every day by parental decree, and progressed steadily until, despite very limited musical talent, I could play "Unchained Melody," "O Sole Mio," and "Hard Day's Night" (oops, I mean Bach, Beethoven, and Bartók) with acceptable accuracy and even some passion. Now, though? I can't even read music.

The highly talented concert pianist Elena Casanova started lessons a couple of years earlier in life than I did. The world-class guitarist Alex de Grassi took up his instrument on his own at about the age I quit studying music. Look where they are today! Obviously, these two legendary musicians possess talent that Grandma noticed was lacking in me, but the secret reveals an essential element without which all the talent in the world cannot manifest and develop.

My brother turned up his nose at piano lessons, and insisted on guitar. Now, 50 years later, he plays for an audience of God and hundreds of the faithful every week at his church in western Washington. Our dear family friend Enrique Henao, a native of Colombia, is an amazingly versatile and accomplished guitarist whose long career spans the globe. He plays regular gigs in Seattle-area restaurants and wineries. To earn extra money? Actually, no.[‡] Enrique tells me he does it for practice, and "to maintain the discipline of my concentration despite noise and distraction around me." He adds, "Sometimes I compose musical pieces in those conditions—something I can't do in concerts when the audience is in total silence." Is *practice* the secret? We're getting warm, but haven't quite unearthed the whole treasure.

In my years of teaching Spanish, I've heard many a student declare, "I'm just not good at languages." Many people refer to some mysterious "flair" for learning foreign language as if it were some magical potion that seeps into the brain (or not). I do think I had a slight advantage for learning foreign language, because I grew up hearing one, even though Dutch wasn't remotely close to the language my mother decided I should study. It's true that some of us have more affinity for mathematics, while others lean

---

‡ The money that does come in from Enrique's gigs is donated to children's medical and educational funds around the world.

more toward language, but the bottom line is this: The real difference among people who set out to become bilingual is that the ones who persist do; and the ones who stop do not.

Now, this may not be the satisfyingly earth-shaking, life-changing, wave-the-magic-wand kind of answer we all hope for—but it's the truth. As life coach Tris Thorp quipped, "If spiritual progress were fast and easy, we'd all be enlightened by now, God would get bored, and the game would be over." The same goes for you-name-it: becoming bilingual, learning a musical instrument, getting in shape, painting a masterpiece, improving relationships, and anything else one might dream of or desire. Knowing what to do is so very simple; actually doing it is where over 95% of us fall short. Don't lose heart, though. Now that our shovel has struck the chest of buried treasure, we have only to dig a bit more to release it.

During my last years of teaching college, I began to learn Italian, first from dear Emma of Ravenna, Italy, then on my own and during a short stint at the Dante Alighieri Institute in Tuscany. Experiencing anew the struggle of learning foreign language after having taught one for decades was humbling, but I thought I was immune to the most common pitfall. I returned from Italy full of pasta, gelato, and the inspired commitment to break through to higher levels of mastery. I organized my notes, made flash cards, stuffed a binder full of handouts, and then . . . got distracted, busy, harried, and overwhelmed by life and work. And I stopped.

The fall semester was coming to an end, but the good news was that most of my students planned to continue to the next level of Spanish. The down*slide* was the five weeks of winter break when they would lose proficiency simply from lack of contact with Spanish, just like my experience with Italian. I devised a contract, as much for my benefit as for theirs, and we committed to do something in our target language every single day. What did "something" mean? It meant *anything.* Sure, they could practice irregular verbs daily, but just as valid—and probably more fun and engaging—were learning the words to a song, ordering lunch in Spanish at local Mexican eateries, writing an email, sticking Post-its on the furniture, or even opting for a Spanish transaction at the ATM. The length of time invested was not part of the contract, but frequency, consistency, and challenge mattered. Eureka! The secret is revealed and, yes, we really have known it all along.

Daily contact with a foreign language (or tennis ball, paint brush on canvas, piano keys, exercise mat, etc.) has a dramatic effect on body (physiology) and mind (imagination). On the flipside, so does daily absence. Every day separated from our dream makes it harder to return, and easier to give up altogether. We only imagine that we "don't remember a thing" from those old Spanish classes or piano lessons because the learning isn't readily accessible anymore. Physiologically, the only way to keep that learning center in the brain refreshed and lit up is to plug it in every day.

That's it. That's the secret to success in foreign language, sports, art, fitness, finance, publishing a book, playing the castanets, everything. Even relationships with loved ones require consistent practice, and that usually means daily.

There will be sub-secrets to the secret in the next section, but for now, I propose this first step in the contract: Name something you've always wanted to get good at; dust off an important but neglected dream; or pick an area of your life where you'd like to create improvement. Lovingly hold that in your heart and mind while you move to the next page to read a few more lines about "The Secret to Everything."

The Secret to Everything, Part II

You have taken the first step to mastery of a skill or realization of a dream by choosing what to focus on, and holding it in your heart and mind. I decided to practice the secret I preach with a daily program of CBS: core, balance, and stretching. Now, after 30 early mornings of 15 minutes on the floor, do I have six-pack abs? Can I walk a tightrope? Have I regained the inch of height I lost somewhere in the last decade? No. But I can hold a plank position for three times as long, move with less pain in my lower back and neck, and brush my teeth standing on one foot. Imagine where I'll be in another 30 (or 365) days!

There are dozens of things I'd like to be good at: tango, Italian, meditation, using eBay, singing opera (okay, some things really do require talent and another lifetime), cycling, throwing a party, playing the castanets, and multiple etceteras. That said, why did I choose CBS as my daily practice to illustrate the secret to everything? Because taking on all the aforementioned learning curves at once is a recipe for failure, as amply demonstrated by my past lists of New Year's resolutions; because fitness is what we all intend to practice in some form; and especially because of the age thing. If you're under 40, you may not relate to this now—but try, because you eventually will.

You know how people age? We're young, strong, invincible . . . and then, suddenly, the seams begin to unravel. Joints ache, the middle spreads, bones are thinning, and we've got an appointment with the orthopedic surgeon to talk new knees. By the time this happens, we're way behind the eight ball, and more likely to opt for meds and surgery than a CBS program because . . . well, because we're just too busy to exercise and, besides, this is the era of pharmasurgical flash miracles, not daily sweat equity for the long haul. We know we've let it go too long—but look around, America! Everyone is in the same sinking boat, except for those two to five people out of 100 who made a different choice.

The secret to everything is to practice *every day* what we want to master in the future. It sounds so seductively simple, but it is dastardly difficult; we are a society of instant gratification. We want the end result—the tightrope balance, virtuosity on the violin, fluid brain-tongue connection in a foreign language—and we want it *now*. I chose core strength, flexibility, and balance because, 20 years from now, I want to be a) alive, b) upright and walking, c) as pain-free as possible, and d) moving with stability and a bit of zing. Oh, and did I mention living independently?

* * *

Let's dig into the treasure chest for four sub-secrets to the secret to everything:

Sub-secret #1: Patience

Not only does it not happen overnight, but don't expect to see positive results day-to-day, or even week-to-week. You replace bagels and donuts with broccoli and kale, and start drinking eight glasses of water a day. What if, in a month, you still look and feel the same? The human body is miraculously resilient and finely responsive but, like the Titanic, it doesn't have a tight-turning radius. Hold that new course, though, and change will manifest.

Becoming bilingual is not something you can accomplish quickly, despite ads saying, "Learn Spanish in a Weekend." Let's say you're taking a class, studying online, and practicing faithfully. When a month or a year goes by, and you're just not very fluent, you get disheartened. You give it up, thinking, "I wasn't really getting very far anyway." Don't! It's not about short-term results. The point is to stay the course, gaining small, even imperceptible, but incrementally compounding benefits, day-by-day.

"The darkest hour is right before dawn" says the popular expression. Sometimes, before bed, I do the crossword puzzle in the newspaper instead of reading. Of course it's entertaining, but here's what I really get from it: There often comes a moment when I think to myself, "This one is too hard. I can't do it. I should give it up." But I don't, and I keep training myself over and over that if I persist, there will be a breakthrough. Funny how it always comes when I'm feeling the most convinced that I'll *never* get it, that I might as well quit. Nothing manifests without persistence. A dream stuffed in a corner of the basement gathers dust and goes dormant, but never really dies.

Sub-secret #2: Perseverance

You're exercising daily, eating well, sleeping seven to nine hours, practicing Spanish 10 minutes a day, and everything is going tickety-tock like a smoothly running clock. Then, life happens: an unplanned trip, a demanding project, a bad cold, final exams, a family emergency, causing your successful practices to fall away precisely when you're under stress and need them the most. "It's only for a day or two," you say, but somehow weeks, months, even years go by before you pick it up again. Simply stated, when the going gets tough, we *can* choose to hang in with good choices that propel us beyond just surviving and into thriving.

Discipline can become our default. The achiever of the dream is the person who completed those seemingly small, incremental actions over time to make it happen—consistently, wholeheartedly, and with an abiding sense of purpose. How familiar we all are with overwhelm, breakdown, and nonstop life under high-level stress, but this approach cuts to the ultimate chase in personal responsibility. The mind screams, "No! I can't! I'm just too overloaded. It's not my fault!" and we spend our days searching for the ever-elusive "round tuit," unable to countenance that overwhelm is an excuse for not pursuing what we really want and need.

I say this without any self-righteousness because it is precisely my biggest challenge in life. It comes as no surprise that the going *always* gets tough—yet we can come prepared with our own personally devised strategy to help us stay the course when it does.

Sub-secret #3: Practice

Take Nike's advice: Just do it! Throughout my years of teaching adults, I noticed that some of my students believed they shouldn't actually try to *speak* Spanish with anyone until they were "better" at it. It's that kind of thinking that keeps me taking tango classes and going to practice sessions to improve my skill before I'll be willing to venture out to a real dance where someone might actually lead me onto the floor.

Maybe you won't play your ukulele at a party until you learn more chords, or you postpone signing up for a 5K race until you lose a few more pounds and speed up your pace. This is one of the deepest, most seductive pitfalls to achieving real progress: we perpetuate the status of beginner, opting to play it safe. Stepping up to the plate is scary, and temptation beckons us to settle into the fleecy comfort of low-level challenge, long-term infancy, and easy forgiveness for being a novice.

Spanish has a wonderful folk saying: "An ounce of practice is worth more than a pound of grammar." 10 minutes of sweating bullets in conversation with a Spanish speaker will move you further than a week of silent study. An evening of dancing with good leaders will test my nerves but take me farther than 10 hours of online tango classes. I have to keep telling myself, "So what if my palms sweat, if I don't follow well, or even if someone says, 'She's not a very good dancer'—So what?" There is no dress rehearsal.

Get out there and just do it already! Do it often, and while making mistakes!—daring, audacious, stellar, unforgettable, and even *(eek!)* embarrassing ones. Who cares? People will remember you for enthusiasm and willingness, not for your slip-ups. Being precedes doing. Own yourself as a (you-name-it)—then go out and do what a (you-name-it) does.

Subsecret #4: Perspective

Install a rear-view mirror. If you are looking forward to that time when you will be fluent in Spanish, formidable on the tennis court, pain-free when walking, or a ragtime virtuoso at the piano, you'll never feel that you've arrived.

On the other hand, if you train yourself to look back to where you were and acknowledge that you *have* come a way, baby, you'll be more likely to persist in the project because you will be viewing your progress rather than gazing dazed and downhearted at an endless road ahead. There *is* no final destination, only the path and the sometimes-imperceptible 1% increments. *No hay destino, sólo camino.* ("There is no destination, only the path.")

* * *

In Sonoma County, California, Steve Brumme offers a course for individuals who have no art training. Many of his students believe they have no talent. He has them practice under his guidance for 15 minutes a day and promises that, by the end of the course, they will have re-created "a painting by any master who ever lived" and have a life they love in the areas of health/fitness, relationships, and career. His students replicate masterpiece paintings by Vermeer *(Girl with a Pearl Earring),* Frida Kahlo, or Michelangelo, and color the canvas of their lives in the process.

Reading this, you might be understandably dubious, but let me add that Steve is not only an accomplished painter but also a gold-medal martial artist in multiple disciplines, as well as an inspirational speaker, language-learner, rock-climber, horse-rider, traveler, author, and master storyteller. He recently completed a 900-mile bike ride for End Polio Now, and published a book about it called *Moving Fast, Sitting Still.* He pedaled this daunting distance with his arms because he suffered polio as an infant and has never had the use of his legs. Steve is an inspiring example of one who keeps his dreams alive by nurturing them and practicing them daily against any and all odds.

So now—yes, *right now*—take up one thing you care deeply about, and commit to a breakthrough year getting better at it, 1% at a time, by investing at least five minutes a day toward your dream. Those daily increments may be imperceptible in producing visible results, but they translate into over 300% improvement at realizing your heart's desire in just one year's time. At that 365-day anniversary, you will either say, "I'm glad I did!" or "I wish I had!"

Around the World in Cupid's Quiver

Valentine's Day is approaching as I write this, but I'm not one to give relationship advice on how to find the perfect mate, woo them, rekindle that flame, or glue a broken relationship back together. Nor would I wish to hold forth on 50 ways to leave your lover.

What I propose here are novel ideas on what you might whisper into your loved one's ear at the breakfast table over Belgian waffles, juicy strawberries, and freshly brewed coffee; over a languorous lunch that starts with a flute of sparkly and continues with oysters on the half-shell, and more; when you reunite to debrief after a hard day's work; or when you're snuggling in for a long winter's nap.

What lassoes a humble writer into launching this conversation on the precipice of Valentine's Day is the *possibility* always alive in every relationship—whether new, seasoned or diminished—for more listening, tuned-in attention, a compassionate hand extended to take the hill together, or an opening to find something beyond what is "already and always" known about a partner, child, parent, or friend.

Now back to those waffles and oysters—though preferably not in the same meal—and the whisper of magic words, perhaps more adventurous than "Honey," "Baby," "Sweetie," or "Boo" (slang for "boyfriend/girlfriend," from the French *beau).* It has been suggested by research—and I can confirm based on personal experience—that people can manifest a different personality in each language they speak. Is it too great a leap to say that terms of endearment might sound more seductive in a foreign language, and the speaker might notice a shift in persona beyond the spoken word?

Speakers of romance languages are stereotypically legendary for their ardent purrings of love. If that sweet murmur is *"Mi Amor"* instead of the American colloquial "Babe," both the speaker and the receiver might experience a romantic surge. Other options in Spanish can be *Mi Vida* ("My Life"), *Mi Corazón* ("My Heart"), *Mi Cielo* ("My Heaven"), *Mi Rey/Reina* ("My King/Queen"), *Tesoro* ("Treasure"), or *Cariña/-o* ("Dear One").

An Italian woman might entice a man to come hither with *Vita Mia* ("My Life"), *Cuore Mio* ("My Heart"), *Caro* ("Dear One"), or *Polpetto* ("Meatball"—don't ask! This is love, not logic. Besides, who doesn't love a good, juicy meatball?). He will melt her heart with *Belissima* ("Most Beautiful One"), *Dolcezza* ("Sweetness"), *Principessa* ("Princess"), *Carina* (Cutie), *Fragolina* ("Little Strawberry"), or *Microbino Mio* ("My Little Microbe").

As you might guess, the French language is also a rich mine of gems when it comes to terms of endearment. We all know *Ma Chérie* thanks to Stevie Wonder's "Ma Chérie Amour," and the odor-able cartoon skunk Pepé le Pew. A sampling of pet names for the *moitié* ("other half") include *Mon Dou Dou* ("Cuddles or Pookie"), *Mon Petit Chou* ("My Little Cabbage"), *Ma Puce* ("My Flea"), and a zoo of other pet names inspired by the animal kingdom including rabbit, quail, hen, duckling, chicken, and shrimp—sounds like a full menu of add-ons for a dish of chow mein! He can be *Mon Nounours* ("My Teddy Bear"), and she can be *Mon Oisillon* ("My Little Birdie") or *Mon Chaton* ("My Kitten"), but even careful pronunciation may not ensure the desired effect with *Ma Biche* ("My Doe").

Turning now towards northern languages, I don't think my Dutch father ever called my mother *Mijn Poepie* ("My Poopsie") or *Bolleke* ("Little Round Thing"), but he might have nuzzled her ear with *Schatje* ("Little Treasure")—yes, as in Ukiah's own Schat's Bakery (founded by the scion of a Dutch baker family). In German, the diminutive terms for bear, hare, mouse, sparrow and deer are preferred pet names for a loved one: respectively, *Bärchen, Häschen, Mäuschen, Spätzchen,* and *Rehlein.* An oddly heartwarming endearment I also came across is *Mausbär,* a creative combo that adds to the diminutive concept of "mouse" with a big "bear" hug. And the winner in the cutesy category is *Schnuckiputzi,* linking words, as German is wont to do, to form something like "Sweet Cutie-Pie."

In Sweden, your lover might swoon as you intone *S*ötnos ("Sweet Nose"). In Ireland, the heart will quicken to the rhythm of Riverdance at the sound of *Mo Chuisle* ("My "Heartbeat"). The Polish key to a willing heart might be *Kruszynko* ("Breadcrumb"). In Denmark, *Min Guldklump* suggests a love cherished over all the "gold nuggets" in the bank vault.

Whether it's the Arabic *Laki uyounul ghazal* ("Eyes of a Gazelle"), Spanish *Mi Media Naranja* ("The Other Half of My Orange"), Tibetan *Nyingdu-La* ("Most Honored Poison of My Heart"), or Russian *Rybka* ("Little Fish"), these all translate to the same thing: affection and devotion, worth more than all the *klumps* of *guld* on the planet.

Now, still in search of that prize, we follow Cupid's arrow for a brief world tour of the customs of courtship and love. In Mexico, February 14 is *El Día del Amor y la Amistad* (The Day of Love and Friendship) and is celebrated with balloons, roses, and cards. But before you say "ho-hum" about this convention, fast-forward to Saint Anthony's feast day on June 13, when single women flip the saint's statue on its head until he manifests their mate. Brazilians opt for "Lover's Day" on June 12th, and singles undertake their own rites and offerings to implore *Santo Antônio* to materialize the mate of their dreams.

I've read that in France of yesteryear, after happy couples united on Valentine's Day and wandered off into *les cafés* to begin their life together, bonfires were lit on the streets, and single women burned images of lost loves and shouted insults into the inferno to voice their blazing rage against the unfaithful ones. In time, this custom was banned by the French government because it became increasingly incendiary each year.

In South Korea, Valentine's variations are observed from February through April, beginning with the women's task of seducing the men with candies and flowers. On March 14, known as White Day, the tables turn, and it's the men who must ante up with chocolates, bouquets, and gifts. Then there's Black Day, April 14, when the so-called unlucky ones eat black bean-paste noodles, called *jajangmyeon,* out of black bowls to lament their lonely status.

In Wales, there's no Saint Valentine, but Saint Dwynwen is celebrated on January 25th as the finder of mates and protector of lovers. On that day, a man carves a small but elaborate wooden spoon and gifts it as a token of dedication to his intended. In the Philippines, hundreds of couples come together at malls and other roomy public sites to take or renew marriage vows in huge ceremonies with thousands of family, friends, and well-wishers in attendance.

When I was a child, Valentine's Day meant a special breakfast before school: waffles with strawberries and whipped cream instead of the usual porridge or runny egg. It meant a little basket of chocolates on my plate, cards to be delivered to my classmates, and anticipation of the cards I'd receive in return. One website states: "In the USA, there have been many varieties of cards given over the years, some of which have often been rude or quite cruel in their humor." Why are those the ones I remember?

Chris was my sixth-grade heartthrob, so I was thrilled to see his name on the envelope. Side one of the card made my pulse quicken: "I love the way your hair hangs down your back . . ." Unfortunately, the message on the flip side was not so heart-fluttering: "Too bad it doesn't grow on your head!!" and a cartoon of a girl with a huge mane but a bald crown and bulging eyes. It still leaves me with the silly vestige of a heartbreak, after all these years.

* * *

It's not about what words are said, or the language in which they are spoken. It's about the emotion, the sentiment, the *feeling* that propels them from heart to mind to voice, and into the eager ear of the one you love. It can be as seductive as *Mia Vita* ("My Life"), as silly as *Ma Puce* ("My Flea"), or as simple as a "Hello" motivated by interest and intimacy; a cheerful "Hey . . ." as one open heart invites another; an "Ouch!" followed by a playful pillow fight; the simple opener "What about . . ." that allows a suppressed thought or idea to finally find a voice; or just, "Whoa! I'm so grateful to see your fabulous self on this special day!"—and every day.

Mary and the Merry Month of May

Spring's beauty unfolds as wildflowers delight woodland walkers, new foliage glistens on trees, and another wave of blooms graces backyard shrubs. May is the month for patio parties, the dilemma of having to choose from six musical and fundraising events on the same weekend, and colorful festivals all over the world. What follows is a short list of these festivals that you just might consider adding to your bucket list:

In Cocullo, a tiny village in the Abruzzo province of Italy, the first Thursday in May is the Feast of Saint Domenic, for which snakes are collected from the environs during the previous six weeks. On the big day, the serpents are festooned over the head and shoulders of the larger-than-life statue of San Domenico, and the writhing assemblage is then paraded through the streets of the hamlet, promising believers immunity from snakebites for yet another year. In olden times, they then cooked and ate the snakes after the procession, but these days, they release the de-fanged reptiles to slither back into the forest.

Jerez de la Frontera in Andalucía, the Spanish capital of sherry, flamenco dancing, and horses, celebrates the annual *Feria del Caballo* (Horse Fair) in which a million people converge to indulge their love of all three for seven days of parades, horse competitions, flamenco, and the kind of revelry Spaniards are famous for.

In France, the glitterati make their May pilgrimage to the Cannes Film Festival. In Hong Kong, 60-foot towers are constructed and covered with thousands of sacred buns. Revelers, willing to make the challenging climb, grab and eat one for good luck during the

Cheung Chau Bun Festival on Buddha's birthday. In southern India, for the annual festival of Thrissur Pooram, a procession of elaborately decorated elephants and their riders treks along for 36 hours, accompanied by drumming and festive fireworks.

In Brockworth, England, a seven-pound wheel of cheese is set in motion down the steep grassy slope of Cooper's Hill, and hundreds of people race or tumble down after it. The *Lonely Planet* travel guide says, "It's like a spin-dry cycle to the bottom." The first to grab the cheese gets to keep it, and all get to nurse their bruises and scrapes. Five cheeses are rolled at 20-minute intervals, in this now-international competition that grows in popularity every year despite the number of cheese fans who end up in the hospital. (Ambulances are parked at the bottom of the hill, always at the ready.)

Belgium holds an annual Dragon-Slaying Festival, with St. George on his black steed daring onlookers to get close enough to pull the dragon's tail. It's all great fun and games, as humanity celebrates the new flowering of life and the resurgence of hope and hormones.

The sense of rebirth and renewal comes from a deep, spiritual well. For Christians, the resurrection of Christ on Easter Sunday (between late March and late April) holds the promise of redemption, and in the Catholic tradition, the month of May is dedicated to Mother Mary. At St. Francis Elementary School, each of us kids in the fourth-grade class was to bring a tiny wreath of fresh flowers on our assigned day in May to place on the head of the statue of Mary, who prayed for us sinners from the back of the classroom. It was a big honor that kids, parents, and the nuns took quite seriously, and woe to the child who showed up empty-handed.

Some of the floral crowns were so large they slipped straight down to circle the statue's feet, and Sister Mary Irene had to raid a couple of lunchboxes in the cloakroom for tinfoil to mold a headpiece inside the twined stems. Some were so small that they sailed off the ceramic brow at the first breeze, and found their escape through the window. I was sure we sang a special song each day to accompany the crowning, and also sure I didn't remember it. Quite miraculously, it popped into my head as I was writing this, and an online check tells me that indeed it is the May crowning song: "Hail, Holy Queen enthroned above, ohhh Maa-rii-a . . . ."

In the Catholic Church, Mary holds dozens of titles: Blessed Mother, Queen of Heaven, Advocate of Sinners, and about 250 more, according to *Wikipedia.* My motive for exploring all this was to trace the source of traditional female names in Spanish. Why would parents name their baby "Dolores" if it means "pains and sorrows," or "Soledad," signifying "solitude and loneliness"? These names and many others belong to Mary, as in "Our Lady of . . ." : *Nuestra Señora de la Soledad, Nuestra Señora de Dolores,* and more to come in the next paragraphs.

The Virgin Mary has many manifestations in history and the hearts of the faithful, and several of the more famous have long been popular female names: "Lourdes" (France, 1858), "Fátima" (Portugal, 1917), and "Guadalupe" (Mexico, 1531). Our Lady of Guadalupe is the patron saint of Mexico, and countless Mexican people carry her name. I didn't realize that men too were named "Guadalupe" until, in a citywide teachers' conference, the chairperson called upon "Lupe," and my head whipped around when a deep male voice replied from the back of the room. In Spanish-speaking countries, men might be given "María" as a second name: *José María, Jesús María, Alberto María,* and so on. I remember being deeply puzzled as a child when I came across a book in my father's collection authored by the Bohemian-born Austrian poet

Rainier Maria Rilke. My mind was unable to grasp how he could possibly have a girl's name.

"Dolores," then, is *María de Dolores*—if not officially by baptism, then at least conceptually; "Soledad" is *María de la Soledad,* perhaps shortened to *Marisol;* "Mercedes" comes from *Nuestra Señora de las Mercedes* (Our Lady of Mercies); the beautiful name "Nieves" is from Our Lady of the Snows; and "Rocío" is from *La Virgen del Rocío,* the Virgin of the Morning Dew.

Mary is also the Patroness of Spain, invoked by the name of *Nuestra Señora del Pilar,* our Lady of the Pillar. On my first trip to Spain, the daughter of the family I stayed with was named "María del Pilar," and everyone called her "Maripili," or just "Pili" for short. The popular name "Carmen" comes from *Nuestra Señora del Carmen* (Our Lady of Mount Carmel), and the number of Spanish women named "María del Carmen," or "Maricarmen" for short, is legion. Other titles for the Virgin Mary have given us the traditional Spanish names (with or without "María de") *Socorro* ("help"), *Refugio* ("refuge"), *Remedios* ("remedies"), *Imaculada* ("immaculate"), *Concepción* ("immaculate conception"), *Consuelo* ("comfort"), *Rosario* ("rosary"), and *Luz* ("light"). A woman I knew in Sacramento named *Amparo* ("shelter") was unfortunately nicknamed "Umpy" by her friends who couldn't pronounce that beautiful word.

In her many guises as Our Lady of . . . (so many different manifestations), Mary is honored worldwide and year-round, but especially in the lovely month of May. My mother continues a lifelong devotion to her Mother Mary, having lost her own mom early in life. In the month of May and every day, love to her and all the mothers of the world.

The Yodeling Dutchman: A Father's Day Tribute

In the nationalistic mood of the postwar 50s, neither my mother nor my father even considered teaching us their native languages. Mom learned English when she started school in her Italian neighborhood in the Bronx. Dad wanted only to become all things American, and leave everything Dutch behind. Despite this zeal, it took him years to learn to like avocados, and he never did lose his accent. With the advance of technology in the 60s, he heard a recording of his own voice for the first time and was appalled to discover he didn't sound like a native of his adopted country: "Vell, der was just no vay around dis and dat."

When I was 12, the budding linguist in me yearned to write his birthday card in Dutch, so I found his well-worn Dutch dictionary and started my search for the right words. *Dear*... *Father*... That was easy enough, and I thought this was coming together quite nicely. On April 12, I presented my card to him with confident excitement, watching his face carefully to see his reaction as he read aloud, *"Duur Vader, . . ."* I can still see his furrowed brow in that moment of confusion, and then he laughed at being saluted as "Expensive Father." That was my first lesson in the pitfalls of language lost in translation but, honestly, I think Dad enjoyed it all the more for my gaffe.

I loved him fiercely, and feared him enough. Now that he has been gone over 25 years, I miss him still. I admire the person he was, and feel proud of all he did. I love to tell the story of how he lied about his age so that he could join the Dutch Merchant

Marines a few months before his 18th birthday in 1940. As the Nazis advanced in early May, his was one of the last ships to leave free Holland, carrying Queen Wilhelmina to safe haven in England. He spent the war years in the boiler rooms of transport ships that carried troops and supplies for the Allies. I know from snatches of conversations not meant for my ears that those vessels with my future dad onboard took torpedo hits, but he never once told us kids any war stories.

Though I had always felt close to my Dad, I was stunned at his funeral to hear people talk about a man it suddenly and irrevocably seemed I'd hardly gotten to know. Bob Kerry, former U.S. Senator and recipient of the Congressional Medal of Honor said, "A hero is someone who over and over does the right thing even though no one is there to witness it." I taped that quote to the frame of his photograph because that was my Dad: a quiet hero. The people he'd worked with at the company and in the service club to which he gave his lifelong loyalty had witnessed some of that, and they spoke of all those he helped, always with open hand and heart.

My Dad lived what some might call a small-time life. He passed up a transfer to a more high-powered job that would have meant moving us back to Los Angeles, and opted to stay with a family-owned company in the Central Valley, convinced it was a better place to raise kids. He provided well, but never got rich. His dream of a family trip to the European homeland never materialized. Instead, we enjoyed homey vacations camping in Yosemite, or renting a beach bungalow in southern California.

On winter weekends, we went for drives to see the snow, and in spring to see the wildflowers. In summer, Mom packed picnic lunches while Dad hooked the sailboat trailer to the family car for Saturdays at Lake Woolomes in nearby Delano, where we practiced port and starboard, close haul and tack. Dad taught us how to ice-skate, and delighted us with his yodeling. I've never met anyone else who can yodel, and I wonder if anyone practices that entertaining vocal art anymore. I remember a camping trip in the Sequoias when he yodeled for us little kids until he was hoarse, as we tried to figure out the magic of his melody echoing back from the facing mountains.

Dinnertime was always at six o'clock sharp, and that meant no TV, no answering the phone, and active participation in the family conversation. My parents had plenty of friends, but company at dinner was a rarity, and they almost never spent an evening out. One night a week, though, Dad left after dinner to pick up one of the several Little Brothers he had over the years to take him bowling or to a movie. Only his own experience of losing his father too early in life could have motivated a man with five kids at home to become a Big Brother. A boy who grew up in a foster home in Holland, and a girl who was taken in by an Italian aunt after her mother died when she was only 12, became parents who cherished their family above all else. It was a simple life in which we were always loved and always cared for, and there is nothing small about that. It is the greatest gift parents can give the children they bring into the world.

As teen angst would have it, in my adolescent years it all seemed so strict—stifling, almost—and way too old-fashioned. "Why can't I go to a drive-in movie? And why does the music always have to be that classical stuff?" We laughed at Daddy for being such a worrywart when he hung wind chimes from the ceiling right above his bed. (He calculated that would give him a few seconds' advantage to save his family in case of a major earthquake.) Suddenly, Dad's yodeling concert from our front porch at midnight on New Year's Eve seemed a little too quaint, even if it was a years-long tradition, and even if he was mostly drowned out by Mr. Lemucchi shooting off his pistol, Mr. Nicolletti banging assorted pots and pans, and Mr. Cleaver bellowing out his best Arkansas hog call.

Those were the breakaway years—a time when I knew I had all the answers, and foolishly thought I was the one who had invented the questions. But deeper than all that, and forevermore, I've been thankful for a childhood woven of stable love and firm convictions from the two people who raised us without benefit of parental models of their own.

Dad lingered long enough in his last illness to put family and personal affairs in order. I was the only duck not quite lined up in that row of attempted stable security, since I didn't have a husband to look after me and was still creating my own financial turbulence. When I visited for the 1990–91 holidays, Dad was in the same hospital bed he'd been confined to for two years, ever since the cancer had rendered him paraplegic. On a sunny winter afternoon, I answered a knock at the front door. I didn't have a clue who the tall, handsome young man with a big yellow dog could possibly be. The holidays were over, I was getting ready to drive home, and we weren't expecting visitors. In one of the most serendipitous and touching moments I've known—one that I still cannot talk about without choking up—that former Little Brother of Dad's happened to stop by with his dog, 15 years later to say hello to the man who had showed up to be his friend when his own dad could not. He had no idea that Dad was on his deathbed, but I have always wondered what deep knowingness drew him to our door that year, on that day.

* * *

I was packed and ready to start the long drive to Bakersfield for spring break when I got the call that Sunday morning. Dad died on Easter of 1991, having already passed through the valley of the shadow of death, and fearing no evil. I'd had a phone call with him a few days before, and in luminous words and voice, he had told me so. I think he knows, through all these years since, that I am okay and that my life is good—if not to the letter of his vision for me, then certainly to the spirit. I meet him often while listening to Rachmaninoff and Beethoven, under sail on the open ocean, or painting a room in my house. In my memory's imagination, Daddy still yodels to the mountains at his beloved cabin in the woods.

Despite many visits with Dad's sisters in Holland and Belgium, I never did learn more than a phrase or two in Dutch, but now I can navigate a bilingual dictionary confidently enough to attempt that salutation to my dad again, in closing:

Lief Vader,
Happy Father's Day.
Love always.

AN AFTERWORD OR TWO

In my home office, there are books, binders, and dictionaries occupying the three walls that surround my desk. At the time of this writing, a friend just called to say he's gifting me two boxes of volumes on words and language. I can't pass them up, but wonder where I'll shoehorn dozens more books into this crowded space. Hmm . . . has anyone yet invented book storage that hangs from the ceiling? At Mendocino College, our tiny faculty offices had books shelved seven feet high on the walls behind and in front of our desks. Colleagues and I used to joke about how (and whether) they would dig us out in the event of an earthquake.

I don't have a lot of novels on my shelves, but the few I indulge in are memorable. It's nonfiction that always beckons irresistibly, and the wisdom, humor, and self-revelation of writers like Lynne Truss *(Eats Shoots and Leaves),* Richard Lederer *(Anguished English),* Bill Bryson *(The Mother Tongue),* John McWhorter *(The Power of Babel),* Alan Alda *(Never Have Your Dog Stuffed)*—and many more I would love to name—sing the siren song I must follow.

I deeply admire authors like Elizabeth Gilbert, Anna Quindlen, and Joan Didion, who write bestselling novels as well as unforgettable nonfiction. I'm well convinced I don't have a novel in me, though I've learned from life's unexpected turns to "never say never." A short story, at least? I don't think so, and neither is there a slim volume of poetry about to burst from my breast. I'm still brimming with ideas and musings on words, language, and cultures, and these chapters of *Wordstruck!* are just the first yellow pad of thoughts and ideas that have been fully fleshed out. Grateful for the discipline that deadlines provide as well as feedback from readers near and far, I keep up this "fleshing" in my bimonthly column in the *Ukiah Daily Journal.*

There's a growing pile of scribbled notes atop the filing cabinet, waiting to find their way to a fresh yellow pad and from there eventually into print. The umbrella theme of words and language still holds but—like most of the subjects in *Wordstruck!*—the topics are all over the board and the world. Another fat file will soon become a handbook for intermediate and advanced Spanish learners. I have finally heeded the call of a notebook of travel stories from four months of mostly stranger-than-fiction adventures in South America, and that will be published in early 2019.

No, I don't think I'll produce a novel in this lifetime, any more than I think I'll write a symphony, pilot a jet, or sing my opera at the Met. That said, the possibilities are unlimited, and I will *still* never say "never."

ACKNOWLEDGMENTS

MY DEEP APPRECIATION:

To *Ukiah Daily Journal* editor K.C. Meadows for affording me the column space and the deadlines to produce a few thousand words a month.

To Tris Thorp, for coaching, wisdom, and guidance in helping me envision and achieve the steps to turn dreams into reality. I continue to be guided.

To editor Mary Buckley, for landing lightly and at the perfect moment onto these pages with wisdom, clarity, and speed to turn what seemed like Mount Everest into a sunny hillside.

To Jerry Dorris and AuthorSupport.com, in appreciation for design and formatting as well as the calm and patience extended to this tech-challenged author prone to making frequent changes.

To Steve Harrison, for the Quantum Leap Program, and to all the amazing QL coaches, especially Martha Bullen, Geoffrey Berwind, and Gail Snyder.

To Jonathan Dooley, for many hours of help with my tech issues, delivered with endless equanimity and sharp attention to detail.

To Dan Barth and Ronald Ford, two of my favorite poets, for detailed reading of my text and valuable comments.

To every one of my family members, friends, and readers for following my newspaper column, tuning in to my blog and Facebook page, and offering cheer, appreciation, and ideas for new forays into yet uncharted territories of words, language, and cultures. There are too many of you to list here, but your names are written in my memory and on my heart.

Reaching back in time, to all the nuns at St. Francis Elementary and Garces High School, to Mrs. Domínguez, my first Spanish teacher, and to my dear graduate-school *compañeros,* to whom I owe my bilingualism and—especially to Dr. Liz Ginsburg—my career. Forever thanks.

To Wikipedia, for the ease and accuracy of readily-available information. I'll keep sending an annual donation in appreciation for all I am able to access throughout the year.

To powers and energies beyond words and the five senses where intuition, inspiration, and endless possibility dwell.

REFERENCES

CHAPTER ONE—Life and Language in the USA

The Tower of Scrabble Babel

"New Scrabble Dictionary to Include 5,000 New Words," *CBS DC*, August 4, 2014. http://washington.cbslocal.com/2014/08/05/new-scrabble-dictionary-to-include-5000-new-words/

Oliver Roeder, "The New Scrabble Dictionary Disrespects the Game," *FiveThirtyEight*, October 18, 2014. http://fivethirtyeight.com/features/new-scrabble-dictionary-disrepects-the-game/

You Say Goodbye and I Say Hello

"Hello," "Goodbye," *Online Etymology Dictionary*. Accessed January 11, 2015. https://www.etymonline.com/search?q=hello and https://www.etymonline.com/search?q=goodbye

William Grimes, "Great 'Hello' Mystery Is Solved," *New York Times*, March 5, 1992. http://www.nytimes.com/1992/03/05/garden/great-hello-mystery-is-solved.html

"Terminator 2: Judgment Day," *Wikipedia*. Accessed January 11, 2015. https://en.wikipedia.org/wiki/Terminator_2:_Judgment_Day

The "U.S. and Them" View of the World

"Metrication in the United States," *Wikipedia*. Accessed May 15, 2015. https://en.wikipedia.org/wiki/Metrication_in_the_United_States

Minding the Metaphor, Part I

Jane Hirshfield, "The Art of Metaphor," *TedBlog*. Accessed October 17, 2015. http://blog.ted.com/the-best-of-ted-ed-the-art-of-the-metaphor/

"Metaphor," *The Oxford Companion to the English Language* (Oxford University Press, 1992), pp. 653–655.

Minding the Metaphor, Part II

"How 'Texas' Became Norwegian for 'crazy,'" *The Washington Post*. Accessed October 29, 2015. https://www.washingtonpost.com/news/morning-mix/wp/2015/10/26/how-texas-became-norwegian-for-crazy/

Nancy Harris McClelland. Quotes reprinted with permission. http://www.writingfromspace.com/

Douglas Van Praet, "Why Metaphors Beat the Snot Out of Facts When It Comes to Motivating Action," *Co.Create.com*. Accessed October 27, 2015. https://www.fastcocreate.com/3048817/why-metaphors-beat-the-snot-out-of-facts-when-it-comes-to-motivating-action

Jim Carlton, "My Favorite Mixed Metaphors." Accessed October 27, 2015. http://www.jimcarlton.com/my_favorite_mixed_metaphors.htm

"Mixed Metaphors," *The Russler*. Accessed October 27, 2015. http://therussler.tripod.com/dtps/mixed_metaphors.html

Pants on Fire

Kathy Benjamin, "60% of People Can't Go 10 Minutes Without Lying," *Mental Floss,* May 7, 2012. http://mentalfloss.com/article/30609/60-people-cant-go-10-minutes-without-lying

Tanya Basu, "It's Almost Weirder if You Don't Lie on Your Online-Dating Profile," *Science of Us,* February 26, 2016. http://nymag.com/scienceofus/2016/02/its-almost-weirder-if-you-dont-lie-on-your-online-dating-profile.html

Natalie White, "10 Verbal and Non-Verbal Signs to Spot a Liar at Work," *Stanford Graduate School of Business*. Accessed

April 1, 2016. http://stanfordbusiness.tumblr.com/post/54109702521/10-verbal-and-non-verbal-signs-to-spot-a-liar-at

"Signs of Lying: How to Catch a Liar," *Way of the Mind*. Accessed April 1, 2016. http://www.way-of-the-mind.com/signs-of-lying.html

"Bill Clinton Lies About His Affair with Monica Lewinsky," *YouTube*. Accessed April 2, 2016. https://www.youtube.com/watch?v=JUDppdVXeMw

"Pants on Fire," *Politifact*. Accessed April 2, 2016. http://www.politifact.com/truth-o-meter/rulings/pants-fire/

CHAPTER TWO—Whence These Words?

The Herd Mentality

"List of English Terms of Venery, by Animal," *Wikipedia*. Accessed July 13, 2014. https://en.wikipedia.org/wiki/List_of_English_terms_of_venery,_by_animal

"Book of Saint Albans," *Wikipedia*. Accessed July 13, 2014. https://en.wikipedia.org/wiki/Book_of_Saint_Albans

"Collective Nouns for People," *Collective Nouns*. Accessed July 14, 2014. http://www.collectivenouns.biz/list-of-collective-nouns/collective-nouns-people/

Shakespeare: The Legacy in His Lines, Part I

Georg Autenrieth, *A Homeric Dictionary* (Focus Publishing/R. Pullins Co., Inc., Massachusetts, 2001), page vi.

"Shakespeare's Influence," *Wikipedia*. Accessed August 8, 2014. https://en.wikipedia.org/wiki/Shakespeare%27s_influence

"Words Shakespeare Invented," *Shakespeare Online*. Accessed August 8, 2014. http://www.shakespeare-online.com/biography/wordsinvented.html

Shakespeare: The Legacy in His Lines, Part II

"Knock, knock! Who's there?" *eNotes*. Accessed August 22, 2014. http://www.enotes.com/shakespeare-quotes/knock-knock-whos-there

"Christopher Marlowe credited as Shakespeare's co-writer," *BBC News*. Accessed May 14, 2017. http://www.bbc.com/news/entertainment-arts-37750558

William Shakespeare Quotes and Quotations. Accessed August 22, 2014. http://www.william-shakespeare.info/william-shakespeare-quotes.htm

"45 Everyday Phrases Coined by Shakespeare," *Anglophenia.* Accessed August 22, 2014. http://www.bbcamerica.com/anglophenia/2014/04/45-phrases-coined-shakespeare-450th-birthday

"Idioms from Shakespeare," *Learn English.* Accessed August 23, 2014. http://www.ecenglish.com/learnenglish/lessons/idioms-shakespeare

Mr. William Shakespeare's Insult Generator. Accessed August 23, 2014. Great fun—it works kind of like a slot machine. http://insult.dream40.org/

"Wordplay Masters Invitational," *The Washington Post.* Accessed July 27, 2014. http://www.washingtonpostsmensainvitational.com/

Jeff Brechlin, "The Hokey-Pokey, Shakespearean Style." Reprinted with permission from the author.

On the Trail of Word Origins, Parts I, II, and III

Online Etymology Dictionary. Accessed March 7, 2015. http://www.etymonline.com/

Jordan Almond, *Dictionary of Word Origins: A History of the Words, Expressions, and Cliches We Use* (New York: Kensington Publishing Corp., 1985).

Willard R. Espy, *O Thou Improper, Thou Uncommon Noun* (Clarkson N. Potter, Inc., 1988).

B. Jowett, "Alcibiades I," *The Dialogues of Plato* (New York: Charles Scribner's Sons, 1897), p. 512.

Bill Bryson, *The Mother Tongue: English and How It Got That Way* (New York: Avon Books, 1990).

The Familiarity of Foreign

"Toodeloo," *Wiktionary.* Accessed March 19, 2014. https://en.wiktionary.org/wiki/toodle-oo

"Mayday," *Wikipedia.* Accessed March 19, 2014. https://en.wikipedia.org/wiki/Mayday

"Poppycock," *Online Etymology Dictionary.* Accessed

March 19, 2014. http://www.etymonline.com/index.php?allowed_in_frame=0&search=poppycock

The Scholar's Ink and the Martyr's Blood

"Moors," *Wikipedia*. Accessed June 27, 2015. https://en.wikipedia.org/wiki/Moors

"Arabic Language Influence on the Spanish Language," *Wikipedia*. Accessed June 27, 2015. https://en.wikipedia.org/wiki/Arabic_language_influence_on_the_Spanish_language

"Which Everyday English Words Came from Arabic?" *Oxford Words Blog*. Accessed June 26, 2015. http://blog.oxforddictionaries.com/2014/08/which-everyday-english-words-came-from-arabic/

Mohamed Elmasry, "Ink of a scholar is more holier than the blood of a martyr," *IslamaCity*. Accessed June 27, 2015. http://www.islamicity.org/3137/ink-of-a-scholar-is-more-holier-than-the-blood-of-a-martyr/

"Seeking Knowledge," *Islamweb.net*. Accessed June 27, 2015. http://www.islamweb.net/en/article/167239/seeking-knowledge

Nick Snelling, "What did the Moors do for us? A history of the Moors in Spain," *Culture Spain*. Accessed June 27, 2015. Quoted with permission of the author. http://www.culturespain.com/2012/03/02/what-did-the-moors-do-for-us/

CHAPTER THREE—Grammar Grievances, Malaprop Muddles, and Pronunciation Pickles

Inconstant Consonants and Sudden Vowel Movements

"Norman conquest of England," *Wikipedia*. Accessed February 6, 2016. https://en.wikipedia.org/wiki/Norman_conquest_of_England

"Anglo-Norman language," *Wikipedia*. Accessed February 6, 2016. https://en.wikipedia.org/wiki/Anglo-Norman_language

Grammurder in the First Degree

John McWhorter, "Freedom From, Freedom To: Yes You Can End a Sentence in a Preposition," *New Republic*. Accessed September 20, 2014. https://newrepublic.com/article/113187/grumpy-grammarian-dangling-preposition-myth

"Preposition stranding," *Wikipedia*. Accessed September 20, 2014. https://en.wikipedia.org/wiki/Preposition_stranding

"Can You End a Sentence with a Preposition?" *Oxford Dictionaries Blog*. Accessed September 20, 2014. http://blog.oxforddictionaries.com/2011/11/grammar-myths-prepositions/

John Donne, "No Man is an Island." http://www.poemhunter.com/poem/no-man-is-an-island/

The Abdominal Snowman on the Cal-Can Highway

"Famous Malapropisms," *Fun-With-Words.com*. Accessed June 13, 2015. http://www.fun-with-words.com/mala_famous.html

"Bushism," *Wikipedia*. Accessed June 13, 2015. https://en.wikipedia.org/wiki/Bushism

"Dan Quayle," *Wikiquote*. Accessed June 13, 2015. https://en.wikiquote.org/wiki/Dan_Quayle

"GED Test (Actual Answers)," *City-Data.com*. Accessed June 13, 2016. http://www.city-data.com/forum/other-topics/1013936-ged-test-actual-answers-funny-but.html

Richard Lederer, *Fractured English* (New York: Pocket Books, 1996), p. 14.

Into the Prepositional Fray

"List of Romance Languages and Dialects," *Ethnologue*. Accessed August 14, 2016. http://www.orbilat.com/General_Survey/List_of_Romance_Languages.html

CHAPTER FOUR—Windows on the World

It's All Bubble and Squeak to Me

"Preface to Pygmalion," *Bartleby.com*. Accessed April 16, 2016. http://www.bartleby.com/138/0.html

"Famous Cockneys," *TheBrits.com*. Accessed April 15, 2016. http://www.thebrits.com/famous-cockneys/

"What is Cockney Rhyming Slang?" *Cockney Rhyming Slang*. Accessed April 16, 2016. http://www.cockneyrhymingslang.co.uk/blog/what-is-cockney-rhyming-slang/

"Language: Top 100 Cockney Rhyming Slang Words and

Phrases," *The Anglotopia Magazine*. Accessed April 16, 2016. http://londontopia.net/londonism/fun-london/language-top-100-cockney-rhyming-slang-words-and-phrases/

"The Ultimate Guide to Cockney Rhyming Slang," *EF English Live*. Accessed April 17, 2016. http://englishlive.ef.com/blog/the-ultimate-guide-to-cockney-rhyming-slang/

"Learn the Cockney Accent with Jason Statham," *YouTube*. Accessed April 16, 2016. https://www.youtube.com/watch?v=1WvIwkL8oLc

Lost (But Not Forgotten) in Translation

Justin Boyle, "Interpreters and translators salary and career outlook," *Schools.com*, July 31, 2014. http://www.schools.com/news/interpreters-and-translators-salary-career-outlook.html

"Nova Don't Go" *Snopes.com*. Accessed November 14, 2015. http://www.snopes.com/business/misxlate/nova.asp

Robert Farago, "Ten Most Unfortunate Car Names," *The Truth About Cars*, July 14, 2009. http://www.thetruthaboutcars.com/2009/07/ten-most-unfortunate-car-names/

Eric Qualman, "13 Marketing Translations Gone Wrong," *Socialnomics.net*. Accessed November 14, 2015. http://socialnomics.net/2011/03/29/13-marketing-translations-gone-wrong/

Nick Vehr, "Selling across cultures can be treacherous business," *Vehr Communications*, May 14, 2014. http://www.vehrcommunications.com/selling-across-cultures-can-be-treacherous-business/

"35 Hilarious Chinese Translation Fails," *Bored Panda*. Accessed November 14, 2015. http://www.boredpanda.com/funny-chinese-translation-fails/

We Don't Have a Word for It, Part I

Howard Rheingold, *They Have a Word for It* (Kentucky: Sarabande Books, 1988).

Katie Mather, "45 Beautiful Untranslatable Words that Describe Exactly How You're Feeling," *Thought Catalogue*. Accessed January 24, 2015. http://thoughtcatalog.com/katie-mather/2015/07/45-beautiful-untranslatable-words-that-describe-exactly-how-youre-feeling/

"Translating the Untranslatable" (review and excerpt of *In Other Words* by Christopher J. Moore), *NPR Books*. Accessed August 21, 2016.

http://www.npr.org/templates/story/story.php?storyId=4457805

We Don't Have a Word for It, Part II

"Duende (art)," *Wikipedia*. Accessed February 8, 2015. https://en.wikipedia.org/wiki/Duende_(art)

News from the World of Words

For further description of Foreign Accent Syndrome:

Beck, Julie, "The Mysteries of Foreign Accent Syndrome," *The Atlantic*. Accessed December 15, 2017.

https://www.theatlantic.com/health/archive/2016/01/the-mysteries-of-foreign-accent-syndrome/429276/

"Texas Mom Wakes Up from Surgery with a British Accent," *ABC News*. Accessed July 2, 2016. http://abcnews.go.com/Health/texas-mom-wakes-jaw-surgery-british-accent/story?id=40065999

"Tenn. judge: Parents can name their baby 'Messiah,'" *USA Today,* September 16, 2013. http://www.usatoday.com/story/news/nation/2013/09/18/tenn-parents-baby-name-messiah/2830999/

"French court stops child from being named Nutella," *BBC News*. Accessed May 19, 2015. http://www.bbc.com/news/world-europe-30993608

John McWhorter, *The Power of Babel* (New York: HarperCollins, 2001).

"Who, What, Why: Why do some countries regulate baby names?" *BBC News,* February 1, 2013. http://www.bbc.com/news/magazine-21229475

Rosemarie Ostler, "Disappearing Languages," *Whole Earth Catalogue*, Spring 2000. Accessed May 30, 2016. http://www.wholeearth.com/issue/2100/article/138/disappearing.languages

"Endangered languages: the full list," *DATABLOG*. Accessed May 30, 2016. http://www.theguardian.com/news/datablog/2011/apr/15/language-extinct-endangered

"List of last known speakers of languages," *Wikipedia*. Accessed May 30, 2015. https://en.wikipedia.org/wiki/List_of_last_known_speakers_of_languages

"Italian call to use less English," *BBC News,* September 10, 2008. http://news.bbc.co.uk/2/hi/europe/7608860.stm

Alice Philipson, "Rome finally abandons 'too complicated' Roman numerals," *The Telegraph,* July 23, 2015. http://www.telegraph.co.uk/news/worldnews/europe/italy/11758563/Rome-finally-abandons-too-complicated-Roman-numerals.html

"Indigenous languages are fundamental to development," *New Era,* October 30, 2015. https://www.newera.com.na/2015/10/30/indigenous-languages-fundamental-development/

"Donald Trump tells Jeb Bush 'speak English,' not Spanish, if he wants to be president," *Fox 32,* September 3, 2015. http://www.fox32chicago.com/news/dont-miss/donald-trump-tells-jeb-bush-speak-english-not-spanish-if-he-wants-to-be-president–/search;query=donald trump tells jeb bush

"Carly Fiorina Thinks English Is the Official Language. It's Not," *Huffington Post,* September 3, 2015. http://www.huffingtonpost.com/entry/carly-fiorina-english-official-language_us_55e85f23e4b0c818f61ae02d

Kim Willsher, "The French Scrabble champion who doesn't speak French," *The Guardian,* July 21, 2015. https://www.theguardian.com/lifeandstyle/2015/jul/21/new-french-scrabble-champion-nigel-richards-doesnt-speak-french

Anthony Rivas, "7th Grader Builds 'Braigo,' a Braille Printer Made out of LEGOS," *Medical Daily,* February 25, 2014. http://www.medicaldaily.com/7th-grader-builds-braigo-braille-printer-made-out-legos-270004

Pigments of Our Imagination

"Cultural Meanings of Color and Color Symbolism," *Psychology.com.* Accessed August 1, 2015. http://www.empower-yourself-with-color-psychology.com/cultural-color.html

"What Colors Mean in Other Cultures," *The Huffington Post.* Accessed August 1, 2015. http://www.huffingtonpost.com/smartertravel/what-colors-mean-in-other_b_9078674.html

"Color and Cultural Design Considerations," *Web Designer Depot.* Accessed August 1, 2015. http://www.webdesignerdepot.com/2012/06/color-and-cultural-design-considerations/

"Color Wheel Pro: See Color Theory in Action," *Color Wheel Pro.* Accessed August 1, 2015. http://www.color-wheel-pro.com/color-meaning.html

John Roach, "In Sports, Red is Winning Color, Study Says," *National Geographic News*. Accessed August 1, 2015. http://news.nationalgeographic.com/news/2005/05/0518_050518_redsports.html

The Language Police

Real Academia Española. Accessed July 9, 2016. http://www.rae.es/

"The 'High' and 'Low' of the German Dialect," *NDSU Libraries*. Accessed July 9, 2016. https://library.ndsu.edu/grhc/articles/newspapers/news/dialect.html

"Languages of the World," *Ethnologue*. Accessed July 9, 2016. https://www.ethnologue.com/

"Languages of China," *Wikipedia*. Accessed July 9, 2016. https://en.wikipedia.org/wiki/Languages_of_China

"List of language regulators," *Wikipedia*. Accessed July 9, 2016. https://en.wikipedia.org/wiki/List_of_language_regulators

"French say *'non'* to the term 'hashtag' in battle to stop English words violating their language," *Daily Mail*, January 26, 2013. http://www.dailymail.co.uk/news/article-2268722/Zut-alors-The-French-banned-world-hashtag—email-blog-English-intrusions-beloved-language.html

James Badcock, "Spain launches 'anti-English' campaign to drive out foreign words," *The Telegraph*, May 25, 2016. http://www.telegraph.co.uk/news/2016/05/25/spain-launches-anti-english-campaign-to-drive-out-foreign-words/

"La RAE contra el inglés," *La Semana*. Accessed July 9, 2016. http://www.semana.com/cultura/multimedia/la-real-academia-de-la-lengua-espanola-lanza-una-campana-contra-el-uso-excesivo-de-anglicismos/474200

Rum and Revolution, Part I

"Dissidents say as many as 200 arrested in Cuba," *Daily Mail*, February 23, 2015. http://www.dailymail.co.uk/wires/ap/article-2965891/Dissidents-say-200-arrested-Cuba.html

Rum and Revolution, Part II

Jared Romey, *Quick Guide to Cuban Spanish*, presented by *http://www.SpeakingLatino.com*

CHAPTER FIVE—The Wonders of the Bilingual Brain

Riding the Silver Tsunami

"The Search for Alzheimer's Causes and Risk Factors," *Alzheimer's Association*. Accessed July 11, 2015. http://www.alz.org/research/science/alzheimers_disease_causes.asp

Clark Boyd and Rob Hugh-Jones, "Melting down hips and knees: The afterlife of implants," *BBC News,* February 21, 2012. http://www.bbc.com/news/magazine-16877393

Shanna Freeman, "Top 10 Myths About the Brain," *How Stuff Works.* Accessed July 11, 2016. http://science.howstuffworks.com/life/inside-the-mind/human-brain/10-brain-myths9.htm

"Brain Myth: Drinking alcohol kills brain cells," *Brain HQ.* Accessed July 11, 2016. http://www.brainhq.com/brain-resources/brain-facts-myths/brain-mythology/brain-myth-alcohol-kills-brain-cells

Dovey, Dana, "How Learning a New Language Changes Your Brain and Your Perception," *Medical Daily,* November 24, 2015. http://www.medicaldaily.com/pulse/how-learning-new-language-changes-your-brain-and-your-perception-362872

Jean Carper, 100 Simple Things You Can Do to Prevent Alzheimer's (New York: Little, Brown and Co., 2012).

"Language learning makes the brain grow, Swedish study suggests," *Science Daily,* October 8, 2012. https://www.sciencedaily.com/releases/2012/10/121008082953.htm

The Best Brain Elixir

Christina Sarich, "6 Herbs to Help Boost Your Brain Power," *Natural Society,* December 2, 2014. http://naturalsociety.com/6-herbs-boost-brain-power-genius/

Dean Alban, "12 Brain Foods that Supercharge Your Memory, Focus & Mood," *Be Brain Fit*. Accessed May 14, 2016. http://bebrainfit.com/brain-foods/

Heidi Godman, "Regular exercise changes the brain to improve memory, thinking skills," *Harvard Health Publications,* April 9, 2014. http://www.health.harvard.edu/blog/regular-exercise-changes-brain-improve-memory-thinking-skills-201404097110

Robina Dam, "Why a walking workout is good for your body," *Daily Mail.* Accessed May 14, 2016. http://www.dailymail.co.uk/health/article-122898/Why-walking-workout-good-body.html

Dan Stone, "The Bigger Brains of London Taxi Drivers," *National Geographic.* Accessed April 27, 2016. http://voices.nationalgeographic.com/2013/05/29/the-bigger-brains-of-london-taxi-drivers/

Katie Drummond, "Baby talk: newborns recall words heard in the womb, research shows," *The Verge.* Accessed May 14, 2016. http://www.theverge.com/2013/8/26/4661368/newborns-recall-words-heard-in-the-womb-research-shows

Beth Skwarecki, "Babies Learn to Recognize Words in the Womb," *Science AAAS.* Accessed May 14, 2016. http://www.sciencemag.org/news/2013/08/babies-learn-recognize-words-womb

"3 Areas of Executive Function," *Understood.org.* Accessed May 14, 2016. https://www.understood.org/en/learning-attention-issues/child-learning-disabilities/executive-functioning-issues/key-executive-functioning-skills-explained

Laura Flynn McCarthy, "What Babies Learn in the Womb," *Parenting.* Accessed May 14, 2016. http://www.parenting.com/article/what-babies-learn-in-the-womb

"Bilingual children ARE smarter: Babies who grow up listening to two languages have better problem-solving skills even before they can talk," *Daily Mail,* April 5, 2016. http://www.dailymail.co.uk/sciencetech/article-3524180/Bilingual-babies-smarter-Children-grow-listening-two-languages-better-memory-problem-solving-skills.html

Molly McElroy, "Bilingual baby brains show increased activity in executive function regions," *University of Washington,* April 4, 2016. http://www.washington.edu/news/2016/04/04/bilingual-baby-brains-show-increased-activity-in-executive-function-regions/

The Blooming Brain

Naja Ferjan Ramirez, "Why the baby brain can learn two languages at the same time," *The Conversation,* April 15, 2016. https://theconversation.com/why-the-baby-brain-can-learn-two-languages-at-the-same-time-57470

Colleen Flaherty, "Not a Small World After All," *Inside Higher Ed.*, February 11, 2015. https://

www.insidehighered.com/news/2015/02/11/mla-report-shows-declines-enrollment-most-foreign-languages

The Tongue May Stumble, But the Brain Purrs

François Grosjean, PhD, "Who is Bilingual?" *Life as a Bilingual* blog *(Psychology Today).* October 21, 2010. https://www.psychologytoday.com/blog/life-bilingual/201010/who-is-bilingual

Mario D. Garrett, PhD, "Brain Plasticity in Older Adults," *Psychology Today*. Accessed June 2016. https://www.psychologytoday.com/blog/iage/201304/brain-plasticity-in-older-adults

CHAPTER SIX—A Life in Words

Make Love, Not War

"Kent State Shooting," *History.com*. Accessed July 8, 2016. http://www.history.com/topics/vietnam-war/kent-state

Ez Dakite Euskaraz Hitz Egiten Duzu?

"Basque Americans," *Wikipedia*. Accessed February 13, 2016. https://en.wikipedia.org/wiki/Basque_Americans

The Cure by Feeding of Earworms

"Earworm," *Wikipedia*. Accessed August 28, 2015. https://en.wikipedia.org/wiki/Earworm

"Ten readers' cures for earworms," *BBC News*. Accessed August 29, 2015. http://www.bbc.com/news/magazine-17302237

In Megahurtz, but Knotfurlong

"Math jokes," *Cool Science*. http://www.coolscience.org

A Girl (Not) Named Sue

"Do Catholic Children Have to be Given Saints' Names?" *Canon Law Made Easy*. Accessed July 30, 2016. http://canonlawmadeeasy.com/2011/10/25/do-catholic-children-have-to-be-given-saints-names/

"Saint's name," *Wikipedia*. Last modified July 25, 2017. https://en.wikipedia.org/wiki/Saint%27s_name

"Top names of the 1950s," *Social Security*. Accessed July 30, 2016. https://www.ssa.gov/oact/babynames/decades/names1950s.html

CHAPTER SEVEN—Marking Moments in the Year

Have a Feliz Navidad and a "Diglot" New Year!

Anu Garg, *The Dord, the Diglot, and an Avocado or Two: The Hidden Lives and Strange Origins of Common and Not-So-Common Words* (South Africa: Penguin Books, 2007).

"The Night Before Christmas, Latin Style," *NPR,* December 24, 2005. http://www.npr.org/templates/story/story.php?storyId=5068774

May Your Days Be Merry and Bright

"Best Fruit Cake Ever," *Indigo.org.* Accessed December 6, 2014. http://indigo.org/humor/fruit.html

"Sex of Santa's Reindeer," *Snopes.com*. Accessed December 6, 2014. http://www.snopes.com/holidays/christmas/santa/reindeer.asp

Christine Dell'Amore, "100-Year-Old Fruitcake Found in Antarctica Is 'Almost' Edible," *National Geographic,* August 10, 2017. https://news.nationalgeographic.com/2017/08/antarctica-fruitcake-scott-terra-nova/

High Notes on Highway 99

"Central Valley (California)," *Wikipedia*. Accessed January 2, 2016. https://en.wikipedia.org/wiki/Central_Valley_(California)

And the Word of the Year Is…

"Word of the year," *Wikipedia*. https://en.wikipedia.org/wiki/Word_of_the_year

"Reach Out and Open Your Kimono": A Lexical Review

"Australia makes 'captain's call' on best words of 2015," *BBC News,* January 20, 2016. http://www.bbc.com/news/world-australia-35368063

"Why Corporate Executives Talk About 'Opening Their Kimonos'," *NPR Code Switch,* November 2, 2014. http://

www.npr.org/sections/codeswitch/2014/11/02/360479744/why-corporate-executives-talk-about-opening-their-kimonos

'Words of the Year 2015," *World Wide Words*. January 9, 2016. http://www.worldwidewords.org/articles/ar-wor4.htm

Curzan, Anne, "Words of the Year, 2016," *Chronicle of Higher Education*. January 8, 2017. https://www.chronicle.com/blogs/linguafranca/2017/01/08/words-of-the-year-2016/

"Word of the Year 2017 Is . . ." *Oxford Dictionaries*. Accessed December 17, 2017. https://en.oxforddictionaries.com/word-of-the-year/word-of-the-year-2017

"Merriam-Webster's 2017 Words of the Year," *Merriam-Webster*. Accessed December 17, 2017. https://www.merriam-webster.com/words-at-play/word-of-the-year-2017-feminism

"Word of the Year 2017," *Dictionary.com*. Accessed December 17, 2017. http://www.dictionary.com/e/word-of-the-year-2017/

"The Collins Word of the Year 2017 Is . . . " *Collins Dictionary*. Accessed December 17, 2017. https://www.collinsdictionary.com/us/woty

The Secret to Everything, Part II

Steve Brummé, *Moving Fast Sitting Still*. http://www.movingfastsittingstill.net/

Around the World in Cupid's Quiver

Claire Fallon, "62 Pet Names Your Honeycake Deserves to Hear on Valentine's Day," *Huffington Post*, February 12, 2016. https://www.huffingtonpost.com/entry/pet-names-foreign-languages_us_56bbbede4b0c3c5505005ab

Viator, "10 Valentine's Day Traditions All Around the World," *Huffington Post*, February 8, 2016. https://www.huffingtonpost.com/viator/10-valentines-day-traditi_b_9190888.html

Mary and the Merry Month of May

"Festivals of the world: where to go in May," *Lonely Planet*. Accessed April 23, 2016. https://www.lonelyplanet.com/search?q=travel-tips-and-articles%2F77164

"Titles of Mary," *Roman Catholic Saints*. Accessed April 24, 2016. http://www.roman-catholic-saints.com/titles-of-mary.html

INDEX

C

D

E

F

G

J

K

L

N

O

P

Q

R

S

T

U

V

W

Y

Z

ABOUT THE AUTHOR

Susanna Janssen is a foreign-language educator, author, speaker, and newspaper columnist on all things about words, language, cultures, and travel. She is a passionate advocate for second-language learning at any age to benefit one's brain, career, bank account, and worldview; and for developing a lifelong devotion to reading—a love affair that promises to be ever fresh and stimulating. She resides in Northern California, where magnificent redwood trees, legendary wines, a rich culture of the arts, and great friendships are a source of wonder, inspiration, and joy. *Wordstruck! The Fun and Fascination of Language* was declared the Winner in Humor/Comedy, and Finalist in Education/Academic by the 2017 Next Generation Indie Book Awards; as well as Finalist in Reference by the 2017 National Indie Excellence Awards.

CPSIA information can be obtained
at www.ICGtesting.com
Printed in the USA
LVHW05s2352011018
592102LV00008B/279/P

9 780998 304823